THE MONKEY BOX

BY

ART RODRIQUEZ

To Claudia!
Enjoy!

Dream House

ACKNOWLEDGEMENTS

I would like to thank all who read *East Side Dreams* and encouraged me to write another book. Thank you, also to illustrator Hiram Duran Alvarez, and Margarita Maestas-Flores, my editor; both were very easy to work with and were very helpful in assisting me to finalize this book. My father and uncles are no longer alive, but if it had not been for all of the stories they shared with me, this book would not have been possible.

Copyright 1999
Art Rodriquez
Publishing date January 2000
Published by Dream House Press
P.O. Box 13211, Coyote, CA 95013
E-mail: dreamhousepress@yahoo.com

ISBN: 0-9671555-1-7
Library of Congress
Catalog Card Number: 99-93258

Edited by
Margarita Maestas-Flores

Cover Illustration and Production by
Alvarez Design & Illustration
CasaRaza@pacbell.net

DEDICATION

This book is dedicated to my wife Flora and my mother Mildred, as well as to my children: Tito, Gina, Artie, Daniel, Lisi, Marina, Desiree, and Ramiro. In addition this dedication is shared with my brothers and sister: Eddie, Mildred, and Victor. I really appreciate all of your encouraging words.

CONTENTS

LYDIA

In the early part of the 1800s, a family of noblemen of the highest hereditary rank lived in Spain. The family Fuentes originated from lineage of royalty and wealth. They also had numerous children. One of these children became a Catholic priest. The priest was not agreeable with a life of celibacy. He met a young woman and fell in love with her, and the romance continued on until the year of 1850 when the young woman became pregnant. Nine months later she bore a baby girl whom they named Lydia. The priest and the young woman decided to try to keep the affair and pregnancy quiet, since they knew it would be disastrous for the priest's family name. Shortly after little Lydia's mother gave birth, she became very sick and died. At that time it became public knowledge the priest was the father of baby Lydia. It was no small matter that the priest was having an affair with a young lady.

In the best interest of the family's name, it was decided the priest would leave the country with his young daughter. With him would go his portion of the family inheritance, his documents of the family name of royal descent, and proof of his title of duke.

The priest gave up his priesthood and boarded a ship destined for the Americas; it took several weeks to cross the Atlantic Ocean. He and his young daughter docked in Vera Cruz, a coastal city in México.

During that time the Spaniards were still immigrating to México. The priest traveled from Vera Cruz to the pueblo of San Bartolomé de los Llanos (Llanos means tall grassy plane. Ll in Spanish has a 'Y' sound, 'Yanos') in the state of Chiapas. Today the pueblo of San Bartolomé de los Llanos is now called Venustiano Carranza, Carranza for short.

San Bartolomé de los Llanos was a small, beautiful pueblo with cobblestone streets. It sat on a bluff halfway elevated on a small, cen-

1

turies-old, dormant volcano in the Grijalva River Valley. It was surrounded by green jungle. The pueblo could be seen for miles before approaching it, as the houses were made of whitewashed adobe that glistened in the sun. When it rained in San Bartolomé de los Llanos, it rained with such a downpour that the streets turned into rivers. The inhabitants were prospering with the land, a very fertile region. Of course there were the Indians, descendants of the Mayan, who also lived in the region.

In the pueblo of San Bartolomé de los Llanos, the priest had friends whom he knew back in his country of Spain. He had written and informed them he was traveling to México with his daughter Lydia. Since he had to leave Spain in a hurry because of his family's embarrassment and ridicule, he did not wait for a reply. He did not know what his friends were going to say in regard to his situation, but he would soon find out.

Arriving in San Bartolomé de los Llanos, his friend, Dr. Miguel Gonzales, had already heard of the situation and was disappointed with regard to his priesthood and what he did to his family's reputation. The priest noticed this as soon as he entered their home. The greetings of the family were not what they should have been. These people, whom the priest called his friends before they immigrated to México from Spain, looked at the priest with high regard because of his representation of people in God's name.

A few days after arriving, the priest spoke to his friend the doctor and told him what he had decided to do about himself and his little child. He asked his friend if he and his family were willing to take on the responsibility of caring for and nourishing little Lydia. He told him they would be well compensated for their work in caring and raising the child. In reply his friend told the priest they would find pleasure in caring for his young child. The Gonzales' had two children of their own, and one more would not be a burden on the family.

The priest left enough money to care for his daughter for many years. In addition, he paid them in advance what he thought would be a sufficient amount for their work in raising and educating her. He also left the documents indicating her family's heritage. He left the portion of her inheritance she would receive when she became of age. The priest then left and said he would return periodically to see how his young daughter was doing. Once he left, he never returned and was never seen or heard from again.

Everything went well from the start of the relationship with the young girl and the Gonzales family. Young Lydia enjoyed being raised by Dr. Gonzales and his wife and growing up in the beautiful pueblo of San Bartolomé de los Llanos.

Lydia grew to be a very beautiful young girl. She was a rubia (light complexion with light hair and blue eyes). She was also very respectful, since this was the way the family taught her to be.

Lydia was now sixteen years old. During that time there was a family in the state of Sonora by the name of Rodriguez. One of the sons, Francisco Rodriguez, wanted to travel south to a territory about which he had heard so much. Francisco was a very large and strong man, bigger than the average Mexican. He had broad shoulders and was a good looking man who stood tall, having excellent posture. He was twenty-six years old then and considered himself to be a man. He was old in comparison to sixteen-year-old Lydia. In México, oftentimes, older men took young girls for their wives.

Francisco arrived in the pueblo of San Bartolomé de los Llanos to work. He was there for only two months. One Sunday afternoon he was walking through the town. He often walked in this particular direction after visiting his friends. He turned a corner and caught sight of a beautiful, young sixteen-year-old girl with blue eyes. Francisco was a man who appreciated beauty.

Lydia was standing in front of her friend's house, chatting with two other girls about small matters, when she saw Francisco walking towards her. He caught her attention.

Francisco slowed his pace. He smiled at Lydia. Lydia did not know if she should return his smile. She had seen Francisco around town and thought he was good looking; however, she had never been formally introduced to him. She could not help herself and returned his smile. "Hey, Lydia," Rosa, one of Lydia's neighbors who was also her best friend, asked, "Who is that? Do you know him?"

At first Lydia did not answer, staring in a trance at Francisco. Francisco was walking away and turned his head in order not to take his eyes off Lydia.

"No, but I have seen him a few times," Lydia replied.

"What do you mean, you have seen him? Have you talked to him?" Rosa asked, thinking it was not a good idea for Lydia to be friendly with someone whom she did not know.

Lydia continued looking at Francisco and said in a low voice, "No, I have not spoken to him yet."

The following day in late evening, Francisco walked through town and looked for the same blue-eyed girl. He did not see her anywhere in the street. He felt she was the most beautiful girl he had ever seen. He wanted to get to know her and was not going to let the chance get away from him.

Every evening during the week he went to see his same friend, Ramiro, hoping to see Lydia. Ramiro was a person he had met when he first arrived in Chiapas. On Friday he saw her in front of one of the homes talking to the same girl. Upon seeing her, he stopped in his tracks and stepped over to the side near the buildings. He mixed in with others who were standing around and visiting with one another. Francisco squatted down, leaning against a wall to observe Lydia. He saw her smile and gesture with her arms. His thoughts were of her beauty. He then watched while her friend spoke. He saw Lydia concentrating on her friend's every word, her eyes staring, in deep thought, and taking in every syllable that was being spoken to her. Francisco felt his heart flutter. He had to get to know her. He just had to!

Francisco stood up and walked in their direction, across the street, two homes away. Just as he was approaching, another girl ran up to Lydia, pulling on her dress and hurriedly telling her something. Lydia turned, told her something, turned back, patted her friend on the shoulder, and walked away with the girl who came for her. Just as she was leaving, she saw Francisco walking towards her. She stopped; she knew this man had something she had never seen in any other man in all her life. Francisco smiled at her again and moved his head up as if he were greeting her. Lydia returned his smile. She wanted to stay and talk to him. The girl who came for her pulled on her dress again and said, "Come on, Lydia! You are going to get in trouble if you do not hurry!"

Lydia kept up with her but at the same time looked back at Francisco, smiling as she turned the corner in another direction. At least now he knew her name. He repeated her name many times in his mind for the next two days.

The following Sunday Francisco again hoped he would catch a glimpse of beautiful Lydia. He walked the same street he had walked the last few days.

He did not know Lydia was waiting for him, hoping he would walk by. She was talking to her friends in front of the same house as the previous week. As Francisco approached, their eyes met. He gave Lydia a smile, and she returned the smile. He knew instantly that she was not just any girl. This was the girl he had often imagined in his dreams; he knew someday he would find her.

"Could this be her?" he thought.

This was why at twenty-six years of age he had never been interested in any other woman. He had seen this girl's light hair dancing in his dreams, but Francisco was never able to see her face. When Lydia smiled at him, he knew she was the one.

"This has to be her," he thought.

This was going to be the girl with whom he would spend the rest of his life. He just knew it.

Lydia felt as if she knew this man. Suddenly, as she returned his smile, she realized she was in love.

She wondered, "Is it true one can fall in love right away?" As he approached, she felt she already knew him.

"Oíga chamaca (Hey girl), what's your name?" Francisco asked, acting as if he did not know it.

"Lydia," she answered, wondering why this good-looking, older man was asking her. She wondered if he felt as she did.

"Lydia, do you live around here?" Francisco asked as he took a few steps toward her, admiring her beauty.

"Yes, I live with the familia Gonzales. He is the doctor of the pueblo," she answered, pointing a few doors down.

"And who is your father?" Francisco wanted to know since he might recognize the family name.

"My father does not live here, but our familia's name is Fuentes."

"And who, may I ask, are you, señor?" Lydia asked as she took a few steps toward him, wondering why she was doing this and knowing she usually was a very shy girl.

"Francisco Rodriguez. I am from the state of Sonora," Francisco answered proudly. He continued, "and I came all this way to meet you." He took off his hat and had a serious smile on his face.

Lydia giggled and said, "How did you know I lived here in this pueblo, Señor Francisco?" she asked, knowing Francisco was his first name and not his last.

"That's Rodriguez. Francisco is my first name," he corrected her. Both started taking a few steps toward each other as if they knew one another.

"Well, nice to meet you, Señor Francisco Rodriguez. Where are you from? I have not seen you around here. Well, I saw you walk through here but only this week."

"I am from the state of Sonora as I have said. I heard so much about Chiapas, I wanted to come and see if it is as beautiful as I was told."

Lydia smiled at Francisco, now feeling comfortable talking to him. "Well, is it as beautiful as you heard?"

"Oh no, it is not. It is ten times as beautiful as I was told. I love the state and really love this pueblo (town)."

They both came to a stop. Lydia knew she could not continue to walk with him, although she wished she could.

"Listen, Lydia, I would like to come back this evening and ask your parents if I can take you for a walk to the Calvario. Would you like to come?" Francisco asked, hoping she would accept. The Calvario (Calvary) was on top of the old volcano. It was given this name because a cross was erected there. The people of San Bartolomé de los Llanos would go to the top of the mountain and see the beauty of the area. They never tired of the sights.

Francisco knew if she accepted she would be the girl who was going to be his wife.

In the next few seconds as she was thinking of her answer, Francisco admired her facial expressions, the way she spoke, and the way she pulled her hair back over her shoulder. Her beauty was indescribable to him. "How can I write my familia and describe this beauty to them?" he thought.

"That would be nice, Francisco. I would like to go with you, but I need to take a chaperon," Lydia answered, knowing this charming man was going to be her choice.

"That will be fine. I would insist on it," Francisco commented, trying to impress her.

"My friends and familia call me Chico. If you would like to call me Chico (Little), or if you want to call me Francisco, you may. Whatever you prefer."

In these short, few seconds, he felt a strong closeness develop for her. He had never felt this for any woman or girl.

"Why do they call you Chico when you are so big?" she wanted to know.

"Believe it or not, I was not always this big. I used to be chico," he answered jokingly.

"I do not believe a big man like you could have ever been chico," she said in an admiring way.

"May I come for you at your home around seven?"

"That will be fine. I will be waiting for you," she answered as she turned back and took a few steps toward her friends.

"Oh, Lydia, where do you live?" Chico asked as he turned and walked backwards a few steps.

Lydia pointed in the direction she had pointed earlier. "Two houses down the street." It was in the same direction that Chico was walking. She continued, "Over there, on your right, at the corner house, the home with the doctor's name on the top of the door."

"All right, Lydia. I will see you later," Chico responded, not wanting to take his eyes off her.

As Lydia walked back to her friends Rosa and Martha, she was in a daze, not knowing what came over her and liking and admiring this older man whose name was Chico.

"Who was that, Lydia, your grandfather?" one of the girls asked, teasing her.

Lydia did not hear what her friend said. She was thinking of Chico's smile and the words he used. She repeated them in her mind and heart.

"Rosa, what are you doing this evening?" Lydia asked.

"I do not know. Why?"

"Would you like to come with me to the Calvario?" Lydia asked, hoping she would accept.

"Yes, Lydia. I will go with you. But why?"

"I just want you to go with me; that is all."

Lydia did not say much more about going to the Calvario. She went home not saying much of anything else to her friends.

When she arrived home, she went to her room to read what the doctor assigned her. To study and to read everyday was part of her formal education. Lydia was a humble girl. She had been told of her family's heritage and the money she was going to receive when she became of age. Lydia did not think much of it; it just was not important to her. She often wondered what she would do with so much money, knowing she was happy without it. "Why would I need anymore than I am able to earn?" she thought.

That evening at dinner the Gonzales family sat down together to eat as they did every day. Lydia sat in her regular chair, poking at her food. She did not have an appetite. She just could not get Francisco out of her mind.

"Who was he? Why did he show so much interest in me? He was very good looking. He was sure to have his pick of all the women in this pueblo," she thought.

"Lydia, are you all right? You are not eating. Do you feel well?" the doctor asked, sitting at the other end of the table. The doctor was very good with her. In fact, if she did not know better, she would think this man was her real father. Dr. Miguel Gonzales was an older man in his forties. He was moderately bald and on the heavy side.

"I am fine, sir. I was just wondering if I could have your permission to go for a walk with my friend Rosa and another friend this evening?"

"Sure you can. Why do you ask? You often take walks. Is the other friend who is going with you a muchacho (boy)?" the doctor asked, wondering if that was the reason for her request.

"Yes, kind of a muchacho," she answered, not knowing how the doctor would react if she told him the boy was a man.

"What do you mean 'kind of a muchacho'?" the doctor asked, looking at Lydia in an odd way.

Señora Lupe Gonzales interrupted, "Who is this muchacho whom you are going to go for a walk with, hija?" she wanted to know, since she practically knew all the boys in town. Señora Gonzales was a school teacher. She was an attractive woman in her forties, even though she did not look a day older than thirty-five. She had long, black hair and big, brown eyes.

Lydia thought it over and reasoned to herself that it was best not to say anything about Francisco's not really being a boy.

"He is just a friend. His name is Francisco Rodriguez, and he is a very nice person."

"Francisco Rodriguez?" Señora Gonzales said in a low voice with her finger on her lip as if she were in deep thought. She continued, "I do not think I know who he is. Is his familia the familia Rodriguez who live in Tuxla Gutierrez?" Tuxla Gutierrez was a big town about a two-day ride on horseback from their home.

"I do not know," answered Lydia, hoping they would stop trying to figure out who he was.

"Fine. You may go, Lydia. But you need to be very careful because, as I told you many times, you are a special muchacha with a special familia," the doctor reminded her in a serious and proud way.

That evening at exactly seven o'clock, there was a knock at the door. Señora Gonzales went to see who it was, anticipating Lydia's new friend. When she opened the door, she saw a young man holding his hat. She thought maybe Lydia's friend could not take her for a walk and he had sent a messenger to inform Lydia what had happened.

"Señora, my name is Francisco; and I came to ask if Lydia and her friend can take a walk with me to the Calvario," he said, thinking this woman was very pretty for being the older doctor's wife. He had seen the doctor around town and thought he was in his fifties.

"You are Francisco?" Señora Gonzales asked, showing her surprise.

"Yes. I wanted to ask if I may take Lydia for a walk to the Calvario."

"Yes. She asked us. Come in, young man, and have a seat. I will tell Lydia that you are here," Señora Gonzales stated as she pointed to a chair by the front door.

Señora Gonzales thought as she walked away, "No wonder Lydia said he was, 'kind of a muchacho.' "

Lydia's room was toward the back of the house. The doctor and his family lived in one of the biggest homes in town. Here in this part of México, the weather was tropical. From the street the houses were lined up side-by-side with very few alleyways, just as any other small town in México at that time. Most of the homes were built with rooms of three walls only. The fourth wall was opened to the enclosed yard outside. Lydia's room had beads hanging on her door for privacy.

"Lydia, your friend is here," Señora Gonzales said in a tone of disapproval.

She thought as she was walking away from Lydia's room, "The young man is much too old for our Lydia; and more than that, he is just a ranch hand. A laborer at that!" Señora Gonzales knew this by the way he dressed.

She walked away from Lydia's room toward her bedroom where she thought her husband awaited her. In a low voice she said to herself, "Lydia cannot have a muchacho friend who is a ranch hand! She has special blood! 'Blue Blood'!"

She needed to inform her husband about the situation and see what he was going to do about it. She approached their bedroom and looked inside. He was not there.

"He would either be in this room or in his small doctor's office next door," she thought. The house was connected to the small office by a door.

She thought that if she could reach the doctor right away he would stop it right then, before they left on their walk. The doctor was a strict man. When he saw something that was not proper, he put a stop to it immediately. She stepped into the doctor's office and said, "Are you here, Miguel?" She waited for a reply.

"Yes, over here," the doctor answered.

The doctor's office had two rooms. One room was to see the patients; and the other room had three beds for the sick who had to stay, since there was no hospital in San Bartolomé de los Llanos. His office was the hospital.

"Miguel, you need to come right away! Lydia's boyfriend is not a muchacho friend but a man friend! Not only that, he is a ranch hand!" Señora Gonzales exclaimed, attempting to rush the doctor.

"How do you know that, Lupe?" he asked with a suspicious expression in his eyes.

"Because I just met him at the front door. He came to get Lydia!" she exclaimed, wanting him to run to where the young man sat.

The doctor looked down at his patient, who was lying on the bed, and said, "I will be back in just a few minutes."

He started walking behind his wife as she started for the front part of the house.

"Hi, Rosa. Are you ready?" Lydia asked, with Chico standing next to her.

Rosa was a short, sweet-looking, seventeen-year-old girl. She had a round face with a small nose; brown eyes; and short, black curly hair.

"Is this all right with the doctor, Lydia?" Rosa asked, wondering if they were going to get into trouble for having the young man with them.

"Rosa, I want you to meet my friend Chico. Chico, this is my friend Rosa."

"It is an honor to meet a friend of Lydia's," Chico said, removing his hat.

"It is nice to meet you too, Chico," Rosa replied, looking at Lydia and still wondering what the doctor and Lupe would say.

"Do not worry, Rosa. I asked the doctor and Lupe at dinner, and they said it was all right."

Rosa thought, "That sure does not sound like the doctor to let Lydia go with this man, even though he is a good-looking man and very well mannered."

As they started their walk to the Calvario, Lydia looked up at Chico and thought, "What a big, handsome man for having a name like Chico (little)."

Chico felt her eyes examining him.

"So, Lydia, tell me about yourself? How long have you been with the doctor and his wife?"

As Lydia started to tell Chico the story the doctor and Lupe had told her about her father, Chico was listening intently and asking questions periodically.

"So, Lydia, you have not seen your father since you were a small baby, right?"

"Yes, that is right, Chico," she answered as they climbed the steep trail.

Rosa was quiet during the walk. She was also enjoying her story about the family and the priest.

"Have you tried to find out where your father went, if he went back to Spain?" Chico asked.

"No, not really. I do not have any reason to. I feel that if my father were back in Spain he would have tried to contact me, and he has not."

Rosa finally asked a question, "What about your familia in Spain? Have you heard from them?"

"No. If you think about it, they are the ones who sent me away when they sent my father away."

"But," feeling confused, Chico said, "they really don't know where you are; and, besides, at the time they really had no choice. It was your father's mistake, not your grandparents."

Lydia thought it best not to say anything about the money she was going to receive when she became of age.

As they approached the top of the trail, Rosa leaped ahead of them and ran to the top of the hill.

Once Rosa was out of sight, Chico and Lydia stopped their walk and sat on the side of the trail on the tall grass. At first they both sat, not knowing what to say, both feeling the same way inside. They wanted to say how much they liked each other, but they did not want to be presumptuous or assume the other felt the same way.

"Chico, what about your familia? Were they always from the state of Sonora?"

"As far as I know. My father owns a big rancho there. I could work with my father and brothers, but I wanted to make my own way."

"How long has your father owned his own rancho?" Lydia asked, thinking if his family owned their own rancho, it would make it a little easier for the doctor and Lupe to accept Chico.

"All my life. My grandfather started the rancho, and my father took it over when my grandfather passed away. Now my father and the rest of my familia work it. It has many steers, so many I cannot even tell you how many they own."

"Well, if your familia has so much, then it might be best for you to work with them. Do you not think so, Chico?"

"As I said, I want to make my own life here in this beautiful place. My familia thought I was loco for wanting to come here without knowing anyone. But I do not mind. I want to do things my way. If I stayed there with my father, I would have to do things his way; and his way is not my way. Do you understand Lydia?" Chico asked, reaching for her hand.

Lydia felt his hand touch hers. She did not resist. She felt close to Chico when he touched her; she never wanted that moment to stop. Here she was, learning about someone she was rapidly falling in love with, and now he was showing he felt the same way as she did.

Thoughts were roaring through her mind, "I wish Chico would hold me in his muscular arms right now."

Chico's eyes looked into hers, and he thought, "Am I doing something I should not do? Am I moving too fast for this young and beautiful angel? All I want now is to feel her lips press against mine."

"Lydia! Chico!" Rosa yelled as she ran down the trail.

Lydia stood up, "What is it, Rosa? What is wrong?"

"Ay, Dios (Oh God)! You scared me. I was walking with both of you. I thought you were right behind me. The next thing I knew, you were both gone! What will I tell the doctor if something happens? I am supposed to be watching you and taking care of you. I am a bad chaperon, leaving you both here all by yourselves. Anything could have happened!" Rosa exclaimed, trying to hold back tears.

"It is all right, Rosa. Nothing happened. You found us, and we are fine! We were just talking; that is all! Come on; let's walk the rest of the way up," Lydia said, putting her arm around Rosa.

Chico thought to himself that it was a good thing Rosa came back when she did. He could have gone too far and kissed Lydia; this could have been disastrous for their relationship.

As they reached the top of the old volcano, they all stopped. Chico wanted to hold Lydia's hand again but thought it would be a bad idea. "There will be many more opportunities in the future," he thought.

From their vantage point at the Calvario, they could see 50 to 60 kilometers away, a beautiful scene. Everything on the jungle floor was a gorgeous green. Adding to the beauty were the rolling, small hills. In the distance one could see a lone, thick, black cloud with rays of lightning flashing under it. Chico realized he had never seen such a beautiful setting in all his life.

"Look," said Chico, pointing out past the town a few kilometers away. "That is where I want to build my home and have my rancho, away from the pueblo but not too far to come up for supplies."

"You want to build your rancho here in San Bartolomé de los Llanos?" Lydia asked, anticipating a pleasant feeling if Chico's answer was yes. She felt a joy in her heart that Chico had plans of owning his own rancho and not just being a ranch hand.

"Yes."

"You want to buy your own rancho, Chico?" Lydia asked excitedly, wanting confirmation of what she had just heard.

"Yes, someday. Soon. As soon as I can. I will work hard, and I will have the money to start."

"And where are you going to get the money, Chico?" Rosa interrupted, thinking he was just talking as many other boys usually did.

"I save all the money I earn. I nearly have enough to buy a small place right now and could make a deal to buy a few steers if I wanted, Rosa. But I am not quite ready, just a little while longer," Chico said, now looking at Lydia as if he were going to buy it for her.

Lydia did not say anything for a while. She just gazed down and looked at her future home.

Rosa looked at Lydia and knew something pretty serious was occurring.

For the next half hour, they talked about small things, pointing things out they could see from where they stood.

They arrived back at Lydia and Rosa's street. Chico and Lydia did not want the evening to end. They both wished they could stay together from this point forward.

When they were five houses from Lydia's home, which was the closest to them, Rosa took off running, "¡Hasta luego, Lydia y Chico! I will see you tomorrow!"

"Wait, Rosa! What is your hurry? Come back here!" Lydia yelled out, wanting Rosa to stop. She wanted for Rosa to walk her home, so the doctor and Lupe would see a chaperon had been with them the entire time they were at the Calvario.

"She must have been in a hurry to get home," Chico said as he slowed his pace.

"Yes, she must have been," Lydia answered as she stopped and faced Chico, not wanting to return home just yet.

"Lydia, I want to tell you. In all my life I have never enjoyed an evening like this one. And I... I... I want us to see each other all the time," Chico said as he tried to put his feelings into words. He continued, "I feel something very special for you. I feel as if I have known you all my life and have been waiting to meet you for the longest time."

"Ay, Chico," Lydia replied as she reached for his hand. "I know exactly how you feel. I feel the same," Lydia said, surprising herself. She would have never imagined she would tell a boy, let alone a man, something like this.

"May I come and visit you tomorrow?" Chico asked, looking deep into her eyes.

"Ay, Chico. I would find pleasure in that."

"But for now let me take you home, so the doctor does not get upset that I brought you back too late," he said as they both turned and started their walk toward her house.

They stopped at the front door, "Hasta mañana, Lydia. I had such a nice evening."

Just as Lydia was going to return the compliment, Lupe came to the door.

"Lydia! Where is your chaperon? You were going to have one! And you, señor! What are you doing with our little girl without a chaperon? Do you not have any manners?" Señora Gonzales vented, not wanting an answer.

"But Doña Gonzales," Chico replied, trying to explain they did have a chaperon.

"Do not 'but' me, señor! There is no excuse for this!"

Just as Lydia was going to speak up and clarify her questions, the doctor approached behind his wife.

"What is going on here? Why are you talking to my wife like this? Why are you bringing back our Lydia so late?"

Chico wanted to answer, if he were only given a chance; but as soon as he tried to open his mouth, the doctor continued, "Lydia, get into the house right now!"

Lydia, now crying, did not know what to say or do. The short time she knew Chico, she felt as if she wanted to be loyal to him more than to the doctor.

"Lydia! I said get in here right now!" the doctor repeated.

Lydia looked at Chico in an apologetic way as if the whole affair were her fault.

"It is all right, Lydia. Do as the doctor said," Chico stated, trying to make it easier on her.

She wanted to take Chico into her arms right there on the spot, not caring about the doctor or Señora Gonzales' statements.

Lydia stepped into the house. The doctor and Señora Gonzales also stepped inside and closed the door.

That night Chico lay on his bed and wondered what went wrong with his first contact with his true love. He had his mind made up that he was not going to stop seeing Lydia. He did not care if the doctor and his wife disapproved.

Chico thought it over and decided what he was going to do. First, he would try to talk to the doctor and his wife, if they were willing to speak to him. He wanted to do things right.

He thought to himself, "The doctor should listen since he should be a reasonable man and since he is well educated. Doña Gonzales, well, that is another matter. The way she jumped all over me right away, without knowing the situation, was something else. I will have to get around her if I speak to the doctor. What I will do is go see the doctor as if I were sick and speak to him then. This way the señora will not bother us as we speak. And if the doctor refuses to see things my way, if he is not a reasonable man, then I will have to do things behind his back. Ay, ay, ay," Chico rolled over on his bed sighing. "I sure hope this does not turn into a big mess."

Chico's thoughts started to fade. Before he went to sleep, he saw Lydia smile at him.

CHICO

T he next day after Chico finished working for his employer, he went home and cleaned up, changing his clothes. He was on his way to see the doctor. Throughout the entire day he could not think of anything but Lydia and what happened the previous night. He knew what he was going to say and how he was going to express it. "Now if it only works," he thought.

Halfway up from Lydia's street, there was a marketplace where people sold their produce, staples, and meats in small booths or on tables. As Chico approached the street, he saw townspeople walking about and taking care of their business, buying their food for their evening meal. Chico stopped halfway down the street to see if Lydia was anywhere in sight. He did not see her or Señora Gonzales. He continued his walk, keeping his eyes on the lookout for Señora Gonzales, not wanting to be caught by her again. He stepped up to the doctor's opened door and looked inside. He was expecting to see a girl working behind a small desk that was at one end of the room.

"Doctor?" Chico called out not too loudly. He did not want his voice to reach the house.

"Doctor, are you here?" Chico called out again. He was now a few steps into the office.

"Yes, I will be with you in just one minute," the doctor called out from the other room. "Have a seat."

Chico looked around the room. There were two chairs against the wall next to the door.

Chico was the type of person who was not afraid of anything. As he was growing up, he was taught to never look for trouble. "However," his father would say, "if trouble comes your way, defend yourself." He could remember many times when he was in situations where he could have lost his life. Chico never backed out of a fight. He sat in the chair wondering why he was now so scared. He was so frightened that his stomach hurt. The palms of his hands were perspiring, and he was biting down on his teeth. He felt as if he wanted to get up and run away.

"I will be all right. I will just talk to the doctor like a man, as I planned, and tell him how it is going to be," he thought.

Chico looked up. He thought he heard Lydia's voice coming from the main house. He was so nervous that he stood up, anticipating Lydia would walk in and see him in the doctor's office.

"Yes, what can I do for you?" the doctor asked as he walked in from the other room. He looked downward as he wiped his hands with a cloth. He had not looked up yet.

"Doctor, I want to talk to you about Lydia and me," Chico said, trying to sound as if he was not afraid of the doctor.

The doctor looked up, after rubbing his hands with the cloth, and said, "Oh, it is you!" Dr. Gonzales looked at Chico and frowned. "What do you want, señor? Are you sick?" he asked as if he were going to throw Chico out if he were not.

"No, Doctor. As I said, I wanted to speak to you about Lydia and me."

Before Chico could get anything else out, the doctor interrupted. "You want to talk to me about Lydia and you? What do you mean Lydia and you? What do you have to do with Lydia, señor?" the doctor vented angrily.

"Doctor, I want to continue to see Lydia with your permission. I know she wants to have your blessing for our relationship," Chico explained, trying to be persuasive.

"Your relationship? What relationship? You do not have any relationship with Lydia! You take Lydia without a chaperon, and you want my blessing? And what is an older man like you doing wanting to see a young girl like Lydia? I do not know if that is what your familia taught you, but around here it is inexcusable! We will not allow it!" the doctor replied, raising his voice.

"Doctor, you need not bring my familia into this. And as far as last evening, we did have a chaperon. Rosa went home as soon as we approached your door. She was with us the whole time we were gone," Chico explained, feeling good about himself, finally telling Dr. Gonzales what really happened the evening before. Chico noticed his nervousness was gone. "And what is more, Doctor, I will see Lydia if you want me to or not; but I would prefer to have your and Doña Gonzales' blessing."

"You will see Lydia only if I want you to! Go! Go! Get out of here! You are not to come back to my house again, and I will forbid Lydia from seeing you!"

Chico stood there listening to the doctor. This is not what he had planned. He wanted him to see things his way.

"Doctor, may we talk?" Chico asked, trying to get him to calm down.

"Talk? We did our talking! Now, out!" he demanded, raising his voice. He took a few steps and forced Chico to walk backwards toward the door.

Chico raised his hands to waist level and with his palms facing up said, "Doctor, be reasonable. All I want is to see Lydia. And I want to get to know you and your wife. That is all," Chico declared, trying to be mild and persuasive.

Chico was now stepping backwards as he moved out of the office with the doctor right in front of him. The doctor's finger was pointing in Chico's chest. He continued, "How dare you come to my office and tell me what you are going to do with my Lydia. No one talks to me like that in this pueblo (town)! Now go! Get out of here!"

The doctor went back into his office. Chico stood by the front door and waited for a few seconds, wondering what was going to be his next move. Chico turned and started to walk back up the street in the direction he came. He walked slowly down the street. When he was a half block down, he went to the side of the street and stood against a building. He stood there in deep thought, wondering what went wrong.

"Did I come on too strong for the old man? Should I go back and apologize to him? No matter what, I am not going to stop seeing Lydia," he thought.

There was much activity around him. People were coming and going. He turned his head as he saw people pass him. Some were walking around the corner on the next street. Upon seeing Lydia walking around the corner carrying a sack, he stood up straight. Chico took a few steps to intercept her. Lydia's eyes caught his, and she felt her heart move. She picked up her pace to approach him.

"Hola, Chico," Lydia greeted in a warm voice as she came to a stop and put her sack down. She felt as if she wanted to embrace him; but that was out of the question, since she really did not know Chico as well as she should. Besides, there were a lot of people present. What would they say?

"Lydia, how are you?" he inquired as he raised his hand and gently moved her hair from the front of her shoulder to the back.

"Chico, I am so sorry about last night. Rosa should have stayed with us. I talked to Rosa this morning, and she said she was going to talk to Lupe and tell her she was with us the whole time we were together," Lydia said sadly.

"Oh, I think it is too late for that. I tried to talk to the doctor. Things did not turn out the way they should have. He was very upset with me."

"When did this happen?"

"Right now. I just left there. He forbids me from seeing you. He said he never wanted me in his house again."

Lydia's eyes started to tear up, and she put her head down. She wanted things to turn out well for them.

"Ay, Lydia, do not cry," Chico said, feeling bad for her, knowing how she felt, and knowing he felt the same. He had the urge to cry, but his father always told him and his brothers that men do not show their emotion. It would show their weakness. His father taught him and his brothers that it is all right when a woman cries. God made woman with a lot of tears; but if a man loses his, it takes away his strength.

Chico wanted to take Lydia into his arms and give her a hug. Instead he reached for her hand and said, "Can you go for a walk with me, Lydia; so we can talk?"

Lydia did not say anything. She nodded her head affirmatively. Picking up her sack and turning with him, Lydia walked with Chico in the direction she came from, both not saying much of anything for awhile. They came to the small clearing where the people met in the Town Square. The Town Square was a small park. People gathered there to chat, and they brought their children to play. As they approached the square, some of the people looked at Lydia and Chico, wondering what relationship existed between them. In a small town like San Bartolomé de los Llanos, all the people knew one another, especially the doctor's family. As people passed by, they greeted Lydia, "Hola, Lydia." Every so often someone would stop and ask for Señora Gonzales and the doctor. "How are they? Tell them hola for us."

They sat on a bench. "Lydia," Chico said. He took her hand and knew people would see this and wonder why he was holding her hand. Lydia and Chico both did not care what people thought at this point. Chico continued, "I know we just met, but I feel more for you than I have ever felt for anyone else."

Lydia's eyes looked into his. She felt a great joy inside of her heart. Chico went on, "I want to see you no matter what the doctor said. I know you love the doctor and his wife. I know you have the proper respect for them. So I think we should give it some time to try to get them to change their thinking about me. I do not know why they feel this way. I noticed it when I went to your house and Doña Gonzales looked at me. I knew she disapproved of me from the start."

"I sense they believe you are much too old for me," Lydia stated. Her tears were now gone, and she had regained her composure. "I am sixteen years old. How old are you, Chico?"

"I am twenty-six years old. Yes, I think that is the reason too. But is not the doctor much older than Doña Gonzales?" Chico asked, looking puzzled.

"The doctor is forty-eight, and Lupe is forty-two. The doctor looks much older, I know. Everybody thinks he married a child. It is just that Lupe looks young for her age."

"Well, that is a six-year difference."

Lydia smiled and said, "Yes, that is true. Do you want me to talk to Lupe, Chico? I will do whatever you request. I have to say that I feel the same as you do."

"What will you do if the doctor prohibits you from seeing me, Lydia," Chico asked, gripping her hand a little tighter. He hoped he would hear the answer he wanted.

"I will listen to him. I will not tell him I will not see you anymore. I will just listen," Lydia said in a matter-of-fact way.

Chico felt a wonderful feeling inside. Now he knew in fact that this was his true love, and he knew she felt the same as he did. Chico and Lydia stayed in the square for another hour talking and telling each other stories about one another, things they experienced throughout their lives.

"Lydia, Lydia!" someone called from a distance.

Chico and Lydia turned when they heard the call. It was Rosa, walking hurriedly towards them.

"Lydia, ay, ay, ay Lydia, what are you doing? Do you know that

Doña Gonzales is looking for you?" Rosa turned and said to Chico, "Hola, Chico, how are you today?"

"Fine, Rosa," Chico replied in a low voice as he smiled.

Rosa's eyes glanced down; she saw they were holding hands. She knew this must be a serious relationship for them to be holding hands in public.

"Doña Gonzales came to my house and asked if you were there. You were supposed to be back with the frijoles (beans) an hour ago. She wanted to start cooking them, and you have not returned."

"How did you know I was here, Rosa?" Lydia questioned.

"Everybody knows you are here. I do not know why Doña Gonzales does not know. Everybody in the street is talking about you and the young man who is your boyfriend. Does the doctor know Chico is your boyfriend, Lydia?" Rosa wanted to know, thinking it was really odd the doctor approved of this.

"Yes, he knows Rosa; and he does not like it. As I told you this morning, he thinks that when we went to the Calvario last evening we did not have a chaperon," Lydia answered, not intending to make Rosa feel bad.

"Ay, I am sorry, Lydia. I did not even think about that. I just wanted to leave you and Chico alone, thinking it was all right because you were on our street and almost at your house. I am really sorry. I feel really bad."

"Oh, do not worry about it, Rosa. It is not your fault. I think Miguel and Lupe already did not like Chico because they think he is much too old for me."

"And what is wrong with that? Is not the doctor much too old for Doña Lupe?" Rosa asked in a sassy way.

Lydia did not answer the question but said, "Well, I better get back before the doctor gets his friends to come after you and me, Chico."

"All right," Rosa said as she turned and started home. "I will see you later. Be careful, Lydia. I hope everything goes well for you."

"Well, Chico, I better get these frijoles back to Lupe before she sends an army out to get me. She probably knows I am with you by now, especially if she knows you talked to Miguel."

"Lydia, can we meet here tomorrow at the same time?" Chico asked, looking deep into Lydia's eyes.

"Yes, Chico," she answered, knowing how things could change at home. She continued, "But if something were to happen, then I will meet you here the next day. If something were to happen then, you could look for me on the following day after that. Who knows what could happen," Lydia responded, not wanting Chico to give up on her.

"That will be fine, Lydia. I will be thinking about you every minute until the next time I see you," Chico said as his fingers combed her light-colored hair back over her shoulder. "I will walk you to the corner at least."

Both of them stood and started their walk, not saying a word. Once they reached the corner, they turned to face each other. Chico thought he was in love with this princess, and he had not kissed her yet. He knew that was out of the question, to do such a thing in public; but he thought it was a good idea anyway.

"Adios, Chico, I hope I will see you tomorrow," Lydia said with her sad, blue eyes, thinking she would not see Chico until the next day.

"Lydia, I will be here tomorrow, the next day, the day after that, and forever, if that is what it takes!" Chico exclaimed with a tone of determination.

CHAPTER THREE

THE RANCH HAND

“**L**ydia! Where have you been?” Lupe demanded an answer.

“I was bringing the frijoles as you asked, Lupe. Why?” Lydia questioned, as if it was not a big deal.

“I want to ask you a question, Lydia; and I want you to answer the truth to me muchacha (girl). Were you with the ranch hand?” Lupe asked, looking at her straight in the eye.

Lydia did not like the way Lupe posed her question. She did not feel it was a bad thing for a man to be a ranch hand. “Lupe wants me to marry a man who comes from a special familia,” she thought.

“What ranch hand, Lupe?” Lydia asked in a smart tone.

“What do you mean what ranch hand? You know what ranch hand I am talking about. Francisco!” Lupe vented, raising her voice.

“¿Qué pasa aquí (what's happening here)?” the doctor asked, as he walked into the front room where they were talking.

“Miguel, I told you this muchacha was with that ranch hand! Miguel, what are you going to do about this?”

Lydia stood there with the saddest expression on her face, worrying that the family was really going to give her a difficult time.

“Ay, Lydia, come in here and sit down with me for a few minutes,” the doctor said, pointing to the parlor where they had a few chairs for use when guests arrived. “Mujer (Woman),” the doctor said, speaking to his wife, “Why don't you go and start the frijoles while Lydia and I speak.”

Señora Gonzales knew the doctor always had a way with Lydia, even when she was a baby. She would cry for attention, and Señora Gonzales did not know how to give the baby love as she did her own children. The doctor would wake in the middle of the night to hold baby Lydia. He would rock her back and forth to sleep. As a young girl when

Lydia was growing up, she always found pleasure in being with the doctor. As far as she could remember, there was always a wedge between her and Lupe. Lydia never could put her finger on the reason for it. She thought maybe Lupe was jealous for her own children. However, the doctor treated his own children just as well, if not better.

"All right, Miguel, but you talk some sense into this muchacha," Señora Gonzales said as she walked toward the kitchen.

With his arm around Lydia, the doctor took a few steps into the parlor. Both of them sat across from each other. They did not say anything for the first few seconds. The doctor put his elbow on his knee, placed his finger on his lip, and took a deep breath, wondering how he was going to tell Lydia that she was not allowed to see the disrespectful ranch hand anymore.

"Lydia, Señor Rodriguez is not a good person for you. You are a young girl, and you have a lot to learn. I do not want you to see this young man anymore."

"Oh, Miguel, Francisco is a fine man. He did not do anything wrong; and, what is more, his familia is very wealthy," Lydia said, trying to focus the doctor's attention on Francisco's wealth.

"Wealthy? What do you mean wealthy? I thought he was a ranch hand," the doctor asked, reconsidering what he had said.

"Yes, his familia owns one of the biggest ranchos in the state of Sonora. He came here to look at the land and to work it. He is doing this because his familia wants to invest here in San Bartolomé de los Llanos," Lydia said, trying to sound convincing. She knew what she told the doctor was not exactly the truth, but she had to do something to convince him Chico was all right.

The doctor sat in the chair in deep thought for a minute and then said, "Is that right? Well, I need to check into this. But in the meantime, I do not want you to see him until I give you permission," the doctor stated, knowing that with his connections it was not going to take him long to find out. All he really needed to do was ask his friend, the governor, to find the information for him. The governor would have his people look into it.

Lydia was silent, since the doctor was in deep meditation. The doctor looked up at Lydia, realizing she did not respond to his demand, "Do you understand, Lydia?"

"Do I understand what, Miguel?" she asked, trying to avoid the question.

"Do you understand I do not want you to see the young man Francisco until I say you can?" the doctor asked again, this time wanting an answer right away.

Lydia thought about what she told Chico with regard to listening to the doctor but not going along with him. She was feeling better, since the doctor sounded a little promising and because he was going to check out Chico.

"Yes, I do understand what you are asking, sir."

"All right, I trust that you will obey me and do as I wish."

Lydia thought to herself, "I did not say I would do it. I said I understood you."

"Now go and help Lupe in the kitchen!" the doctor exclaimed, getting up from his chair. He thought of the people waiting in his office, "No end to it, we need another doctor in this pueblo!"

As soon as Lydia stepped into the kitchen, Señora Gonzales started, "I hope Miguel talked some sense into you, Lydia. Do you know how much work it has been taking care of you all these years? It was not easy, you know. Start cleaning the frijoles on the table," she insisted, pointing to the table and continuing to speak. "To have you here in this house took a lot of extra work. We really did not want to do this, but we felt sorry for you when your father brought you here. And now you want to waste everything and see a ranch hand!"

"What if you were to marry a ranch hand? Do you know what it would mean? Do you understand what it is like being a ranch hand's wife? All day you will be making tortillas for other people, washing other people's clothes as a service, trying to make ends meet. And your husband will always be gone. By the time he gets home, it will be too late to talk to him. Then he will have to get up early in the morning and be gone again. And forget about the weekends. Forget about going to the iglesia (church) with him. The animals on the rancho do not take the weekends off so the ranch hands can go to the iglesia with their families. Yes, Lydia, you will be worse off than a widow!" Señora Gonzales kept right on talking, and Lydia did not say a word. She just did her work and listened.

As Lupe was talking, Lydia did have her own thoughts. She thought about her money, the money she was supposed to receive when she became of age. She wondered if Lupe was planning on keeping it. If

Lydia did receive it, then she did not have to worry about anything Lupe was saying. She thought to herself, "With the money I will take care of my true love."

The next day Lydia asked Lupe if she wanted her to run some errands. It was getting close to six o'clock, and she knew Chico would be waiting for her at the corner.

"No, Lydia, the doctor does not want you going anywhere today. He wants you to stay home."

"Stay home? Why? Now I cannot go to the market or go to my friend Rosa's house? I do not understand!"

"You do not have to understand. You just have to do as you are told!" Lupe declared harshly.

Lydia was upset. She knew she could not fight about it. Once the doctor said something, Lupe was not going to change it. Lydia stepped to the front door and looked to see if she could see Chico from where she was standing.

"No sight of him yet," she thought. If she could only see him, she felt it would make her happy.

"Lydia! Come here! I want you to help me prepare supper. And I do not want you by the door!"

"What is wrong, Lupe? Why are you acting this way with me? What did I do wrong?" Lydia asked, trying to hold back her tears. She was hurt that Lupe and the doctor were treating her badly.

"Maybe it is because they do not love me, since I am not their real daughter," she thought.

Six o'clock came and went, and she was not able to see Chico on that day.

Chico went home feeling ill late in the evening, not being able to see the girl of his dreams.

He thought, "Maybe tomorrow I will be able to talk to her or see her."

On the second day it was the same for Chico. He went home wondering what the problem was. He thought the doctor was making an extra effort to stop Lydia from seeing him.

On the third day Chico arrived home to clean up. He was in a hurry to get to Lydia's street. As soon as his employer told him he could leave, Chico left in a hurry. His job at the rancho consisted of maintaining the food stock for all the steers. It did not require that he stay late into the evening as the other hands who were on the range minding the steers. All he could think about all day was Lydia, hoping he would be able to see her on the street. He prepared himself just in case she was not there again. He knew he was not going to give up and would be waiting for her every day, no matter how long it took. If her family thought she was too young for Chico, he was willing to wait a few years until she got older. He knew it would not be a problem because of the way he felt about her.

Chico was out of the door in no time. It was now 6:30 in the evening. If he were going to be there at the same time they met on the first day, he would need to be there within half an hour. That would be no problem. He would be there early, just in case she was there prematurely waiting for him.

As he came out of his door, he saw two policemen. The policemen were part of the federal government. Their uniforms were khaki in color and lightweight with short sleeves because of the hot and humid weather.

"Señor Rodriguez?" one of the police called.

Chico was in a hurry and really did not want to talk to them. He had never had any run-ins with the law. Back home his family owned the police in the area. They took care of them with mordidas (bribes). His grandfather learned many years ago that you get the law on your side with the mordida. It was a common thing in México. Only those who could afford the law were able to make it work for them.

"Yes, I am Señor Rodriguez," Chico answered in a tone as if he were saying, "Make it fast; I'm in a hurry."

"You need to come with us. We would like to ask you some questions," the taller police officer demanded.

Chico thought, "Now what? Of all the days these huevones (eggheads) want to talk to me, they pick one of the most important days in my life."

"What is this about? I am in a hurry."

"You will have to come with us, señor," the shorter police officer insisted, sounding irritated.

Chico knew he did not do anything wrong in this area nor in any other place. All he did was work, go to his new friend's home, drink a little beer, and play cards.

"I am sorry, señores; but I really cannot go with you right now. I will come and see you in a little while. I need to take care of some important business first. Where would you like me to meet you in about one or two hours?" Chico asked, hoping the police would agree with him.

"No, señor, we have orders from the chief director who is waiting at the police station. He came from San Cristóbal de Las Casas to speak to you. He has some important questions to ask you."

Chico thought, "Important questions to ask me? About what? I do not know anyone around here to respond with any important answers."

Chico now took a few steps towards them, "What kind of questions does he want to ask me? What is this about? May I ask?" Chico now lightened up, since the chief director was the one who came from a long distance to speak to him. Chico knew he was an important man. "Whatever it was about, it must be very important for this man to take his time and come here to this small pueblo to speak to me. And sending these two polecias to get me shows this is not a social call," Chico reasoned.

The thought of Lydia waiting on the corner went through his mind, but he had no control over the situation.

"All right, let us see what the director has to ask," Chico said to both of the policemen.

As Chico walked with the police, one on each side of him, the town's people turned and looked, as if he were a criminal caught by the law. Chico did not like the feeling.

As he entered the station, which consisted of a small room in one of the buildings, he saw the director sitting on a chair behind an old table that was supposed to be a desk. He was not doing anything, just waiting for Chico to arrive. Chico did not say anything, still annoyed that they took him away from his appointment with Lydia.

"Señor Rodriguez, have a seat," an older, heavy, bald man said, as if he was an old friend. "My name is Señor Chávez, the Chief Director of Public Affairs here in the state of Chiapas."

"Yes, Señor Chávez, I know who you are. I would like to know why I was brought here and not given a choice. Have I done anything to disturb the peace?" Chico asked in a demanding way.

"Oh, by all means, no, señor. What gives you that idea? Did my polecia tell you that you did something wrong? Have they mishandled you in anyway? Because if they did, I will get them in here right now and have them apologize to you, Señor Rodriguez." The director stood up as if he were going to go outside to call the two policemen and bring them inside.

"No, they did not tell me I did anything wrong; and they did not mishandle me. They said you wanted to ask me some questions; that is all," Chico replied, not wanting to make a bigger issue than it already was.

Chico thought, "The chief director will be gone tomorrow, and I will have to live with the polecia once he leaves."

"What is it that I can answer for you, Señor Chávez?"

"Yes," he said, sitting back down in his chair. "Well, there is a rumor that your familia in the state of Sonora is looking to buy land here and build a rancho in Chiapas." The director stopped speaking, wanting Chico to pick up the conversation and tell him what he wanted to know.

Chico's mind went into first gear, thinking, "Why is he asking me this? What gives him the idea my familia is looking into property here in San Bartolomé de los Llanos? The only ones that I ever told in the last two months were Lydia and Rosa. I told them I wanted to buy my rancho here. Now the chief director is asking me if it is true. The story is changed a little by putting my familia into it."

"May I ask, señor, of what concern it is to the state if my familia is looking into buying a rancho here?" Chico asked, not wanting to give too much away. Chico continued, "Where did you hear this rumor, Señor Chávez?"

The director did not like being asked questions. He felt he should be the one asking, not the young hired hand. He wished the governor had not asked him to come to this small town to try to find out information from this young man. The director knew he owed the governor a lot of favors; however, it bothered him to ask this young man questions just for the sake of finding out something that did not matter either way.

"If your familia wants to buy land here," he picked up his hand and pointed down, "they have to come to our office in San Cristóbal de Las Casas, you know. Now if it is only a little acreage, that is another matter. However, if it is an enormous portion of land, we will want to make sure your familia is doing things right when they come to the state of Chiapas," the chief director explained, not really telling the truth. Señor Chávez knew the state welcomed any business and money from other parts of México, even if things were not done right. It would mean more wealth for him and more for the people who lived in his state. The director was trying to sound convincing.

Chico thought as Señor Chávez spoke, "Liar. The government does not get involved when one is going to purchase land, especially if the familia is already known in other parts of México. There has to be another reason for this meeting."

The meeting continued, and the director kept asking Chico questions. Where was he planning to buy land? Why was he working as a hired hand if he was going to buy a lot of land? When was his family coming to look over the land he had scouted out, and from whom did he want to buy the land? Chico was very careful how he answered the questions. He had no idea why the director was conducting this investigation.

Chico thought, "There is no law that says a man cannot buy land in the state of Chiapas or in any other state for that matter. And besides, there is no law that states a man cannot come to a state and prospect for land and, as he is prospecting, work for a living."

Finally, after an hour the director stood up and said, "All right, Señor Rodriguez, you may go. You can relay a message to your familia. They are welcome here, and I look forward to meeting them." The director extended his hand to shake Chico's.

He stood up with the director and put his hand out, still wondering why they had the meeting. "Thank you, señor, for your time. It was a pleasure meeting you," Chico responded, thinking he should be on good terms with this elderly and rich man. "Who knows," he thought, "I might need his services in the future." Chico wanted to keep things right with the director.

"If your familia needs anything and they want to contact me, come to San Cristóbal de Las Casas. I will see if I can help."

Chico was walking towards the door with the old man behind him. "Thank you, señor, I will. When I buy my rancho, if I have any problems, I will call on you."

"Oh, so you are buying a rancho here?" the director asked, surprised, finally getting a confirmation from the young man.

Chico wanted to kick himself. He did not know why this man was asking all the questions, but there was a reason for it. "In time, señor, if my father decides not to, I more than likely will," Chico said as he continued walking out the door, trying to get away before the director continued his probe.

"When will that be, señor?" the director called out as Chico began walking down the street.

"In time, Señor Chávez. In time."

As Chico walked away, he thought of Lydia waiting for him. He looked up at the sky and realized it was about 7:30. "Too late to see Lydia. I will just walk by her street. I just might catch a glimpse of her."

When Chico arrived on Lydia's street, it was still busy with activity, people coming and going. The street seemed to be one of the busiest in the small town.

"That looks like Lydia," Chico thought, as he saw three girls talking on the porch of one of the houses on the street.

As he approached, he knew it was she. Just then Lydia turned, as she had been doing the last hour, hoping Chico would come around the corner. Their eyes met. Chico stopped his walk as he focused his eyes down the street, a few houses from where Lydia was standing. He thought it best not to walk to where she was. He did not want Señora Gonzales to walk out of her house or appear from down the street. Chico motioned with his head and a hand motion for Lydia to follow him. He turned and walked back in the direction he had just left. Now, after everything that happened, Chico knew he had to be more discreet than he was in the past. He knew if he was not, it could mean not being able to see Lydia for a long time. He knew the doctor meant business when he said he did not want him to see Lydia.

When Chico arrived at the Town Square, he walked past it and down another quiet street. Chico turned a few times to make sure Lydia was following him. At the next corner he turned and stopped. It was a poorer neighborhood. He could hear a man and a woman arguing. In a distance he could hear a baby crying. Chico stood against the wall of the building waiting for Lydia. As she came around the corner, she stood right in front of Chico. Chico could not resist the temptation. He put his arms around her and held her for a few seconds. Lydia did not know what to do. She had never been held like this by anyone before, not even the doctor or Lupe. In those few seconds she felt a bond with Chico that she had never felt for anyone else. She did not want him to release her.

Chico released her and stood back a few inches, "Lydia, it seems like a lifetime that I have not seen you."

"Yes, the doctor and Lupe have been keeping me in the house. Just as you said he told you, he instructed me also, forbidding me from seeing you, Chico. Ay, Chico, I don't know why they feel this way. What are we going to do?"

"Is there somewhere we could meet without anybody knowing, Lydia? I would like to see you without the doctor and Doña Gonzales knowing; but I would like to have a chaperon with us when we do, for our protection," Chico answered. He thought about Lydia's father, the priest, and what he had experienced. He did not want Lydia to go through the same thing.

"Chico, let's meet here every two days. I will ask Rosa if she will come with us. I am sure she will not mind. Rosa is a nice girl, and she likes you. She thinks you are a very nice person."

"How long can you stay with me now before they notice you are gone?" Chico asked, standing right in front of her and holding both of her hands.

"Just a little while. Lupe thinks I am in front of the house, talking with the muchachas (girls)."

"I will come back in two days. If you are not here in two days, I will be waiting for you the next day. And if you are not here that day, I will be here the following day. Until you come, I will be here waiting."

"I was expecting you to come today at 6:00. When you did not show up, I thought maybe you got tired of coming because I was not there."

"No, Lydia, I would never get tired of waiting for you. What happened to me today is that the chief director of public affairs had two policemen come and get me. They took me to the police station, and the director questioned me."

"Questioned you? About what, Chico?"

"I do not know why they took me in or why the director came all the way from San Cristóbal de Las Casas to ask a lot of questions about my familia's plans to buy a rancho. I do not know how or from where he got that information."

"Ay, Chico, I think I know why. I think it came from me."

"You? What do you mean?" Chico asked, trying to put together the questions from the director and Lydia.

"Yes, when Miguel told me I could not see you anymore, I told him you are rich and that you are here to look for land for your familia to buy a rancho. I am sorry, Chico; but I thought Miguel would let me see you because you are rich. But I guess he told his friends to check on it. Miguel has some important friends. I hope they were nice to you."

"Nothing that I could not handle, Lydia," Chico said, trying not to worry her.

They turned and walked down the quiet street. Chico went on to tell Lydia things about his childhood and places he had been. Things went well for them the next hour. When Lydia went home that evening, the doctor and Lupe did not know she was away.

Two days later Chico was at the quiet corner where he had previously met Lydia. He did not have to wait long; right on time, Lydia came with her chaperon Rosa. They spent an hour-and-a-half with one another and walked up to the Calvario. They talked and told stories, laughed, joked, and played.

CHAPTER FOUR

THE BUSYBODY

As the days went by, they continued to meet, getting to know each other better as time passed. Rosa accompanied them everywhere and enjoyed herself. She felt good, knowing she was contributing to a nice relationship. Chico and Lydia fell in love with one other. No longer was it mere infatuation. At times Rosa would walk away from them, so they could have their private conversations. They talked of what they wanted out of life and how many children they would like to have. They were both careful with respect to talking about things they should not discuss, such as marriage. They both knew the time would come when Chico would ask for Lydia's hand in a proper way. To speak of marriage now would be presumptuous.

Chico had his own horse that he kept at a stable on the edge of town. He did not take it with him when he walked through town because he enjoyed walking alone on the small, beautiful, cobblestone streets. He used his horse when he went to and from his place of employment. At times, since there were other horses at the stable, he borrowed two other horses and took Lydia and Rosa out for rides on the outskirts of town. Lydia and Rosa were getting to know areas around their small town that they never knew. The roads were lined with green foliage; and every so often they would come to an area where the foliage was cleared to make room for a growing, small rancho.

One day as they were leaving the stables, a señora and her three small children came walking down the road.

"Hola, Lydia y Rosa. What are you muchachas doing out here?" Señora Sánchez asked. She was surprised to see the girls out of their everyday surroundings with a young man whom she did not recognize. Señora Sánchez was a woman in her fifties, but she looked as if she were in her sixties. She had a face like an old, dried-up prune, from years of working in the sun and having lived a very difficult life. Her round face had a hard and worn look. The climate was warm; however, the old lady wore an old, dirty bandanna. By wearing the bandanna she would not have to comb her hair. She had a wicked sound in her voice. Her husband died a few years back and left her to take care of herself and her children, cleaning and washing for other people. She was known to be a busybody.

"We are going for a horseback ride, Doña Sánchez," Rosa answered, trying to sound as if this were a minor affair.

Señora Sánchez raised her finger at them and vented in a tone of displeasure, "Do your mothers know you are out here, muchachas?" She did not like it one bit that the young girls were out on the road with a man. To Señora Sánchez, this was not proper, especially for the town-doctor's household.

"Yes, Doña Sánchez, my mother knows I am with Rosa," Lydia answered, not lying.

"But does she know you are with a man?" Señora Sánchez asked with her hard, shrill voice.

Rosa answered this time, as Señora Sánchez was behind them now. They did not stop the horses, so they would not have to keep the conversation going, "Yes, Doña Sánchez, she knows I am with my friends."

Señora Sánchez stood still on the road as she watched them ride around a curve. Chico, Lydia, and Rosa heard her mumble something under her breath.

Lydia yelled out, "Adios, Doña Sánchez, have a nice day!"

Through the whole thing Chico did not say a word. He knew the day was coming when they would be caught, especially in such a small town as this one, where everybody knew everybody. He did not want it to happen so quickly. He knew he loved Lydia and knew he was going to spend the rest of his life with her. He did not want to rush things. He knew Lydia would marry him as soon as he asked her. He was hoping the doctor and Doña Gonzales would come around if they were given more time. He was planning on doing something nice for them to see what would happen. He just wished this vieja (old lady) would not ruin things for them.

Señora Sánchez was a lady who was very strict with her children and everybody else's. She grew up in a small home outside of town. Her father was Indian, and her mother was born in the town of San

Bartolomé de los Llanos. She was raised believing children should have absolute respect for their parents; and parents should have complete authority over their children, even when they became adults. She was going to make sure Señora Gonzales knew about this situation, even if it meant going out of her way to do it.

"If Doña Gonzales knows about this and it is all right with her, I will lose all respect for the familia," she thought.

For the first few minutes, Chico, Lydia, and Rosa did not say anything. They all wondered if Señora Sánchez was going back to town and if she was going to tell their mothers.

"What do you think, Lydia? Should we go back right now?" Rosa asked, not being very sure of herself.

"I think it will be all right. The vieja (old lady) has to go a long way to tell our mothers. If she says anything the next time she goes to the pueblo, we will have made up a story by then. Maybe we can say Chico was one of your brothers, Rosa," Lydia said.

"My brothers? My brothers are too young!"

"That is all right. We can say the vieja (old lady) cannot tell if she really saw a man or a boy who looks like a man," Lydia stated.

"What do you think, Chico?" Rosa questioned. "You have not said anything."

"Well, what if the vieja goes straight to your and Lydia's houses. Then what? What do you think your familia and Lydia's familia will say?" Chico questioned, trying to make them think about turning around and going back.

Lydia looked at Chico, wanting to do whatever he suggested. "What are you saying, Chico? Do you think we should go back?"

"Yes, there will be other days we will be able to go for our rides. If we go now and the vieja goes and tells everybody she saw us, when we get back, there will be nothing but trouble waiting for us."

They all stopped their horses. Lydia looked at Rosa with an expression as if she were saying, "We should go back."

Rosa did not say anything but turned her horse around. She felt a knot in her stomach, thinking of her father waiting for her, knowing she lied to him when she said she was going to be in the Town Square.

Chico felt that if he took the horses back first and then took the girls home later, it might be too late. The vieja would have already gone and told their families. "I will take you to the town's edge first. You can walk the rest of the way home, and then I will return the horses. That will save time. You can get back before the vieja arrives."

"Ay, Chico, do not worry. I think it will be all right. We will all take the horses back, and then we will all walk up to the pueblo," Lydia declared, wanting to stay with Chico as long as she could.

They arrived at the stable in a short time. Pablo, the Indian who worked there, looked up and saw them approach, "¿Qué pasa (What happened), Señor Chico? You did not like the horses? Is there something wrong with them?"

"No, we decided not to go for a ride today, Pablo."

Pablo took the horses by the reins and led them off to the corral. Chico and the girls hurried off towards the town.

Now that they had brought back the horses, it would take forty minutes longer to get to town. It gave Señora Sánchez that much of a head start.

Chico thought, "I should not have let Lydia talk me into returning the horses to the stables. I have a feeling the vieja is up to no good."

Since the pueblo of San Bartolomé de los Llanos was located on a bluff, the road had a few curves. As they were climbing the winding road, they wondered if the old woman went straight to their homes. If she did, then all the families knew who the girls were with and were probably waiting for them.

As Lydia thought about this, she felt her stomach begin to knot. She wondered what she would do if the doctor really put his foot down. He might even send her away to live elsewhere, just to keep Chico and her apart. It was a customary thing to do when such a thing happened to a girl. Rosa's thoughts were also racing, but she knew her parents were not as strict as Lydia's. As they approached the street where Lydia lived, they stopped. Chico wanted to say good-bye to the girls, not knowing if the vieja had told the families that she saw them.

"I think everything will be all right, Lydia," Chico said.

They continued to walk at a slow pace toward Lydia's and Rose's houses. They turned to face each other; Chico looked into Lydia's eyes. He knew by the way Lydia gazed into his eyes that she was in love with him.

There were people all around them, as was typical on that street. It was always crowded.

"Will I see you in two days, Chico?" Lydia asked, gazing at him with her beautiful, blue, sad eyes.

Just as Chico was going to answer, he heard some commotion coming from the direction of Lydia's and Rosa's houses. They all turned their heads in that direction and saw a mob of people walking hurriedly towards them. The principal person who looked as if he were taking the lead was the doctor. The doctor had a large stick or club in his hand. There were other men behind him, also carrying large sticks that looked comparable to bats. Behind them were a few women, including Señora Gonzales and Señora Sánchez. Chico did not know if Rosa's family was in among them, since he had never met them.

"Ay, ay, ay, Chico!" Lydia said in anguish. She continued raising her voice, "Run! Run, Chico! Get out of here, fast!"

Chico stood still, knowing he was outnumbered. "What am I going to do?" he asked himself.

He looked around to see what he could pick up to defend himself, but nothing was in sight. The mob would reach him in a matter of a few seconds. He knew he could not run like a coward. If he ran, he would not be able to live with himself. His father would never approve of his running, no mater how dangerous it was.

"And what is more," he thought, "I will never leave Lydia and Rosa to deal with this all by themselves."

He wondered what the vieja had told them. "She probably told them something that was not true," he thought as his mind continued racing.

"Chico, please run! Get out of here! Please run! I will see you tomorrow! Oh, please, Chico! They will kill you! If you stay here, they will kill you!" Lydia pleaded as she grabbed Chico's shoulder with both hands. Lydia continued, "Then what, Chico? Then what will we do if they kill you?" Lydia was now crying in hysteria. "Please, Chico, go! I'm begging you!"

Once Lydia saw Chico was not going to run, she ran towards the mob. Putting her arms up, waving, and trying to get their attention, Lydia yelled, "Miguel! Stop! Please do not hurt him! I love him! Please!"

They walked right past her. Someone stretched an arm out, pushed her to the side, and knocked her to the ground. Lydia was now on her hands and knees watching everybody trample past her. She looked up and saw Lupe passing by her. Lydia tried unsuccessfully to grab Lupe's dress. "Lupe, please, stop Miguel! Do not let him hurt

Chico!" she yelled. Lupe did not say a word to Lydia. She looked down at her with a disgusted expression, as if she wanted Chico to get what was coming to him, a beating.

Rosa was in shock. In all her life she could never remember anything similar to this happening in her town. As she watched the mob approach and Lydia on the ground crying, she wondered, "Why are they all so angry? All we did was go on a horseback ride."

Miguel was the first one to reach Chico. Chico did not try to speak to the crowd. He knew it was of no use. He saw the expressions on their faces and knew they were crazy with anger.

He looked past them and saw his princess on the ground; he wanted so much to go over and comfort her. He knew he was in for a vicious beating. In fact, he wondered if the crowd was going to kill him, right there in town, the place he wanted to make his home. At that moment the thought crossed his mind of his father telling him he should not leave home. He remembered his father saying, "Things will never be better anywhere else." At the time Chico believed his father was wrong. Now at this instant he conceived that maybe his father was right after all.

"¡Desgraciado (Miserable)!" Miguel yelled with a deformed expression from the hate in his eyes. The doctor took his first swing with his heavy, thick club. Chico quickly took a step back and ducked. The club missed Chico's head.

"The doctor is trying to kill me!" Chico thought. The doctor tried to recoup from the powerful swing he took. At that moment Chico had a chance to swing and to hit the old doctor; however, he decided not to, for Lydia's sake. Just then one of the other men stepped up and swung his club. Chico calculated the movement of the club sailing toward him. He was able to grab it. As his left hand caught the club, his right fist came up and hit the man in the face. As Chico felt the punch hit the man, he saw the man's surprised expression. His head swung back with the blow, and his body fell to the ground.

As Chico tried to turn and face another man, he felt a blow to his right shoulder. He heard a scream come from behind the crowd. He turned, and in an instant he saw a club moving toward him. He reached up and tried unsuccessfully to stop it. Everything turned black momentarily. He swung in the direction of whoever was holding the bat-like club. He felt his fist hit someone, not knowing who it was. He turned and struck another target, connecting solidly.

At that moment he felt another blow to the back of his head. He tried to turn and protect himself, as other blows were connecting to his head and body. As he was turning, he felt numb. His legs were buckling. Chico tried to defend himself, but at that point he was unable to do so. He remembered hitting the ground. He was so exhausted and in so much pain that he could not raise his arms to shield himself. The last thing he remembered were legs scrambling around him and being struck repeatedly.

Chico opened his eyes; he did not know where he was. He tried to move his arms but could not, due to the pain.

"Where am I? What happened to me?" he thought. He could not remember what happened or where he was. His body hurt tremendously. He wondered if he were dead.

Lydia came to his mind. He remembered he dreamed about her. She was there with him, combing his hair with her hand, as his head lay on her lap. His mind was not clear. "Is it a dream, or is it real? Is Lydia here with me now?" he wondered. He tried to reach back to feel her.

As he attempted to reach back, he felt pain all over his body. In a few seconds he remembered what happened to him. He wondered how long he had been there. He wondered who had brought him to the place where he was, and who was taking care of him. Again he tried to move his arms in order to sit up. The harder he tried, the more pain he experienced. He lay still and gave up trying to move any part of his body.

His mind went back to what had happened. He remembered the evil face the doctor had when he tried to strike him. He wondered if the doctor hit him after that first try. Chico reasoned he probably did. He had a difficult time accepting that the doctor would try to take his life. "How could a man who helps people live try to kill me?" he asked himself.

And his Lydia, he wondered if she were all right. If they were able to do this to him, "What would those crazy people do to Lydia and Rosa!"

He thought of the vieja. "She was certainly a troublemaker. Someone should straighten her out, so she cannot get involved with the affairs of other people."

Chico did not know what was wrong with him, but he knew he was hurt badly. His chest was injured. When he tried to take a deep breath, he felt as if it were going to be his last. The pain was almost unbearable.

Chico heard a noise in the room. He tried to talk and ask who was there. His mouth opened; but there where no words, only a groan.

"Ay, señor, you are awake!" a man's strong voice said.

Chico tried to talk again, but nothing came out. He wanted the man to tell him what happened to Lydia. He wanted to know if he was going to die. If not, he wanted to know if he was going to be a cripple.

"Do not move, señor," the old man said. The polecia of the pueblo hired a curandero, Señor Gómez, for a few pesos a week to take care of Chico because the doctor refused to treat him. Miguel Gonzales was the only doctor for many miles. The police had to get the curandero to treat and set Chico's broken bones. (Curandero is a medicine man or a self-made doctor who never went to school to become a licensed doctor.)

Señor Gómez continued, "If you move, you are going to pay for it, señor. Just relax, and do not try to do anything. You will be here for quite a long time. You sure got beat up good, Señor Rodriguez. They say you put up a good fight, and you had a chance to run but did not. People are talking about it all the way over in Tuxla. They say you are a man who is not afraid of anything, not even the worst incident that has happened in this small pueblo for many years. Anyway, señor, I do not know if you understand me; or if you can hear me for that matter. However, we will talk when you get better, if you get better. We thought you would have died by now. We did not think you would make it this long. Four days is a long time to be unconscious without dying. Anyway, we will talk later, maybe," the old man said, not sounding very encouraging.

Chico had wanted the old man to tell him where his true love was and if she had come to see him.

He felt himself drifting in and out of consciousness. Maybe it was because of the drugs or the herbs that the old man was giving him.

"Let us see," the old man said, as he lifted Chico's head, trying to have him drink something. That was the last thing Chico remembered for a while. He went back to sleep and woke periodically when someone fed him. He could not really tell if it was a woman or a man who fed him. At times the person was gentle, and it felt as if it was a woman; other times it felt like a man. Sometimes when he was being fed, he thought he heard Lydia's voice.

One morning he awoke and opened his eyes. His limbs were tied down and were in a great deal of pain. His mind was clear on this day. He noticed he was in a small room. He saw a window at the opposite end of the room. The door was open. He looked down at his body. They had not only put bandages around his legs but also around the whole bed. He recognized the room to be the one where he visited the director of public affairs.

Chico tried to speak. "Hola," he moaned. "Hola, is anyone here?" No one responded.

"Well," Chico thought, "at least I can speak. Whoever is here with me, when they return, I will ask them some questions." He hoped it was Lydia taking care of him. He fell asleep for a short while.

"Wake up, Chico! Wake up!"

Chico opened his eyes and saw Rosa holding a cup and a big wooden spoon, trying to hold up his head. She was about to serve him something. "Chico, I have not seen you open your eyes like this in all these days that you have been here. I am so happy!"

Not being able to speak well, he asked in a low, mumbled voice, "What happened? How bad am I? How is Lydia?" Chico had a lot of questions to ask.

Rosa put the cup down on a small table next to the bed. With the wooden spoon in one hand, she tried lifting Chico's head a little higher to serve him something that appeared like soup.

"Well, first of all, you were beaten up pretty badly, you know. Everybody thought you were dead right there in the street," Rosa stated. Chico was having a difficult time swallowing the broth she was feeding him. She continued, "They broke some of your bones with those clubs. They broke one of your arms, and they broke your legs. That is why we have your legs wrapped around the bed, so you will not move them so much. Also we think they broke some of your ribs, but the curandero (medicine man) was not sure. Those people did not want to stop hitting you. Nobody in this pueblo ever saw people so cruel. I have heard in times past, before my time, that they took people out of the pueblo and hung them. But this is the first time they tried to beat someone to death. Doña Sánchez came to the pueblo and told the familias you and Lydia were in the bushes when she passed by, and she yelled at you to leave the young muchacha alone. Now after all of this, she denies she said that exactly. Now she says everybody misunderstood her. But I don't know, Chico. I do think that vieja could do such a thing, just for the sake of getting involved in other people's business."

"And Lydia, how is she?" Chico asked in pain, coughing up his broth.

Reaching for a cloth on the small table and wiping around Chico's mouth, Rosa said, "Well, the doctor did a pretty bad thing. Even his friend the governor heard about the way they beat you up. He is disturbed at Miguel's actions and for being the leader of the mob. The doctor blames you for being the cause of all the trouble he is having with all his powerful friends. He sent Lydia to San Cristóbal de Las Casas to live and to go to school." (San Cristóbal de Las Casas is about two days horseback ride from San Bartolomé de los Llanos. It is one of the oldest towns in all of México.)

Rosa continued, "Lydia loves you very much, Chico. She told me if I am her good friend, I am to come here every day and help you regain your health. I told Lydia I am her good friend as well as yours. You have been very good and respectful with both of us all the different times we went with you, so I consider it my duty to come and take care of you," Rosa stated in a matter-of-fact way.

"Your father?" Chico asked. He thought, "If all the people think of me as such a bad person, why does Rosa's father let her come to help me?"

"My father said you are a brave man, Chico. He was in the house when all this happened. He came out when it was too late. He said if he had come outside and saw you fighting with all those people, all alone, he would have helped you. Besides, he wanted to know what happened between you and me, what I know about you, and how you treated us. I told him how respectful you were with us and how you handled yourself around us, that you are a gentleman. My father and mother want me to come and help you. My father thinks the doctor is a coward. The doctor will not lift a hand to help you. He tells people he wants God to finish the job he started. No one in this pueblo ever thought the doctor could be so cruel!"

Chico tried to ask another question, but this much talking and listening was too much for him. His eyes started to close.

"Chico, try to rest. The herbs we are giving you are helping you to rest. In a few weeks you will be back on your feet. Lydia told me to tell you that whenever you are ready, she will be ready. I do not know what she meant by that, but she said you would know. So now, Chico, drink some more of this. It will help you," Rosa said as she lifted up his head. This time she used the cup to serve the soup instead of the wooden spoon.

When Rosa was done, she told Chico he looked much better than in days past. Also, since the doctor refused to attend to his injuries, Rosa explained to Chico that a man who works for one of the ranchers, who takes care of the animals, is a curandero (medicine man). He came and set Chico's bones. "He works on people at times too, you know," she said. "He takes care of some of the Indians who work on the ranchos. Also, he takes care of people who cannot afford to go to the doctor."

Chico felt his eyes become heavy. He closed them and thought of what Rosa had said, "Whenever you are ready, she will be ready." He dozed off.

Each day Rosa went and sat with him. The room became Chico's home for the next few weeks. The police said it did not bother them to keep Chico there and thought he was probably going to die from the way he looked. They felt that if Chico were left at home and alone he would die for sure. So he was better off at the police station.

Every evening Rosa brought Chico food that her mother made. Rosa's parents did not know him, but she had described him. Rosa's father felt the doctor was being unreasonable toward Chico. For him to listen to Señora Sánchez was a big mistake. He should have waited and talked to his own girl before relying on the information from a lady to whom he was not related. Rosa said her father wanted Chico to come to his house to visit when he was well.

In a few weeks Chico was able to go home and take care of himself. He had a difficult time, but he managed. He was looking forward to going back to work, but the curandero told him it would be a matter of weeks before he could return.

One evening there was a knock at the door. "Yes."

"Hola, Chico," Rosa greeted, carrying her food as she did everyday at that time.

"Hola, Rosa, what do you have for me today?" Chico asked, looking at the tray covered with a white cloth.

"Oh, my mother made some good frijoles today." Chico loved his frijoles, as did all Mexicans.

"Also, she sent you some of the special qüeso (cheese) she

makes. You know, Chico," Rosa said as she put the tray down on a small table next to the bed, "my mother must like you to send you her precious qüeso."

"She must, to send me food everyday; and she does not even know me. Now that I am starting to walk a little with this stick as an aid," Chico said holding up the stick he was using as a crutch, "I am going to meet your mother and father tomorrow, Rosa. Wait, maybe I better not," Chico said in a puzzled way, looking at Rosa.

"Why not, Chico?" she asked as she sat in a chair against the wall.

"If I go and meet them, they might not like me. I might not get any more suppers!" Chico exclaimed, waiting for Rosa to laugh.

"Ay, Chico," Rosa said with a soft laugh. "No wonder Lydia loves you so much."

"Have you heard from her, Rosa?"

"You ask me that everyday, and it is always the same answer."

"I know, but I need to hear some news from her. I want to go to San Cristóbal de Las Casas to see her as soon as I can ride a horse, which is not going to be very long the way I am going."

Chico stood up with the crutch under his arm. He walked slowly to the other side of the bed where Rosa put the tray down. "Once I take a few steps, I loosen up; and I am able to walk for a little while. If I walk to your house tomorrow and if I walk a little everyday, it will help me to recuperate faster."

"What did the curandero say? Does he think you should be trying to walk yet? Has it been long enough for your body to heal to the point you can go for long walks?" Rosa asked, concerned.

"Yes, he said that when a steer breaks a leg, in just a few days, it is back on its feet. But he also said that when a horse breaks his leg they shoot him!"

"Ay, Chico, you are funny! Chico, I have something for you today. Something you have been waiting for."

"What is it Rosa? News from Lydia? Do you have news from Lydia?"

"Better than news from her," Rosa said as she pulled an envelope out of the pocket of her dress. "I have a letter she sent to my house for you," Rosa answered as she reached over and handed it to Chico. "She wrote me a letter too; and I think she loves you as much as you love her, Chico," Rosa expressed as she stood up to leave. "I have to go; but if you want me to come back for a letter from you tonight, I will. Now that we have her address, we have a place to mail a letter without her father finding out. Would you like me to come back? The mail is leaving tomorrow in the morning about 10 o'clock. The next mail after that will not go out for a few days."

"Yes, come back in about an hour or two," Chico responded, as he glanced at the letter, still in shock. He could not believe he had a letter from Lydia. All the time he had been hoping to hear from his true love. "A letter right here in my hand. In her own handwriting!" he thought.

"All right, Chico, I will come back later. I hope you enjoy your letter, and do not forget about the frijoles my mother made for you!" Rosa exclaimed, knowing that the frijoles did not mean anything to Chico now.

Chico stood up as if he were going to see Rosa out; but as soon as he stood up, Rosa was out the door and gone. Chico went over to the chair where Rosa had been sitting and sat down. He looked at the letter but was in no hurry to open it. He wanted the moment to last. He had been looking forward to hearing from Lydia since he regained consciousness from the beating. He could feel his heart pounding inside his chest. He took a deep breath and opened it slowly, imagining Lydia's smile and her light hair blowing in the wind. His eyes caught the first words. The letter was about a page long with medium-sized writing. He imagined Lydia talking, looking into his eyes with her gaze of love.

To My Dearest Love, Chico,

First of all I want to tell you I am truly sorry for what happened. I blame myself for the whole incident. I put myself in this situation. I wish things could be right.

I hear from people in San Bartolomé de los Llanos that you are recuperating. I am so glad. I hate the doctor and Lupe for doing this to you; I will never forgive them. I am here, so far from you. All I think about is you, all the times we were together, and how much fun it was. I want things to be like that again.

Chico, I love you; and I will go anywhere with you. I want you to know that. When you are ready, my love, I am ready to do whatever you want.

The address where you can write me is at the bottom of the page.

The doctor and Lupe are coming here every weekend. They

know I am angry with them, and they are trying to make it up to me; but I do not want to be with them anymore. The doctor refuses to talk about you. I told him if he does not want to talk about you then I do not want to talk to him or Lupe. He might take me back home in the next few weeks. We will see.

Well, my love, I will look for a letter from you everyday for the rest of my life. Remember, never, never forget I love you with all my heart and will always be waiting for you. Your true love, Lydia

Chico sat in the chair thinking of what his love had written. The statement that stood out in his mind was when she said she would do whatever he wanted.

"What did that mean?" he wondered. "Will she go with me if I went after her? Will she marry me? If I did that, what situation will it leave her in with all the doctor's familia and everybody Lydia knows?"

Chico thought about these things as he read Lydia's letter over and over again. He was going to write her once he calmed down. He knew he was too excited right at this moment. He was willing to marry her on a minute's notice.

"But, where would we live?" Chico thought, looking around the room he called his home. It did not appear nice, not nice enough for someone as special as Lydia. She was used to the finer things the doctor provided. "Will she be able to live in this little home that does not have much?" Chico wondered. Chico thought about the money he had saved up that could get them started off somewhere else. He had enough money to buy a small rancho and a few steers, not many though.

Chico looked over at the food Rosa brought. He did not want to eat. He was not hungry. The only appetite he had at the moment was for his love, Lydia. "I hope Rosa does not mind that I am probably not going to eat much of her food. Maybe later I will eat; but for now, I will write the letter," Chico said to himself.

Chico took out his bottle of ink, paper, and pen. He was used to writing letters. He wrote to his mother every week and told her what was going on in his life. He had already told her he had found the love of his life. He did not tell her of the beating he had received and did not know if he ever would. Chico knew if he told his mother she would tell his father and his brothers. They would then be in San Bartolomé de los

Llanos in a matter of days, to take care of the doctor. Chico did not want this. He wanted to work things out with his Lydia.

He took the pen, dipped it into the ink, and started writing slowly.

My Dearest Lydia,

I received your beautiful letter, and I am so happy you are fine. I was longing to hear some news about you. I needed to know if you still loved me. Now my heart rejoices hearing from you directly.

Yes, I am recuperating. I can see why you are angry with the doctor. He should have never listened to Señora Sánchez and jumped to conclusions, listening to her lies.

Chico stopped writing for a minute and thought about what he wrote. "The doctor did not care for me from the start. And also, Lydia just told me in her letter that he does not want to talk about me. I could kill that man. But, for Lydia's sake, I will not."

Chico looked down at the paper and continued to write.

Once I am well, I will go for you. If you will accept me as your husband, I will come for you. We will be married right away.

Lydia, I did not want our marriage to be this way. I wanted the doctor's blessing. But now I think there is no choice. Try to talk to the doctor again. Maybe he will listen. It will be worse for him if he tries to stop us. I do not want you to receive a bad name because of me.

If you come back to San Bartolomé de los Llanos, I will see you here, and I will make all the arrangements to be married. I love you, Lydia.

Do not worry about me. I am fine and getting better. I will be waiting to hear from you, and I would like to know if you accept my proposal. My heart longs to see your most beautiful, blue eyes and your pretty, soft hair. I will await your reply. Love, Chico.

Chico folded the paper and reached under the bed for his box that contained the envelopes he made. Now all he needed was for Rosa to come back and take the letter to the post office.

As the weeks went by, Chico improved in his walking. He had been by Rosa's house many times. Rosa's father Roberto was a nice man. He was in his thirties, short and thin. He had a bakery a few doors down from his home. The problem Roberto had was that he liked getting drunk almost every day. His wife did not seem to mind it one bit. One could tell his wife loved him; he was good to her and took care of her. And Rosa, she did not know better. All of her life her father was the same; he got up at three in the morning, worked, came home, got drunk, and went to sleep.

Periodically Chico saw the doctor or Lupe, coming or going. Señora Gonzales would look at him resentfully. When he saw the doctor, the doctor looked at Chico as if he objected to his being on the same street. He always looked back to make sure Chico was not running after him. It seemed as if he were afraid that one day Chico would avenge himself.

Rosa told Chico the doctor bought bread from her father's bakery for many years; however, now that he saw Chico go to his house, he walked two blocks to another bakery. She said her father did not care; he did not need the business of a coward.

CHAPTER FIVE

ROSA

Afew weeks passed, and Chico was able to go back to work. He wrote Lydia letters everyday, even though they did not get mailed but twice a week. Lydia returned the number of letters she received.

One day Chico came home. Approaching his house, he saw Rosa sitting by his front doorstep waiting for him.

"Chico!" Rosa yelled as he walked up the street.

"Something must be wrong," he thought, since Rosa never came to wait for him.

Chico picked up his pace to a jogging mode. When he reached Rosa, he asked, "What is it, Rosa? Did something happen to Lydia?" All Chico had done the last few weeks was think of Lydia and how he was going to work things out between them.

"Ay, Chico, I have news for you! Lydia came home today! She is home! I saw her!"

"That is good news, Rosa, really good news!"

"Well, not really good. When I saw her, I wanted to talk to her; so I went and knocked on her door. Lupe came to the door and told me not to come to their house anymore. She said I was not welcome there and could no longer be a friend to Lydia! It cannot be this way." Rosa was sobbing at this point. "Lydia has always been my friend, Chico! Lupe has no right! She is just being mean! What am I going to do?"

"That is all right, Rosa," Chico stated calmly, reaching for her with his arms extended and ready to embrace her. "Señora Gonzales might stop you right now from seeing Lydia. But do not worry. Lydia considers you her best friend, and she will never forget that. You will always be her best friend, Rosa. When I marry Lydia, you will be able to come to our home as much as you like. And what is more, our children will know you as their tía (aunt)!"

Rosa continued, brushing her tears away and taking a deep breath, "Really, Chico? Is that true? Will your and Lydia's children think of me as their tía?"

"Yes, Rosa. So do not feel disappointed that the doctor and his wife are treating you badly. Lydia will not live there forever, even though the doctor would like that. Then again, maybe he will not care after I do what I am going to do," Chico said, thinking of what he intended to do and knowing the doctor would not like it.

"What do you mean, Chico? What are you going to do?" Rosa asked, pulling away from Chico and seeming interested in what he said.

"Well, I am going to go and try to talk to him one last time. Maybe he will listen to me before I take Lydia from his house."

"You are going to go to the doctor's house?" Rosa asked, not believing what she had just heard.

"Yes, I will give the doctor one last chance to come around and see things our way!" Chico declared with conviction.

"But, Chico, he might beat you up again; and this time he might kill you! You'd better not go. It will only make things worse. Are you not scared of the doctor? Look what happened to you the last time."

"The doctor does not scare me, Rosa. The only reason he was able to do what he did is because he had all of his friends with him. When I go to his home, he will be by himself. And what can an old doctor do to me by himself?"

"But what if he goes and gets his friends and comes after you?" Rosa asked, trying to talk Chico out of his plan.

"If he does that and he brings his friends, then I will be waiting for him. This time I will not be the one who will be hurt!" Chico declared, thinking of the gun he had at home. He had always had a gun but never had a reason to take it out. Even after he was beaten up, he did not want to take revenge. When he was a young boy, his father bought him his first gun and gave him and his brothers lessons on how to handle it. He was taught that a man always has to have the proper respect for a firearm. If he were ever to take a gun out in anger, it would turn on him. But if he were to take it out to defend himself, the gun would be a friend. Chico always felt he had learned from the lessons his father had given him. He felt he had the proper respect for his gun.

"Ay, Chico, I know I will not be able to talk you out of going to the doctor's house. But I would like to tell my father; so he can be ready to help you, if you need it."

"You may tell your father, Rosa; but I will not tell you when I plan to do this. I do not want your father to be involved in this. If things are to get nasty and your father helps me, it could ruin his life as well as yours."

"But what about your life, Chico? If something happens to you, it will ruin everybody's lives!"

"Ay, Rosa, leave it! It will be all right. If the doctor does not want to talk to me, that will be fine. If he does, then we will accomplish something."

"All right, Chico; but I sure wish Lydia was here to try to talk some sense into you!"

"I think Lydia will be happy that I am trying to do things right. We will be able to be married properly and with everybody's blessing, and all will be happy."

That is where it stayed. Rosa went home and told her father Chico was going to try to talk to the doctor again. Rosa also told him what Chico had said about not wanting to get Roberto involved, not wishing to ruin his life. That did not go well with Roberto. He felt life was exciting when one could stand up for his friends. Since Chico was a friend of Rosa's, Chico was also a friend of his. He told Rosa to try to find out when Chico was going to do this, so he could stand by.

That evening Chico felt he did not want to put off talking to the doctor. If he waited, he would worry about it all night. His stomach hurt thinking about it. Once he talked to him, Chico would go home and wait to see if the doctor and his friends went to his house.

Chico took the gun out that he had hidden among his clothes. He was sure he was not going to need it, but he did not want to take any chances. He thought of taking the gun with him but thought it over. If he did take it and the doctor really upset Chico, he might take it out and use it. When that thought crossed his mind, he saw his father looking at him with a frown on his face. Then he thought of what the doctor did to him. Thinking again, Chico realized he would have his father's approval to blow off the doctor's head.

Chico took the bullets out of a small box he had made specifically to use for his cartridges. He never kept his gun loaded. He felt if there was trouble, he would have to go into his house, pull his gun out, take out his cartridges, and load the gun. Within that time period, he would cool off. He did not want to shoot anyone if he did not have to.

Once the gun was loaded, he put it under his pillow. He wanted to make sure that if he returned in a rush he would be able to draw it and use it within a drop of a peso. The thought crossed his mind again to take it with him. "What if the doctor draws a gun? Then I will be defenseless without mine. No, if the doctor has a gun in his house, he would have used it when the vieja went and told them the lies."

As Chico left his house, he thought of being at Lydia's home talking to the doctor. If the doctor listened to him, he would still be able to have a relationship with Lydia. However, the way things were going, the doctor and Señora Gonzales were ruining things for themselves as well as for Lydia and her family to be.

Chico was as nervous as he was the last time he spoke to the doctor. As he walked towards the house, he reasoned that this time was different. The first time there was no reason for the doctor to be angry with Chico, nor Chico with him. This time he had a good reason to be angry with the doctor and his wife; they almost killed him. Maybe he should not try to make an effort to talk. What he should do is just go and get Lydia, then that would be it. It would be over.

As he approached Lydia's street, he felt his nervousness disappear. Now he talked himself into being angry. The street had a lot of people as it always did. Chico started to walk up the street.

He walked past the bakery that Rosa's family owned. He knew Rosa's father was not there this late. He had one of Rosa's tías (aunts) working in the evenings. Roberto was probably drunk by this time and was probably getting ready for bed. Because he was a baker, he needed to be up early in the morning.

Just then he saw the door of Lydia's house open. Chico stopped. Señora Gonzales stepped out with a big bag hanging from her arm. She came out by herself and appeared as if she were going to the market to buy something. Señora Gonzales started walking towards Chico. Chico did not want to be seen by her. He wanted to talk to the doctor, not to her. Chico turned and started to walk in the direction from which he had started. When he reached the corner, he walked up to the building, partly facing the wall. A man was there selling oranges.

"Hola, señor," he addressed his greeting to Chico.

Chico looked over at the man who was just a few feet from him and said, "Hola, señor."

"You are a brave man to come back here. I remember what happened to you the last time. You are the one who got into a fight with the doctor. They almost killed you. You really should leave, señor. From the way it appeared last time, the doctor and his friends are loco!" the man exclaimed, concerned for Chico.

Chico thought to himself that the man did not know he had been by this street many times since then. He had come to Rosa's house. Chico answered, "I don't want anymore trouble, señor. I want to make peace; that's all."

Chico saw Señora Gonzales approaching on his side of the street. Chico squatted down, partly facing the man and partly the wall, as if he were a friend of the man. Chico pulled his hat over his forehead and stuck a small stick into his mouth, as if it were a toothpick, holding onto it. He wanted his hand to shield his face.

"Hola, Pepe. I will take five oranges," Señora Gonzales told the man. Chico hoped the man was not going to say anything. Señora Gonzales glanced at Chico, thinking he looked familiar. She did not give him much thought. Most people on this street and in the town looked familiar to her.

Señora Gonzales paid for her oranges and moved on. The man, Pepe, looked over at Chico, knowing Chico was hiding from her. "She is gone, señor."

Chico turned to make sure she had left. She was out of sight and must have walked around the corner. Chico stood up and looked both ways, not wanting any more surprises. It looked all clear in both directions. As he walked away, he turned and looked at the man named Pepe. Pepe had a smile on his face and nodded his head at Chico as if he were telling him, "Good luck!"

Chico walked up the street to Lydia's door. "If the doctor comes to the door, I will ask him only one time to reconsider, only once. If he refuses, I will leave and come back to get her," he thought as he knocked solidly on the door.

He heard noise in the house, as if someone was coming to answer. The door opened. It was his princess, his true love. Her beautiful, sad, blue eyes were staring at him in shock.

"Chico! What are you doing here? The doctor will kill you! He told me that if you came around again he was going to end this and kill you!" At that moment she paused and said, "Are you here to take me with you? Do you want me to come out and go with you right now?" Lydia asked, hoping he was going to say, "Yes."

"Lydia, I came to talk to the doctor one last time. If he does not want to talk to me, this will be the last time. The next time I come, you can go with me."

"No, Chico, you do not understand. Miguel will not talk to you. He is not being reasonable. He will not listen. I have tried so many times! Ay, Chico, I have missed you so much," she declared as she put both of her arms around Chico, embracing him. "Take me with you right now. I will go with you! We will start our life together right now!"

"Lydia, who are you talking to?" the doctor's strong voice vented as he walked towards the door.

Lydia pulled away from Chico, terrified of what Miguel was going to say and do. The door swung open as if the doctor knew to whom she was speaking. "¡Desgraciado (miserable)! What are you doing here, muchacho (boy)! Do you want to meet your death so young? Did not everybody in town tell you that if you came here again I was going to kill you?"

"Doctor, I came to talk about Lydia and me. I do not want to fight with you. You are too old to fight me."

"Talk? Too old? I will never talk to you about Lydia. Do not forget what this old man did to you the last time!" the doctor yelled as he stepped back from the door.

Chico saw he was retreating for a reason. He thought maybe he was getting a club again. He figured that if the doctor was getting a club and was alone, he would be able to defend himself better than the last time. "I will take it away from the old man and beat him with it!" Chico thought.

Lydia was standing inside the door and had turned to look at the doctor. He was out of sight from Chico. Then Lydia screamed, "Miguel! Put the gun back!"

Chico knew he was no match for a gun and started his run down the street. He turned in the opposite direction from which he had come. He felt there were two reasons to run in that direction. First, the corner was closer; and he could get away from the bullets faster. Second, if the doctor took a shot at him with so many people in the street, the bullet was sure to hit an innocent person, even a child; and Chico did not want that.

As Chico pushed his legs into high gear, he heard Lydia screaming at the doctor behind him. His legs were in pain because of the injuries he had received from the beating a few months earlier. "This is no time to cry about pain," he thought. Just as he was nearing the corner, he heard a pop; he heard a bullet buzz by. There was no time to look back to see if the doctor was going to take another shot.

Chico darted around the corner and kept running. He did not want to take a chance and stop. If he did, the doctor could come around the corner. The next bullet might not miss.

Chico did not know if he was using a handgun or a rifle. "If it is a handgun, I will be out of range pretty quickly. If it is a rife, I might be in trouble if he comes around the corner." Chico's mind was racing as fast as his feet.

When Chico arrived home, he went straight for his gun. He opened the chamber to make sure he had loaded bullets in it. He was sure he did, but he wanted to confirm it. He went back to the window and looked out to see if he was being followed. He was still out of breath. Chico pulled a chair over to the window and waited, watching to see if anyone was coming. He wanted to catch his breath and needed to rest before deciding what he was going to do.

He thought about what had happened. "Ay, ay, ay, what a mistake that was. I should have listened to Rosa and not attempted to try to talk to the doctor." But then he thought of Lydia. He felt good that Lydia wanted to go with him right there on the spot. He thought that if he lived through this he would get Lydia to leave with him. They would have a happy future together.

A few minutes went by, and Chico was again breathing normally. He thought he was better off out of the house. If the doctor came with a lot of people, then he was going to be trapped because there was no back door and no back windows. Chico put the gun in his belt and under his shirt. He stepped over to where his cartridges were, took the box out, and put several handfuls of bullets into his pockets. He imagined himself hiding behind something with ten men firing guns at him. He would need a lot of bullets to defend himself. Chico thought, "Maybe I should have told my mother what happened. I would not be by myself now. I would have my brothers and father with me."

Chico opened his door slowly. He looked outside before stepping out to make sure no one was waiting for him. He cautiously stepped out and looked around, hoping a bullet would not strike him. Once he knew he was not going to have to go back into his home to take cover, he started down the street. At fifty yards up the street, he stopped. There was a pile of wood stacked up against a wall. He thought it would be a good place to take cover and wait. He wanted to make sure he had a good view of his front door. If someone went to his house, he was going to take care of him with a bullet.

He noticed kids playing down the street behind him. He thought of a bullet flying in their direction and hitting one of them. "Should I go and tell the kids to go home so nothing happens to them?" he asked himself.

Just then he saw Rosa running around the corner, holding her dress high in order to take longer footsteps. She reached Chico's door and started to bang on it, yelling, "Chico? Chico? Open the door!"

Chico stood up and yelled, "Over here, Rosa!"

Rosa turned and saw him standing, waving at her.

"Ay, Dios, Chico," Rosa stated, running up to him.

"Rosa, what are you doing here? You better get out of here, or you are going to get hurt!" Chico declared.

"Are you all right? Did he shoot you? Answer me, Chico!" Rosa exclaimed, trying to turn him around to examine him for any sign of blood.

"No, he did not shoot me. The old man cannot shoot a gun; or he would have got me, Rosa!"

"The only reason he did not shoot you is because Lydia pushed the doctor, and he almost fell when he pulled the trigger."

Chico looked at Rosa for a few seconds and then asked, "And Lydia? What did the doctor tell her?"

"The doctor did not tell her anything. He just hit her a few times."

"Hit her!" Chico could feel his face turn red with anger.

"Well, he hit her outside from what the people said who were in the street. The doctor took Lydia into the house by the hair, and who knows what happened to her in there!" Rosa shouted. Rosa was as angry as Chico.

"Is the doctor coming over here?" he wanted to know.

"I do not think so, Chico. He is telling everyone he shot you. And he is saying that if he did not shoot you he will next time he sees you."

"Well, that will be right now! If he is not coming over here, then I am going over there, right now!"

"No, you cannot! I know how badly you want to go and fight with the doctor, but he has a gun!" Rosa exclaimed, trying to convince Chico.

"So do I," Chico said, pulling out his big handgun.

"Ay, Chico, if you go over there and fight with the doctor right now, you are going to lose!"

"How do you know that, Rosa? You never saw me shoot a gun before. You do not know how good I am with a pistol!" Chico declared, a little irritated with Rosa for not having confidence in him.

"It does not matter how good you are with a gun. Do you realize that if you lose the gunfight, you will be dead? Your relationship with Lydia will be over! And if you win the gun battle, you will lose anyway! You will have killed the only doctor there is for miles around. How will the people feel about that? Do you think it will go well with them? What about the doctor's friends? Will you kill all of them too? Do you think if you kill the doctor, you can still have a life with Lydia? I do not think so! You will have to leave here and not come back. Then what will happen to Lydia?" Rosa asked, talking rapidly, trying to persuade Chico not to make the biggest mistake of all his life.

Chico listened to Rosa. He felt she was very logical in the things she was saying. She made him take a step back and really think about his options.

Rosa saw she had Chico's attention and wanted to keep going now that she had him thinking. "And if you want to win, Chico, I will tell you how to win, really win. Do you want me to tell you?" Rosa paused and waited, wanting an answer from Chico. "Do you, Chico?" Rosa asked again.

"Tell me, Rosa, how can I really win?" he asked sarcastically, although he really did want to hear what Rosa had to say.

"All right, I will tell you. But listen!"

Rosa continued to have Chico's attention. He had never seen Rosa act like this. She was more resolute than he thought.

"What you do is give it a few days; then wait for Lydia on the street. When you see her, take her with you. Then you will win! That is it, Chico! Take her, and you will WIN!" Rosa declared. She stopped speaking and stood there, staring at Chico.

Chico did not say anything. He knew she was right. If he went and killed the doctor, maybe his life would be over with Lydia.

"All right, Rosa, you are right. That is what I will do," Chico said, lowering his voice, feeling disappointed because he was not going to kill the doctor and rescue Lydia right then. "I am not afraid of the doctor, but I do want to win. I do want Lydia! So I will wait."

Chico went to work the next day. Everything was normal. Some of the men at the rancho where Chico worked heard about him almost getting shot and joked about it. Señor Rios, the owner of the rancho, never went out to where Chico worked. He liked working with the steers on the range, but on this day Señor Rios rode his horse to the area where Chico worked.

Chico was watering some of the horses when he saw him approaching. "Don Rios, how are you?"

"I am fine. And you, Francisco, how are you?" Don Rios asked as he dismounted his horse. Chico took the horse from him and walked it to the water tub.

"Francisco, I came to speak with you. I understand you are having trouble in town with Dr. Gonzales again. Is it true?" Don Rios asked in a nice way.

Chico did not like the way he worded his statement. "No, Don Rios. I am not having trouble with the doctor. He is having trouble with me again. I did not do anything to provoke him. I knocked on his door and wanted to speak to him in a peaceful way. He did not want me there because he does not want me to talk to Lydia, so he pulled his gun out and took a shot at me. I could have shot back at him but chose not to. I do not want to have trouble with anybody," Chico declared, thinking to himself that if the doctor took a shot at him again he would blow his head off for sure!

"I see," Don Rios said as he considered what Chico said.

"I would like to know, Don Rios, why are you asking?" Chico requested. He knew something was bothering him.

"Well, I had a visit from one of the doctor's friends. He came to ask me to return a favor I owe the doctor."

"What is the favor they are asking of you, Don Rios?"

"Well, they want me to let you go; but I do not have a reason to do that. You have not caused any trouble here. And besides, I sent one of my men to check to see what actually happened between you and the doctor. My people told me the last time the doctor and his party beat you up, you did not do anything to deserve it. If it was any other man, they would have gone back and killed the doctor for what he did. So I wanted to come and talk to you and convey what I have decided to do," Don Rios said.

Chico was listening closely and in deep thought. Don Rios continued, "I want you to know I recognize this is not your doing. If you were a person who was trying to start some kind of trouble, then I might consider what my friend wants me to do. But on the contrary, I will not honor the doctor in what he is asking. Francisco, you have been working with me a few months now; and I think you are an honorable man, worthy of my loyalty. Whatever I can do for you, just let me know."

"Thank you, Don Rios. I appreciate everything you are telling me and everything you are doing for me. There is something you can help me with."

"What can I help you with, Francisco?" Don Rios asked in a tone showing he wanted to please.

"I need a few days off from work. I need to go to San Cristóbal de Las Casas to take care of some business," Chico requested, not wanting to tell Don Rios he was going to be married. He did not want to tell Don Rios about his business because he might tell someone, and it might find its way to the doctor. Then the doctor would be waiting for him.

"That will be fine. I will get one of the other men to come here and take your place. And if there is anything else I can do for you, you must let me know, Francisco," Don Rios said as he mounted his horse.

"Thank you very much, Don Rios. I will never forget what kind of man you are."

"You are welcome, Francisco. Be careful," he said as he rode away."

Chico had a plan. He needed to ride to San Cristóbal de Las Casas to make arrangements for Lydia and him.

Early the next morning Chico started off to San Cristóbal de Las Casas. He had never been there, since he was new in the state of Chiapas. On his ride he was able to appreciate the beauty of the area. By nightfall he came to a gorgeous site next to a small river. The green foliage almost engulfed the road and the small river. There was a twenty-foot waterfall. Chico bathed under the waterfall and ate a little of the provisions he had taken. He wanted to reach his destination by the next evening, so he fixed his blanket to lie on it. He did not need much because of the warm weather.

Chico rested on his blanket and thought of all the things that were happening and where he was going. From what Chico heard about San Cristóbal de Las Casas, it was also a beautiful town, larger than San Bartolomé de los Llanos. He did not want to spend a lot of time there; he wanted to return for his true love Lydia.

He had to find a way to make it as easy as possible for her and did not want for things to get out of hand as they had the last time. "I do not want to get shot at again. The next time I see the doctor, I will be sure to have my gun with me," Chico thought as he started to doze off. He heard all the noises that would be heard if one were sleeping in the jungle at night. He felt his gun in his hand; it gave him a sense of security. Chico went to sleep.

Early the next morning he began his ride once again. The pueblo of San Cristóbal de Las Casas had an altitude of approximately 7,000 feet. During the day the scenery changed from a jungle forest to a pine-tree forest.

Chapter Six

The Plan

As Chico entered the town on his horse, people took note of him. Travelers would often go to San Cristóbal de Las Casas, since it was one the largest towns in those parts and was the capital of the state.

The town had cobblestone streets, just as San Bartolomé de los Llanos. San Cristóbal de Las Casas was considered by many the most beautiful colonial town in all of México, located in the valley of Jovel.

Chico took his leather jacket with him. He had been told that because of the elevation it was cooler in San Cristóbal de Las Casas. The average temperature generally was a pleasant 66.2 Fahrenheit.

Chico thought, "First, I will find lodging; then I will make arrangements with the padre (priest) of the iglesia (church)." He stopped and asked a man in the street where he might find an inn. He asked the man if he could direct him to one of the better and more respectable inns in town. Chico wanted to bring Lydia and Rosa to the very same inn in a few days.

He came to a house he was told was an inn. The inns were homes where people lived. They often opened up their homes for visitors like Chico who were traveling through or just wanted to spend the night in San Cristóbal de Las Casas.

Chico knocked on the door. The door opened. A woman who was in her late thirties stood in the doorway. She was dressed in colorful clothing, was very attractive, and had a scarf around her neck. She looked at Chico with an expression of surprise at having a young man at her front door. She had four daughters; the oldest was twenty-one years old. She wondered if this handsome, young man was calling on her unmarried, oldest daughter.

"Yes, señor, may I help you?" she asked with a friendly smile.

"Yes, doña. My name is Francisco Rodriguez; and I am living in

San Bartolomé de los Llanos, originally from the state of Sonora," Chico stated. He was trying to be polite to her since she was known for having one of the better inns in town.

He continued, "I was told I might find a room here. I would like to spend one night, if I may."

The woman smiled and said, "Yes, señor, my name is Olivia Ramos. I have three rooms. I charge two pesos a night, which includes breakfast and dinner. Would you like to see the rooms?"

She opened the door so Chico could enter. As Chico stepped into the house, he said, "Yes, I would."

They stepped through the front parlor room, and she opened a door where the first room was located. The large home was tidy with decorous furnishings. Things appeared spotless. Chico was thinking, as Señora Ramos was showing him the room, "This is going to be a pleasant place to bring Lydia."

Señora Ramos opened the door to the second room. It appeared to be as tidy as the first one. Chico thought, "This woman enjoys her work of entertaining people."

"Let me show you the next room," she stated, as she started to take a few steps in the direction of another door.

"Oh no, doña, this room will be fine. I will take it. It is very nice." As Chico said this, Señora Ramos stood there with a smile and with an expression of pride.

"If you are going to take it, let me get my girls to help you get your things down." She turned and shouted, "¡Muchachas! Come here and help the señor with his things!" Señora Ramos wanted Chico to notice her pretty girls. She did not know Chico's heart was already taken.

"Oh no, Doña Ramos, I do not have much. I will get it down myself," Chico insisted as he turned and walked out the front door.

Señora Ramos called out, "I will have breakfast ready at 7:30 and dinner at 5:00."

Chico re-entered the front parlor room and answered, "Well, I will have breakfast with you but not dinner. You see, I will be here for the day only, and then I will have to leave as soon as I take care of my business."

"I see. Then, as you said, you will actually be spending only the night?"

"Yes, but I am coming back in three to four days and will need two rooms at that time. May I rent them in advance."

"Yes, but who are you bringing with you?" Señora Ramos wanted to know. Chico appeared to be an honorable man, but she wanted to know who else was going to be staying in her house. She was a woman who wanted to ward off trouble before it started.

"Well, I will be bringing my wife. Or should I say, by the time we arrive here at your house, she will be my wife. And the other room will be for our chaperon Rosa."

"I see," Señora Ramos replied in a disappointed way. She continued as soon as she got over the initial surprise, now realizing there was no room for her daughters in his life, "I have never had newlyweds stay here in my house on their first night together. Yes, you can have the rooms. So you are planning your honeymoon here in San Cristóbal de Las Casas?" Señora Ramos asked, now smiling, rubbing her hands together. She thought it a privilege to have newlyweds in her inn. She could not wait to tell her friends. "I will plan to have special meals for you because it will be a special occasion. Where will you be married?" the Señora asked, appearing a little nosy.

Chico thought she might become a little too nosy and wanted to end the subject at that point. He reached into his pocket and pulled out a lot of pesos. "Here, Doña Ramos. Here are two pesos for tonight, and here are four more for when I return with my new wife. In addition, here are another five pesos for the nice meals you are going to prepare for us. And to answer your question, we are getting married here in San Cristóbal de Las Casas. Once I rest up for a few short minutes, I will go to the iglesia and talk to the padre to make arrangements," Chico said, ending the conversation with a smile.

As Chico turned, Señora Ramos called, "Señor, would you like me to get a bath ready for you?" Inns such as this one had a bathroom where the tub was located. The hot water was heated in the kitchen and taken to the bathroom.

"Yes, I have been on the road all day. I do need a bath. But before the bath I will take my horse to the stables I passed down the street," Chico answered as he stepped out of the house.

Once Chico was rested and cleaned up, he left the house for the iglesia (church) to make arrangements with the priest. In a pueblo the size of San Cristóbal de Las Casas, there were a few different iglesias in town. Chico wanted to get married in the largest one in town. He was told by the señora that the nicest, biggest, and oldest was the Iglesia de la Caridad. It was one of the first the Spaniards had built upon arriving in this region.

As Chico entered the iglesia itself, he noted its wealth and the exceptional works of art, as well as the architectural details.

Walking through the aisle inside the building, he admired the walls made with layers of solid gold that was pounded in by hand.

Chico found the priest in his office in the back of the old iglesia. "Padre, I came from San Bartolomé de los Llanos. I want to make arrangements for my wedding."

The priest was a balding man in his fifties. He looked up at Chico, stonefaced, not saying anything for a few seconds. Then he asked, "Your name, young man?" He did not like it that Chico did not introduce himself first, believing that it is impolite for someone not to introduce himself before stating his business.

Chico was embarrassed. He realized this was being disrespectful to the priest. "I am sorry, Padre. My name is Francisco Rodriguez."

"Good to meet you, Señor Rodriguez," he stated, getting up and extending his hand to Chico. "Now, what was it you were saying?" the priest asked, still frowning and not caring for Chico's approach.

"Yes, Padre. I want to be married here in a few days. I came to make arrangements and wanted to make sure you were going to be here."

"Who is it you are going to marry, young man?" the priest asked, starting to soften up.

"Lydia Fuentes. She lives with the Gonzales familia in San Bartolomé de los Llanos. She is a very nice girl, and...."

Before Chico could say anymore, the priest interrupted. "Say no more, young man. I know the familia and the muchacha. There was some trouble with the muchacha Lydia a few months back. I was told she had a boyfriend who was giving the familia some trouble. Do you know of it?" the priest asked, looking at Chico suspiciously, as if he were waiting for Chico to lie.

Chico thought it was not a good idea to tell the priest something that was not true, since he was raised to have the proper respect for the iglesia. He thought for a second and realized why the priest must know Lydia. "Her father was also a padre. I am sure all of them in the area must have heard of the situation," Chico thought. He had forgotten the trouble her father had with the iglesia. Chico reasoned he had to choose his words very carefully with this man.

"What did you hear happened?" Chico asked, thinking he would return the question to him.

But it did not work; the priest vented, "Young man, I asked you!"

Chico was caught in his evasiveness and now had to answer. "I am the boyfriend, Padre, although the trouble was not with me but with the doctor. All I wanted to do was talk with Lydia. Then the doctor and his friends came after me, and they beat me up so badly my leg and arm were broken. I assure you, Padre, I did not do anything to provoke it!"

"Does the doctor know you intend to marry the young muchacha?"

Chico thought, "This padre was not holding back any questions. He is going to want to know all the details."

"No, he does not," Chico answered. "Lydia wants to marry me, and we love each other very much," Chico stated. He hoped the priest was going to be sympathetic towards him.

"I will not marry you and the muchacha Lydia without the consent of my friend, Dr. Gonzales! You should immediately inform him of your intentions; because if you do not, I must! In fact I should send someone to inform him about this. I think I will send someone out first thing in the morning to make sure Dr. Gonzales is aware of this!"

"But, Padre, are you not going to give me a chance to tell him first?" Chico asked, trying to buy some time.

"No, not now. I think that since the doctor is my friend my loyalty is to him. So I will do my part in informing him right away!"

Chico was very disappointed with the priest. This matter was none of his business.

"I am sorry you feel this way. If you will not marry us, then that is the way it will be." Chico turned and started out of the church thinking, "I will go to one of the other iglesias in town. One of the other padres will marry us."

"By the way, Señor Rodriguez," the priest said in a loud voice so Chico was sure to hear him as he walked away, "I will speak to the other padres in our pueblo and inform them of the situation."

Chico returned hurriedly to the room he had rented. On the way back he thought out how he was going to resolve the situation, now that it had changed because of the busybody priest.

He knew he had to leave San Cristóbal de Las Casas on that night, before the priest sent his messenger. He thought of the attractive rooms he had rented.

He felt it best to leave the rooms rented. If the priest inquired of him, he would think Chico and Lydia were returning to San Cristóbal de Las Casas. If the doctor were to follow them once he went for Lydia, he might think they were returning to San Cristóbal de Las Casas. What Chico would do is take Lydia to Tuxla Gutierrez and marry her there, without anyone knowing.

On arriving, he saw Señora Ramos and informed her he was not going to be spending the night that evening, due to some changes. He told her to keep the money and keep the other two rooms reserved for him and the girls. He told her he was looking forward to staying in San Cristóbal de Las Casas for his honeymoon. Chico asked the woman if he could have a few provisions for his return trip. She agreed and went to the kitchen as Chico stepped out to get his horse from the stable.

Upon returning to the inn, he packed his things and put them on his horse. He was tired and was looking forward to having a restful night; however, now that was out of the question. He thought it would be best to ride most of the night, to stop for two hours to sleep, and to continue on to San Bartolomé de los Llanos.

"Thank you, Doña Ramos. I will look forward to bringing my new wife here to stay in your house."

"Thank you, señor, for renting my rooms. I look forward to seeing you in a few days and meeting your new wife and your friend."

With that Chico rode away, knowing he would not return.

It was close to midnight, and Chico was very tired. It was time he stopped and slept as he had planned.

Chico arrived in San Bartolomé de los Llanos late the next evening. He had ridden hard all night, except for the two hours he had slept. He thought if the priest's messenger left twelve or thirteen hours after he did, and did not ride as hard as he had, then he should have a good fifteen to twenty hours ahead of him.

That evening upon arriving in town, he went to talk to Rosa. Chico did not want to take any chances with the doctor. He imagined the doctor waiting for him in front of Rosa's house and putting a bullet in his head. The doctor had many friends in high places. If he killed

Chico, nothing would happen to him as far as the law was concerned. Chico put his gun under his belt and pulled his shirt over it. He was not going to be caught defenseless again.

Chico knocked on Rosa's door.

"Hola, Chico," Roberto said with a slur in his voice.

"Hola, Roberto. How are you today?"

"I am fine, Chico. What are you doing on this street? Do you know what could happen to you? What if the doctor finds you here?"

"I am not afraid of the doctor, Roberto! You know that! I will come to your house whenever I want, and the doctor has no say about that!"

"You must be right because you are here," Roberto said, laughing to himself. Chico knew Roberto thought most things were funny when he was drinking. He wanted to have a good time with everyone.

"Maybe this is why his wife loves him so much," Chico thought.

"Roberto, I came to ask you for a big favor," Chico requested, not knowing if it was a good time, since Roberto was intoxicated.

"What is it you want? Do you want me to go and get the doctor with you or for you? I already told Rosa to tell you I am ready whenever you are! Let's go right now! I am ready!" Roberto stood up with his drink in his hand, taking his last swig before departing to the doctor's home.

"No, Roberto, that is not what I want you to do. If I want to fight with the doctor, I will not have a problem. However, I am not ready right now."

"No? What is it then?" Roberto asked, confused and disappointed. He thought he was finally going to help Chico fight.

"In a few hours I am going to come for Lydia and take her to San Cristóbal de Las Casas to marry her. I do not want us to be by ourselves when we go. I want to ask if Rosa can go with us on our trip as our chaperon. I do not want people ever to say anything bad about Lydia. I want things to be as right as possible." Chico stopped talking, hoping Roberto would agree.

Roberto sat back down and scratched the side of his jaw, thinking about what Chico was requesting.

"¡Vieja (Old lady)! Come here!" Roberto yelled for his wife.

"Yes, Roberto?" she answered as she walked into the room. "Hola, Chico. How are you?"

"I am fine, Blanca, and you?"

"I am fine. I heard you almost lost your life, Chico."

"Well, that is what some say; but it really was not that bad," he answered. Chico called Rosa's mother by her first name because she insisted on it when she first met Chico.

"Vieja, listen to what Chico is asking. Tell her, Chico," Roberto said, not wanting to repeat what he had requested. He would rather have Chico say it again.

Chico repeated himself, trying to sound convincing, hoping they would allow Rosa to be their chaperon.

"What does Rosa say about this?" Blanca asked.

"I have not asked her yet. I wanted to ask your permission first. She will be gone a few days. I promise I will take care of her as if she were my sister!" Chico declared, meaning it.

"Rosa! Rosa, come here!" Roberto yelled.

"Yes, Papá," she answered, entering the room. She saw Chico and greeted, "Hola, Chico, I did not know you were here. The doctor did not see you, did he?" Rosa inquired out of concern.

"Hola, Rosa. I do not think the doctor saw me. Anyway, I am not concerned if he did," Chico responded, a little irritated that everybody thought he was afraid of the doctor.

"Chico, tell Rosa what you asked us," Roberto insisted. It seemed Roberto thought it was funny that Chico was going through this a third time, repeating what he was asking. However, Chico did not mind. He was the one asking the favor.

He repeated to Rosa what he wanted to do. Rosa looked pleased, realizing Chico was doing exactly what she had told him to do. Rosa looked at her father and asked, "Papá, will you let me? This will be a good thing. I will be honored to be able to assist in helping Lydia and Chico in their marriage."

Roberto took another big swallow of his drink and stared at Chico for a minute before talking. Everybody was quiet, waiting for Roberto to speak.

"I will let my Rosa go but only on one condition!" he declared, raising his finger, feeling he was now in control and involved in the fight between the doctor and Chico.

"What is the condition, Roberto?" Chico asked, knowing he really did not have a choice.

"If you are going to take mi hija as a chaperon and you are going to have a crazy doctor after you, I want to help."

"In what way, Roberto?" Chico asked, puzzled. He wondered if Roberto wanted to fight with the doctor before they left. If he did, was it going to be before or after he became drunk?

"When you get Lydia, Rosa and I will wait for you on the road outside the pueblo. That way if the doctor comes after you shooting, I will be able to defend mi hija! I will ride with you for a few hours; and if the doctor does not follow, I will return," Roberto stated, taking another swallow of whatever he was drinking.

Chico hoped Roberto would not drink too much right then. If he did, his next condition might be to go and fight with doctor right away.

"That is fine, Roberto."

"Then that is what we will do!"

Blanca interrupted, "I want to go too!"

"¡Ay, callate, mujer! (Shut up, woman!) You cannot go! This is something we must do. You stay here and have supper prepared for me when I return. Also, you can prepare provisions for Chico and the muchachas for the trip."

Roberto yawned, showing he was becoming sleepy. He stood up, took his last big drink, and said, "I am going to bed. When do you want to do this, Chico?"

"Tomorrow, early in the morning, Roberto," he answered, standing up and showing his respect for Roberto.

"Tomorrow, early?" Roberto repeated. "Good, the sooner the better! All right, give Rosa all the details. I am going to bed. Buenas noches," Roberto said, walking away, not waiting for a reply.

Chico told Rosa to be ready early in the morning at 7:00 a.m.; he wanted Roberto and her to be at the stables where they always went for their rides. He told her he was going to pick up Lydia at that time because he knew the doctor would still be sleeping. Señora Gonzales would be busy getting things ready for the day, preparing to teach children in her home.

"How are you going to get Lydia out of the house, Chico?" Rosa asked, unsure of his plans.

"Do not worry, Rosa. You just make sure you are there waiting for me. When Lydia and I get there, we will not have time to wait. We will need to be on the road right away. If the doctor wants to follow us, we will be long gone. And make sure you do not tell anyone. Do you promise?" Chico asked, knowing how girls like to tell their friends.

"Why would I want to tell anyone, Chico?" Rosa questioned, concerned that he did not trust her.

"I know you will not tell anyone. I just want to make sure. I do not want anything to go wrong, Rosa."

"Mamá, you will not tell anyone, will you?" Rosa asked her mother.

"¡Ay, callate, Rosa! (Shut up Rosa!) You do not tell me what to do!" Blanca vented. Rosa did not say anything in return. She knew she had let her mother know she should not tell anyone either.

The next morning at 6:30 a.m., Chico walked out of his house. Before leaving, he loaded and checked his gun. He did not want to use it, but he was not going to be shot at again. "This time if the doctor shoots at me, he will receive a surprise," Chico thought as he left his house.

The night before, after he left Rosa's house, Chico had gone to the stables and talked to Pablo and made arrangements to use three other horses. He told Pablo one of the horses was going to be back in just a few hours. Roberto did not own his own horse. Most people did not. They were too expensive for someone who lived and worked in town.

Chico rode his horse through town. If he was going to get through this, taking Lydia, he wanted to make a speedy getaway on the horse, especially if the doctor pursued him.

As Chico approached Lydia's street, he felt very nervous. He thought back to when he was a youngster, how at times he and his brothers sneaked out of their house without their father knowing. He would put pillows and blankets under his covers. If his father or mother walked into his room, they thought he was asleep. He remembered walking by his father as he slept. This same uneasiness is what he felt at this time. Chico felt that getting caught by his father was worse than being shot at.

When Chico approached the avenue that crossed Lydia's street, he stopped his horse and dismounted. He walked it over to the side of the road and secured it to a post, not wanting his horse too far away but also not too close. He hoped for a clean getaway with Lydia next to him.

The street was not as busy as the night before when he left Rosa's house. A few people were moving around the street. Some were starting to set up small stands to sell their merchandise. Chico walked toward Lydia's street and stopped next to one of the buildings. He squatted down as if he were waiting for someone, trying to act as if he belonged where he positioned himself. He wanted to observe things for a short while. An older woman walked towards him. She held two chickens by their legs. The chickens were alive but were not fighting her. It seemed as they were enjoying their last walk before being slaughtered for someone's supper.

The woman glanced at Chico and said, "¡Hola, señor!"

"Buenos dias, señora."

The woman turned and looked back in the direction of Lydia's house. Chico thought she must have recognized him. She had an expression as if she knew why he was on that street so early in the morning. Chico did not want to be recognized by anyone else. He pulled his hat down over his forehead and put both of his hands in front of his mouth, rubbing his hands together.

In just a few moments, he saw Roberto walking out of his bakery a few doors down from his house. A few seconds after entering his house, Roberto and Rosa stepped into the street and started walking towards him. Even though Chico thought he was disguised well enough with his hat pulled over his forehead, Rosa spotted him right away. Rosa's eyes looked up and met Chico's. As Rosa and Roberto passed him on the other side of the street, Rosa said in a subdued voice that others could not hear, "Be careful, Chico. You should hide. If Lupe comes outside, she will see you."

Chico refrained from answering. He did not want to draw attention. Roberto kept his eyes straight ahead, not looking at Chico.

They kept walking down the street and turned the corner. Chico felt better after seeing Rosa and Roberto, knowing he was not in this all by himself.

"Should I move farther away so Señora Gonzales cannot see me if she comes outdoors?" he wondered. "No. If Lydia comes out, I am close enough. If she steps out, even for a second, I can get her attention. I'd better stay right here!"

Chico had about a half hour wait before he made his move. He wanted to make sure Rosa and her father had enough time to get to the stables and to have their horses ready.

He started to daydream, thinking of the conversation he had with Roberto the night before. He was not as honest as he should have been with Roberto. He told Roberto he was taking Rosa and Lydia to San Cristóbal de Las Casas to be married. However, he was really taking them to Tuxla Gutierrez. Chico did not want to state the truth because if it reached Señora Gonzales or the doctor, it would ruin everything. His plan was to tell Roberto when they left the stables.

More people started moving around the street, setting up their stands. Chico imagined being married to Lydia and living happily the rest of his life. He wondered how many children they were going to have. He wondered if any of them would have blue eyes and if any were going to look like him. He thought of Lydia's demeanor and felt there could only be one result in being married to her—good! His true love had all the qualities to give Chico a happy life.

"¡Hola, señor! You are a brave man to come back here!" Pepe, the orange man, asserted.

"Hola, Señor Pepe," Chico answered, not knowing if this man was a friend of the doctor. He hoped the man was not going to go and tell the doctor he was here again. Chico remembered how the man covered for him when he tried to talk to the doctor.

Pepe put his things down. He had his stand set up closer to Lydia's house the last time he encountered him. "What are you going to do this time, Señor Rodriguez?" the man asked. Chico wondered how he knew his name. But then again, Chico thought, "I am probably the talk of the street because of the last time I was shot at."

"I have some business here this morning, señor."

Pepe looked over at Lydia's house; and without looking down at Chico, he said, "Just be careful. The doctor does not care if he kills you. Many of us want you to succeed in whatever you are going to do. We do not like the doctor very much. He is not a friend of the common people here, you know."

"I did not know that. Why?" Chico asked, puzzled.

"The doctor is friends with all the rich society, and he does not care about us poor people or our children. He will not treat us when we are sick unless we have the pesos to pay right away. We only go to him if it is life or death and sometimes not even then!" Pepe expressed resentfully.

"I am sorry to hear that, señor."

"Yes, well, I guess that is the way it is when one is poor."

Chico did not say anything. He knew life was difficult. He thought of how his father was always fair with all who worked for him. He also thought of how his father treated the poor, with dignity and respect; but his father could not save the world. "If my father slaughtered all of his steers and gave the meat to the poor, where would that leave him? As far as my father being rich," Chico thought, "it took a lot of work to get what he has. But my father was not like the doctor, if what this man is saying is correct. If my father were a doctor, he would treat the poor; and he would feel compassion for them."

Chico looked up at the sky and realized it was time to make his move.

Chico stood up and said, "Well then, señor, wish me luck! I hope I do not get shot this time!"

Pepe reached down and picked up his bags and said, "I hope and wish you get what you want, Señor Rodriguez! Good luck!"

Chico walked up the street with his hat still pulled over his forehead as much as possible. Lydia's house appeared quiet. He turned and looked at Rosa's house and saw what appeared to be Blanca peeking out of her front door. Chico was now one house away from Lydia's home. He put his hand on the handle of his gun, not to pull it out but just to make sure it was there. Chico laughed to himself, thinking, "Where can my gun go?"

He had the same feeling he had when he was a young boy as he was passing his father's room, sneaking out. He approached the front door, stopped, and stood next to the door. If someone were to open the door, they could not see where he was standing. He was not in a hurry. He did not want to cause a commotion. He really was not sure how he was going to do this, but he just knew he would succeed.

Chico listened very carefully to see if he could hear any noise inside the house. He did not. Two minutes went by, and he thought it was time. He wanted to knock but imagined the doctor answering and a repeat of what happened last time. "If the doctor comes to the door, I will have to shoot him right away and take Lydia with me. Then I will have to go, not to Tuxla, but all the way back home to Sonora. Ay, I do not want that!" Chico thought.

Chico reached over and grabbed the handle of the door. He pushed it a little. The door opened about an inch. He listened. Still no noise. Chico put his ear on the door and waited. As he had his ear on the door, his eyes scanned the street. He noticed all the people standing still and watching him. "Now I have to act," he thought.

THE WICKED LADY

T here was no noise coming from inside the house. He stood up against the door and pushed it. It opened a little. He wondered what he would do if the doctor or Señora Gonzales saw him. He did not know and thought it all depended on how they reacted.

Chico stepped into the house and scanned the parlor. No one was there. There still were no sounds coming from anywhere in the house. Everything was still. Chico closed the door behind him and thought of the people outside. The thought crossed his mind, "What are they thinking of me entering the doctor's home?" He hoped no one would knock on the doctor's door and inform him of the intruder.

Chico took a few steps toward the entrance that led to the rest of the house. He was unfamiliar with the layout of the dwelling, remembering Lydia mentioned her room was toward the back of the house. He thought she had said her room had beads as curtains in the doorway.

As Chico entered the hallway, he noticed all the rooms had curtains hanging over the doorway, except the last one. It had beads hanging. "Did Lydia say her room had beads or the doctor's room had them?" Chico asked himself, feeling confused.

He took a couple of steps toward the back of the house. Chico knew at this point that if the doctor found him, there was going to be big trouble. Chico stopped at the first curtain doorway. He put his hand on the gun under his shirt and his other hand on the curtain very slowly. He drew the curtain back just enough to see who was lying on the bed. It was the other children. He closed the curtain and moved on to the next doorway. Just as he was going to draw the curtain, he heard the doctor's voice coming from inside the room. It sounded as if he was up and ready to walk out of his bedroom.

Chico looked back and saw that there was only one more room

left. It was the one with the beads hanging from the doorway. Chico did not want to get caught by the doctor, so he moved toward the room with the beads as quickly as he could.

Entering the room, he stopped and was satisfied he had found his true love. She was lying in her bed sleeping. He stood there and gazed at her. She slept just as he imagined her, with all her beauty radiating from her beautiful self. Chico looked back at the doorway as he heard Señora Gonzales approaching the room. Lydia's bedroom had no back wall; it opened to the outside backyard. He thought of stepping outside into the yard. This was not a good idea because the doctor or one of the other children might see him from their bedrooms. Chico looked around the room and saw the closet. He slipped behind a drape that was covering the closet and did not move.

"Lydia! Lydia!" Señora Gonzales called out as she opened the beads with one hand and looked into the room. "¡Lydia, muchacha! Time to get up and pronto (fast)! I will need your help more today because Señora Vasquez is bringing her two small children. So get up right now!" She released the beads and started to say something to the doctor as her voice faded.

Lydia was awake now and was lying on her bed with one arm over her forehead. Chico did not know if he should step out of the closet. He hesitated, thinking he might startle Lydia; and it might cause her to scream, not knowing who he was.

"Lydia," Chico whispered.

Lydia put her arm down, thinking she heard someone calling her name.

"Lydia," he whispered again. Chico was watching her through the drapes, observing her surprise that someone was calling her.

Lydia recognized the voice. It sounded as if Chico was calling her. She raised her head and thought it was her imagination.

"Lydia, over here," he called in a whisper.

Lydia now knew for a fact that she was not hearing things. "Where are you, Chico?" she asked, knowing it could not be anyone else but Chico calling her from within her own bedroom. Lydia sat up and first looked outside; then her eyes scanned the closet. Chico pulled the curtains to the side. Lydia's heart started beating with excitement.

"Chico! Chico, I have been waiting for you!" she cried, a little loud. Chico put his finger to his lips, indicating for her to speak more softly. He did not want for the doctor or Señora Gonzales to hear her. Chico thought he heard footsteps outside of her room and drew the curtains back over the closet.

The beads parted. Señora Gonzales looked in the room and scanned it, moving her eyes to the opening to the yard. "Who are you talking to?" Señora Gonzales asked, staring at Lydia. "I asked, who are you talking to, muchacha?"

"I was singing, Lupe. Is it all right if I sing, or I cannot do that either?"

The beads parted next to Lupe. The doctor stood at the doorway next to his wife. "What is it?" he asked, waiting for a response from Lydia.

Chico was sitting in the closet, not moving a muscle. He was trying not to breathe. He did not want them to even suspect he was in the house.

"I heard Lydia talking to someone," Señora Gonzales said. It seemed to Lydia that Lupe was trying to create trouble for her.

The doctor's eyes looked around the room; and he stated, "I do not see anyone here. Who was she talking to? Who were you speaking to, Lydia?"

"I told Lupe I was singing to myself. I guess I'd better not even do that if it is going to get me into trouble."

"Come, Lupe, leave her. Let her sing," the doctor said as he released the curtain beads. Lupe had an expression on her face as if she did not believe Lydia. Before she let the beads fall back, she looked around the room and outside to make sure no one was around. She suspected something. Then, still not satisfied, she let go of the beads and walked away.

Lydia sat there for a few seconds; she stood from her bed and walked to the doorway. She stood on her side of the beads for five seconds, drew the beads away, and looked out. She would not put it past Lupe to be standing on the other side. Once Lydia was satisfied Lupe was not there, she turned and went to where Chico was waiting. She whispered, "Chico, did you come for me?"

"Yes. Get some of your things together and let's go," he stated as he looked at the beads, hoping they would not move.

Lydia put her hands together and looked up to the heavens, saying in a whisper, "¡Gracias (Thanks)!" She turned and walked to her dresser, opened a drawer, and took out a few things. She took a few steps back to where Chico was hiding, reached over his head, and pulled down a traveling bag. She laid it on the bed and started putting a few things in it. She thought to herself that she did not want to take much. She reasoned that in the future she might be able to get the rest of her things. Chico thought about getting out of his hiding place but reasoned it was best not to move until Lydia was ready. Chico peeked out and saw that Lydia was buttoning the bag. He was just about to step out of the closet when the beads opened.

"Lydia! What are you doing? Where do you think you are going?" Señora Gonzales yelled, seeing Lydia preparing the traveling bag. She knew something was not right when she thought she heard Lydia talking to someone.

Lydia turned and saw Lupe standing there, waiting for an answer.

Chico thought maybe he should step out then; but he thought, "What will I do, draw my gun and shoot Señora Gonzales? I'd better stay here for a few short seconds and see what happens."

"I am leaving, Lupe. You have me here as if I were a prisoner; and I am tired of it, Lupe! You are unfair with me and treat me as if you hate me! You are not my mother! And for sure, you certainly do not treat me as if I were one of your daughters!"

"We will see about this!" Lupe yelled, turning around and walking out of the room.

Chico stepped out of the closet and asked Lydia, "Where does the doctor keep the gun?"

She looked at Chico with a hurt expression, thinking he was planning to get the gun and shoot the doctor. "Why, Chico? Why do you want to know where he keeps the gun?"

"I want to hide it! I do not want you or me to get shot! If the doctor knows I am here, I will get shot on the spot! Tell me, where does he keep the gun?" Chico demanded, waiting for a reply. He spoke as if he did not have much time to linger for a response.

"Behind his bedroom door. It is a rifle, Chico; and it has bullets in it all the time," Lydia declared as he walked out of the room through the beads.

"Be careful, Chico!" Lydia exclaimed, as he stepped out of her room.

Chico was not going to get the gun and go after the doctor as

Lydia supposed. He walked into the room and looked behind the door. He took the rifle and put it under the doctor's bed. "If he comes for his gun, he will have a difficult time finding it," Chico said to himself as he stepped back out of the room.

As Chico took a few steps back to Lydia's room, he could hear Señora Gonzales screaming on the other side of the house or in the doctor's office.

Chico stepped inside Lydia's room. Lydia was sitting on her bed as if she were waiting for a gun to go off. "Are you ready, Lydia?" he asked gently, putting his hand out so Lydia could join him.

"Yes, I am ready, Chico," she said with her lovely voice while reaching for his hand.

Chico reached for her traveling bag. Extending his other hand, he pulled her through the beads. Chico knew the quicker they left, the better it was going to be for them.

Just as Chico and Lydia stepped into the parlor, the doctor and Señora Gonzales stepped around the corner from the kitchen.

"What! You again! Here in my house! I will kill you!" the doctor shouted with indignation.

Señora Gonzales yelled at her husband, "Kill him, Miguel! Kill the ranch hand! He deserves it!"

As she said this, Chico thought, "What a wicked lady! No wonder Lydia is willing to leave with me at anytime. I would want to leave too if I had to live with somebody as evil as she!" Chico did not realize Señora Gonzales had never showed that side of her personality to Lydia before Chico came into the picture.

"Let's go, Lydia! Keep walking. Do not stop. Once we get outside, start running towards the Town Square."

The doctor stepped up to Chico. Even though he was an older man, he felt as though he was a young man at heart. He looked at Chico as a kid who needed a good whipping, and he felt he could do it. He swung at Chico. As he swung, he almost lost his balance. Chico could have returned the punch but chose not to. He thought of the relationship he and Lydia had and how much he loved her. He did not want to do anything to make things worse than they were.

He pushed the doctor hard enough that the doctor stumbled to the wall. To the doctor this was a real punch. If it were not, it sure felt like one to him. He did not like being punched by the kid who was complicating his life and the lives of his family.

The doctor regained his composure and came at Chico again. He reached back and swung as hard as he could. This time his punch landed and hit Chico square in the eye. The doctor had not hit anyone so hard since his school days. When his punch struck, he felt Chico's body flow with the blow, falling back.

Chico felt the blow hit him. The punch hit with such force that he knew it was a mistake not to floor the doctor while he had a chance. Chico felt his body giving way to the doctor's heavy punch. He fell back and hit the wall. The next thing he knew, he was on the floor looking up at the doctor. Lydia was already outside, so he was alone with an angry and crazy man. The doctor stepped up to Chico, bent over, and started to swing at him with hefty blows coming from his large solid fists, one blow after the other! Chico had to do something, but he felt defenseless. The doctor was old but strong. Chico was able to grab his leg and hang onto it. Chico raised his leg and placed it into the doctor's crotch. With all his might, he lifted the doctor up, off his feet. The doctor lost his balance and toppled over.

Once the doctor was on the floor, Chico stood up as quickly as he could. The doctor rose as fast as Chico did. Now Chico was ready again for another chance to knock out the doctor. They were both standing. Chico brought his arm back, tightened his fist, and let go as hard as he could. His fist connected with the doctor, hitting him somewhere in the face. Chico was not sure where he hit the old man because his vision was impaired. Chico felt his punch jolt the doctor. The doctor moved back against the other wall with the blow, but the punch did not do what Chico felt it should have. "Any other man would have fallen to the floor with that punch," Chico thought.

At that instant Chico noticed Señora Gonzales had disappeared toward the back of the house. Chico thought of the gun. He did not know if she would look under the bed for it. If she did, she would be back in the parlor in a matter of seconds. At that point Lydia was out of the front door and running toward the Town Square. As she was running, she knew she was never going to return to the doctor and Lupe's house again.

The doctor was bouncing back from Chico's blow. Chico did not want to take a chance and let the doctor come back at him with a harder punch. The doctor was halfway down, trying to stand, hanging onto a chair and a small table. The chair was falling over because of the doctor's weight and his effort to support himself.

Señora Gonzales ran back into the parlor. "Miguel! Are you all right?"

Chico grabbed Lydia's bag that he had dropped, stepped out of the doorway, and stopped. He looked back and thought maybe the punch did more than he imagined. Chico knew he would never have a family relationship with them in the future.

As Chico looked back, Señora Gonzales looked up at him. She was on the floor trying to help her husband. "You are a bad man for hitting the doctor! You are going to pay for this!" Señora Gonzales exclaimed in a vicious tone.

Chico had never before seen that expression on her face or on any other woman's face.

As Lydia was running down the street, she stopped when she noticed Chico was not following her. She wondered if she should return and try to help him. As she took a few steps back towards the house, Chico stepped out of the doorway and stood for a second. She wondered why he had stopped. Chico started running towards her. He yelled at Lydia, "Run, Lydia! Do not wait for me! I will catch up!"

Chico ran fast and was right behind Lydia with her bag in his hand. He had almost lost it due to the scuffle with the doctor. The people on the street were stopped, motionless, watching Chico and Lydia run by them. As Chico passed the orange man, Pepe, he heard him say, "¡Andale, señor! ¡Andale (Hurry)!"

As they approached the corner, Chico called out to Lydia. She was only a few feet in front of him. "Lydia, here, turn right! My horse is there tied up!"

Lydia raced around the corner, having a difficult time running with the sandals she was wearing. Chico stopped at the corner to look back at the doctor's house. He wanted to see if the doctor and Señora Gonzales were following. In that way he knew how quickly they needed to get away. Just as he turned, he saw the doctor and Señora Gonzales exiting the house. The doctor had found his rife and was running with it, ready to shoot. "At least it bought us some time," Chico thought.

Chico saw the doctor catch sight of him. The doctor lowered his rifle to take aim. Chico did not think the doctor would shoot at him with all the people on the street. He turned and ran hard, hoping the doctor would not shoot. Chico heard a pop. As he slipped around the corner and out of the sight of the doctor, he heard another pop. He dashed around the corner as fast has he could where Lydia was waiting next to the horse.

"Stupid doctor," he thought as he untied the horse. He mounted his horse and reached down for Lydia to take his arm. He pulled her up. She was not settled on the horse. Chico did not want to waste any time. He lifted the reign and kicked his legs, so the horse could begin his run.

He knew the doctor would come around the corner in a matter of seconds. If Chico hurried, he could be around the next corner before the doctor took another shot at him and Lydia. As Chico and Lydia approached the next corner, Chico drew his gun. He looked back and anticipated the doctor's moving around the corner at any time. Chico was hoping he did not have to shoot. The horse was moving fast, approaching the next corner. The doctor came around the corner. He slumped down on one knee and raised the rifle. Chico reached back, behind Lydia, with his gun in his hand, and took aim the best that he could. Chico knew he would never hit the doctor with a bullet. He was a good shot and could hit almost any target at a standstill but not moving at that speed and with his gun bouncing from the horse's gallop. Chico reasoned that the shot was not to put a bullet into the doctor but to frighten him.

Chico's revolver fired. Because it was a larger caliber weapon, the blast was much louder than the doctor's rifle. Chico pulled the trigger a second time; and he saw the doctor falling to the ground, taking cover. The doctor did not have time to return the shot. Chico was glad. The worst thing that could have happened was that the doctor could have put a bullet into Lydia's back. He did not know what he would do for the rest of his life if something were to happen to his true love.

Riding his horse through town, he felt Lydia's arms around him. He knew this was it. He finally had his true love and would never let her go. As they were leaving town, Chico saw people motionless in the street. They turned to look at them as Chico and Lydia rode through the streets. Chico wondered how they knew he had just started his new life with the girl of his dreams. He did not realize the people were turning because they were riding through town so rapidly.

Periodically Chico would look over his shoulder to see if he was being followed. He knew the doctor did not have a horse in town.

However, he knew anything could happen at this point.

As he was approaching the stables, he felt Lydia's arms around him and her cheek against his back. Chico felt his back wet. He then heard and felt Lydia sobbing. Chico was sure the doctor would never be able to catch him at this point, so he stopped the horse. As the horse came to a stop, Lydia was crying uncontrollably. Chico turned as much as he could and wondered if Lydia was brokenhearted because he had taken her from her home.

"Lydia, my love, what is it?" Chico asked as he dismounted and reached to help her off the horse. They were only a quarter of a kilometer from the stables and could easily walk the rest of the way.

Lydia was unable to answer, still sobbing. Chico could not tell if it was because of joy or if it was because she realized she had made a mistake.

As Chico embraced her, he said, "What is it, my Lydia? What did I do to you, my love?"

Lydia, now realizing Chico thought he did something to make her cry. Sobbed and said, "I... I cannot believe that Miguel...."

Because she was weeping uncontrollably, she could not finish what she started to say. Chico felt distress for her. He wanted to put himself into her heart and comfort her. He did not know what to do. He squeezed her and said, "Ay, Lydia. I will take care of you. You are with me now, and nothing will happen to you."

Lydia felt Chico's arms tighten around her; she felt comforted, not wanting to be anywhere else at that moment. She stopped weeping but was still breathing heavily.

"Chico, I cannot believe Miguel shot his gun at me! I would have never imagined he would do that!" Lydia exclaimed, starting to sob once more.

"He was not shooting at you, Lydia. He wanted me dead, not you," Chico stated, squeezing Lydia in his arms.

Pulling himself away a little, he looked at Lydia and brushed her hair back with the back of his hand. He continued, "He has only himself to blame. I tried my best to do things right, but he just would not listen. So now this is the way it is for him. Do not worry, my love. You will be happy. I will see to it!"

Lydia, wiping away her tears, looked at Chico, took a deep breath, and smiled. Lydia felt happy at that moment because she was with the man with whom she wanted to spend the rest of her life. No matter what the doctor or Lupe said, they were not going to take her away from Chico.

Lydia started to sob once again. She did not know if it was for joy or the sadness of losing her family, the family she grew so fond of through the years.

Chico said, "Lydia, I will do whatever I can to make you happy. Anything I can."

Chico thought to himself, "I hope I can, despite this situation with the doctor." Chico looked down the road and wondered what the doctor was doing right at that instant.

"Let's go, Lydia. Rosa and Roberto are waiting for us up the road by our stables." Chico felt comfortable referring to the stables as theirs, since they had met there so many times in the past.

"Rosa and Roberto?" Lydia asked, surprised.

"Yes, Roberto wanted to help. He knows how much I love you, and Rosa will go with us to be our chaperon until we are married. I want everything to be as right as possible for us. I do not want anyone to say anything bad about your being with me. The only time we will be alone is now, from the time we leave town until we meet Rosa and her father at the stables, just ahead on the road. Even though people might think otherwise about what is happening right now, the true story will come out later," Chico declared.

"I do not care what people say about us. I want to be with you no matter what people say."

"You might feel that way now, Lydia, but later it might be a different matter. Besides, we want to make sure our children know the truth about how we conducted ourselves," Chico answered, looking into Lydia's blue eyes.

They turned and started walking towards the stables. Chico thought of the doctor again and tried not to walk too slowly. In the next ten minutes, Chico told Lydia of his plans for getting married, which she already knew was going to take place shortly. He also told her of his trip to San Cristóbal de Las Casas to make arrangements, adding what he had told Roberto and Rosa the night before.

Chico thought he heard something behind him and thought it was foolish to walk when they could have an army behind them. "Let us get on the horse, Lydia. I think we should get out of here. We are spending too much time talking when we are going to have the rest of our lives together." They mounted the horse and rode off.

Roberto and Rosa were sitting on top of a large rock when they saw Chico and Lydia. From a distance they seemed to appear relieved.

As Chico and Lydia approached them, Rosa said, "Ay, Lydia and Chico! We were really worried about you! Are you all right? We heard four gun shots coming from town and from two different guns!"

"We are fine, Rosa," Chico answered.

"Ay, Rosa, you are a true friend. You are closer than a sister would be."

"Lydia, you are my best friend and so is Chico. Anyway, I am not doing it for nothing. Chico said that your children will call me tía (aunt)!"

Lydia smiled and said, "That is so. Chico spoke for both of us. I will have it no other way, Rosa."

Up to this point Roberto did not say anything. He listened to his young daughter acting as a grown woman. He then said, "Well, we had better go; or nobody is going to call you tía! We will all be shot!"

They all mounted their horses. Lydia looked at Chico and wanted to ride with him as she did earlier. "Chico, I can ride with you; and we can pull this horse along with us," Lydia said with her dreamy blue eyes.

Chico, knowing they had the rest of their lives to be together, replied, "Lydia, it will be better if you ride that horse for right now. We do not know if the doctor will come around the corner. If he does, we can escape more easily with each one of us on our own horse."

Lydia looked at Chico with an expression of approval, knowing he knew what he was saying.

They had a distance to travel before the road forked, one going in the direction to Tuxla and the other going in the direction of San Cristóbal de Las Casas. Chico was in no rush to tell Roberto where they were really going. He wanted to choose his words carefully so as not to make Roberto and Rosa feel wronged because he had not been honest with them.

After an hour on the road, they spotted a man on horseback. The man on the horse was moving down a hill slowly. Roberto thought it best that Lydia and Chico pull off the road and hide in the thick, green foliage. They did not want this person to report back to the doctor that he had seen Chico and Lydia leaving the area. The person might also report to the doctor and his friends that Roberto and Rosa were accomplices to what happened. Roberto did not mind if the doctor found out. He was willing to fight with the doctor and his friends if it needed to be done. He reasoned, "Why should I if I do not have to."

Roberto was raised in this area and had a number of friends and family as well. He knew if things got out of hand, he would be able to call on them for support if necessary.

As the man approached, Roberto and Rosa did not recognize him. Chico did not see the man closely because he and Lydia had dismounted and walked their horses deep into the jungle. They came to a small stream. They stopped, and Chico told Lydia to sit on one of the rocks by the water with the horses. He was going to return without his horse to make sure the man was out of sight before they returned to the road.

"¡Hola, señor!" Roberto called out.

"Buenos dias, señor y señorita," the man replied.

"May I ask if San Bartolomé de los Llanos is close by? I have been traveling for two days and have never been to the small pueblo."

"Yes. It is just over the next small hill. You will be able to see the pueblo on the side of the mountain, señor," Roberto answered.

"I have been to Tuxla Gutierrez before but never to the small pueblo of San Bartolomé de los Llanos. It sure is hot here. My name is Agusto Bara, and I am from San Cristóbal de Las Casas," Agusto said, fanning himself and extending his hand to shake Roberto's.

"I see," answered Roberto, shaking the man's hand while still mounted on the horse. Roberto wondered why he was going to San Bartolomé de los Llanos, since not too many strangers traveled to the town. Roberto continued, "What is your business in San Bartolomé de los Llanos?"

"I am going to see Dr. Miguel Gonzales."

"Oh, the doctor is my neighbor and my friend. Not only that, but he is my customer as well," Roberto conveyed, wondering why this man was going to see the doctor all the way from San Cristóbal de Las Casas. Roberto knew Chico had just returned from there and was wondering if this had anything to do with him.

"Do you know a young man by the name of Francisco Rodriguez?" the man asked.

"Not really. Are you seeking him also?"

"No, I came to tell the doctor the man has intentions of stealing his young girl and taking her to San Cristóbal de Las Casas to marry her without his permission."

"I see," Roberto replied. He then added, "How do you know this, señor?"

"Well, the boy rented a room at an inn there and told the padre what his intentions were, thinking the padre was going to help him with his scheme. But the padre will have no part in it. He said it must run in their blood."

Roberto, puzzled, asked, "What must run in their blood?"

Rosa knew exactly what he was talking about because she remembered Lydia telling the story of her father.

"Rebellion, señor. The muchacha's father had the same blood. Do you not know the story of the girl's father?"

Roberto, now very curious, asked, "No, tell me."

Roberto remembered years ago when Lydia went to live with the doctor. He had heard the story then. Since the man wanted to tell him, he thought he would let him refresh his memory.

"Well, señor, I really do not have time; but ask your friend, the doctor, to tell you the story. He tells everybody else. Wherever he travels, he relates the story of the girl's father. I had better be on my way. I need to warn the doctor of the boy's and girl's intentions. Buenos dias, señor y señorita," he said as he pulled his horse away from them and rode off.

"Ay, ay, ay, Papá, Chico cannot go to San Cristóbal de Las Casas now! The doctor and his friends will be there and right away," Rosa complained to her father.

"Do you really think the doctor will follow Chico and Lydia? I do not. If I were the doctor and someone came for you, I would put a stop to the friendship right then if I did not like the muchacho. But if you left with him to be married, why should I waste my time? I would know I would not be able to stop it."

"Papá, everybody does not think as you do. The doctor does not like to lose. He only likes to win! You know that. Everybody in pueblo knows that."

"Yes, you may be right. Why should Chico take any chances, especially when he knows this man came to tell the doctor what he intends to do?"

Once Chico saw the man riding away, he returned to where he

had left Lydia. "Lydia, the man left. We can go back now."

"What do you really think, Chico? Do you think everything will be all right? What are we going to do?"

Chico stood as Lydia sat on a large rock. As Lydia sat waiting for an answer, Chico thought, "I never proposed to Lydia in person, only in a letter."

"Lydia," Chico said as he approached her. He kneeled down on one knee and continued, "I want to ask you a question that I really never have been able to ask you in person."

"What is it, Chico?"

"Will you marry me and be my wife for the rest of your life?"

Lydia wanted to laugh because Chico looked funny proposing with his beaten and bruised face and with his eye almost closed from the doctor's punches. Lydia knew he went through a lot to get to this point. He was beat up, had some bones broken, was shot at, and now had been beaten up and shot at again.

Lydia smiled at him and touched his face. She moved her finger around his eye where it looked the worst. She did not answer right away because she wanted the moment to last, knowing she would remember it the rest of her life.

A few seconds went by and Lydia answered as she looked deep into Chico's eyes, "Yes, Chico, I will be your wife forever. I have been dreaming of it for awhile now. The first day I met you, I knew I was going to marry you. I knew you were the one for me. And yes, I will have your children, wash your clothes, cook your food, and go anywhere you would like to take me."

Lydia thought to herself that with her inheritance she would get someone else to do all the work, but it would be the same as if she were doing it.

"Now I will answer your question, Lydia. 'What are we going to do?' Well, now that you will officially marry me, we will go to Tuxla and be married right away. We will wait there a few days so the doctor can cool off. Then we will return to San Bartolomé de los Llanos and start our life together."

Just as Chico finished answering her question, he heard Rosa's voice calling from a distance. Chico looked at Lydia and said, "Why does she always come when things are getting good?"

Lydia laughed and said, "She must. She is our chaperon."

"Chico! Lydia!" Rosa yelled out again.

Chico put his hands around his mouth and yelled back, "We are over here, Rosa!"

In a few seconds Rosa and Roberto came through the foliage. Roberto said, "Ay, you two came way in here. Did you think it was the doctor?" Roberto sounded a little irritated for having to come and look for them.

Chico thought to himself that he was glad Roberto was not their chaperon.

Roberto continued, "The man came from San Cristóbal de Las Casas to report your intentions to the doctor. He said the padre sent him to tell the doctor you are going to San Cristóbal de Las Casas to get married. Now it will not be wise for you to go there. It will be better for you to go to Tuxla Gutierrez. If the doctor wants to stop you from being married, he will definitely go and look for the two of you in San Cristóbal de Las Casas."

Chico was relieved he did not have to tell Roberto he was not going to go to San Cristóbal de Las Casas. He looked over at Lydia. Lydia smiled at him, knowing things were already working out for them. Chico said, "We had better move on. Once we get to the crossroads and head in the direction of Tuxla, we will be safe."

They traveled to where the road met the main highway. It was a small trail with only enough room for a wagon. In that region, if the trail was not used often, the road was covered with vegetation because the jungle grew fast and took over the roadway.

They now headed in the direction to Tuxla. They found a nice place off the road to spend the night. In the morning they started their ride again. An hour later Roberto declared, "I think this will be as far as I will continue. I do not think the doctor will be following now. It will not be long before you reach Tuxla. Chico, you take care of mi hija (my daughter). Do you understand?" Roberto asked as all the horses came to a stop.

"I will take care of her as if she were my sister, Roberto."

Lydia added, "If we know anyone in Tuxla who is going to San Bartolomé de los Llanos, we will send Rosa with them in a few days, unless we decide to return early. But if we do not send her, she will be with us. Do not worry, Roberto; we will only send Rosa with someone who can be trusted with such special merchandise!"

Roberto and Rosa dismounted their horses and embraced each other. "All right, Papá. You have a safe journey back home."

"I have a safe journey? You have a safe journey! I want you to be very careful and not to take any chances. I think it will be best for all of you when you arrive in Tuxla to go and stay with my sister, your tía Anna. She will be happy to see you."

Rosa did not say anything. She knew her tía would be nosy and might not like the situation.

"Adios, Papá," Rosa said as she pulled away from her father.

Roberto mounted his horse and rode away. They were silent for a short while as they rode.

Chapter Eight

Inheritance

By nightfall they entered Tuxla Gutierrez. As they rode into town, Chico appreciated the way the small towns appeared with all their beauty, their cobblestone streets and all. As they moved down the avenue, people sat on their front porches against the flat walls. Children played tag in the moonlight. As they rode by, the people were friendly and greeted them.

"Hola, how are you this evening?" a man asked.

"Hola, señor. Can you tell us where we can find an inn?" Chico inquired.

Earlier, on the road, Rosa expressed to Lydia and Chico that she did not want to stay with her tía. She said she really did not like her tía Anna very much. Also, she really did not know her well because she rarely visited her. Her tía had a lot of money and always had her nose in the air, meaning she felt she was better than others.

This made Lydia think of her inheritance. She never wanted to think she was better than others and wanted to feel this way for the rest of her life. She was going to work on not thinking more of herself than she should. Lydia thought she should tell Chico right away of her inheritance, now that they were going to be married.

One man on the porch stood up from his chair and approached Chico. "You will find an inn just down the street. When you get to the last house, you will find the Chávez home. There is a sign in front that says 'Chávez,' señor."

"Gracias (Thanks), señor," Chico said as they rode away.

The inn they found was nice. Chico paid for two rooms, one for Lydia and Rosa and one for him.

Señor Daniel Chávez and Señora Antonia Chávez owned the inn. Señor Chávez was an older man in his seventies. He was a big man, tall and heavy. He had a round face and did not talk much when more than one person was present. Señora Chávez was also elderly; her face was very wrinkled. She was a feisty old woman who always got her way, but she seemed to always be in a good mood. She had a strong voice and laughed at everything. The couple had lived in Tuxla all of their lives.

Señora Chávez was thrilled to have such young and handsome guests staying with her. She went into the kitchen and prepared frijoles (beans) for them, a very hospitable woman. She called Chico, Lydia, and Rosa into the kitchen as soon as she completed setting the table. As they were having their meal, the old woman inquired as to why they were in Tuxla. Chico was comfortable with Señora Chávez and related the story of the encounters he had with the doctor and of his love for Lydia.

"That is why your face looks the way it does! The doctor should be shot!" she declared. Then Señora Chávez noticed Lydia's sad face. She continued, "Ay, for you, muchacha, he should just be whipped." By her expression Señora Chávez knew Lydia had a lot of love for the doctor and Señora Gonzales.

"The viejo (old man) and I were married when I was thirteen," Señora Chávez said, knowing what it meant to be married young. "And look at us. I am sixty-nine and my viejo is seventy-six."

Changing the subject, she looked at Lydia and asked, "What are you going to get married in, hija? I did not see any big bags, big enough to carry a beautiful dress."

"Ay, Doña Chávez, I did not have time to bring anything with me. I am fortunate to have escaped with myself," Lydia declared.

Chico had a sad expression because he was not providing Lydia with more.

"Well," Señora Chávez said, "I am going to fix that! In the morning I will go out and make sure you are dressed for the occasion. If I cannot buy you a beautiful dress, I will borrow one. And if I cannot borrow one, I will make one in just a few short hours!" Señora Chávez asserted, not really thinking she would be able to make one in such a short time.

"Ay, no, Doña Chávez. That will be too much trouble," Lydia insisted.

"Not for me. It will be my pleasure, muchacha. I am grande (aged), and I have much experience in making dresses. When I was young, that was my occupation. Each day I would make beautiful dresses. So if I was able to make beautiful dresses in my day, I can easily put something together for a pretty muchacha now."

Chico changed the subject again and said with a worried expression on his face, "I hope the padre marries us."

"And why will he not?" asked Señora Chávez harshly.

"Well, in San Cristóbal de Las Casas, the padre would not marry us because he knows the doctor. He was going to tell the other padres in the pueblo not to marry us."

Lydia interrupted and started to relate the story of her father. Once Lydia started the story, Señora Chávez interrupted, "So, you are the young muchacha!" Señora Chávez declared, remembering and hearing of the situation a few years back. She continued, "You do know your father was not a good man. He brought dishonor on God and the iglesia (church)."

"Yes, I know," Lydia said as she bowed her head. She continued, "But it was not my fault. I had nothing to do with it."

"Ay, niña (little girl), we know that," Señora Chávez expressed, feeling sorry for Lydia.

Rosa did not say much. She sat in her chair, eating just a little of the frijoles and listening. She yawned a few times, showing her tiredness.

Señora Chávez did not say much more on the subject. It seemed Señora Chávez was the boss of the house. As Lydia and Señora Chávez sat and talked, Chico looked at the old man. He then glanced at his powerfully voiced wife and wondered if things were different when they were young. He wondered if he was the boss or she had always been.

"Well," Señora Chávez said as she stood up, "let us go to bed. Tomorrow is a big day. For you children it will be the biggest day of your lives!"

It did not take Lydia and Rosa long to fall asleep. Chico lay in his bed wondering how things were going to go in the next few days. He wished he knew what the doctor had done. "If there were a way I could find out," he thought. "If the doctor went to San Cristóbal de Las Casas, he will be returning in about three or four days. That will give us plenty of time. But then again if he did not leave and if he somehow found out we are here, he could be here tomorrow afternoon." Chico sat up, worried about what he had just thought. He sat on the side of his bed and uttered, "What is wrong with me? Why am I worried about what the doctor is going to do? Tomorrow Lydia will be my wife, and there will be nothing he will be able to do!" He lay back down and fell asleep in no time.

Waking up in the morning, Chico stayed in his bed wondering how it had gone with Roberto. He wondered if the doctor found out Roberto had helped them and rode with them part of the way to Tuxla. He hoped it went well. If anything happened to Roberto, Chico felt he would have to be the aggressor with the doctor.

Chico's thoughts went from Roberto to how he was going to marry Lydia. He thought that if he went to the iglesia by himself the same thing could happen as the last time he was in San Cristóbal de Las Casas. He wondered if it would be better to take Lydia with him and be married on the spot. If he were to go and make arrangements, he did not want to lie to the priest. Usually the priests did not marry people on the spot. Chico thought about all of this and made a decision.

"I am going to get up and look for a padre who will marry us before some more unforeseen circumstances take place. Things will then get more complicated."

Chico arose and dressed. The girls were still asleep. They were tired from the trip and all the excitement. The inn was also quiet. "Either Doña Chávez and Don Chávez have left, or they are late sleepers," Chico thought as he left the house.

On the street Chico asked a man for the location of an iglesia and was directed there.

Walking into the iglesia was different than it was in San Cristóbal de Las Casas. The priest was a nice man. He was young and had a friendly demeanor. Chico asked the priest if he could marry his fiancé and him. The priest replied that it would be fine; he would be there the entire day. Chico thought to himself that he did not want this opportunity to go by. "I will go and get Lydia and Rosa before the padre hears something and changes his mind."

Arriving back at the inn, he stepped up to Lydia and Rosa's room and called out to them, "Lydia, Lydia! Rosa!" The girls were still sleeping. "They are tired because of the long journey," Chico thought.

"What is it, Chico. It is still too early," Rosa answered.

"You two have to get up now. Wake Lydia up. We are going to be married this morning. I found a padre who is willing to marry us right away."

"I do not know if Lydia will wake up; she is sound asleep."

"May I come in and wake her?"

"No, Chico! It is not proper for a man to enter a girl's bedroom!" Rosa declared.

"Well then, you need to wake Lydia right away."

"What is your hurry, Chico? We have all day, and we have all of our lives together!" Lydia called out happily, knowing she was waking up to the grandest day of her life.

"Lydia, we do not have time. Suppose the doctor comes to Tuxla. What will happen then? We need not take any chances! Please get up so we can be married this morning!"

Lydia looked at Rosa and smiled. Rosa was lying in bed, holding her head up with her hand, and resting her elbow on the mattress. She was watching Lydia as she was talking to Chico through the drapes hanging on the doorway. Rosa wondered why Lydia was not jumping over her, trying to get dressed for Chico. She knew she would if she were Lydia.

"All right, my love. Rosa and I will be ready in just a few minutes," she stated as she glanced at Rosa. Rosa now felt better and smiled at Lydia.

Chico stepped out on the front porch to wait for them. He sat on one of the chairs against the wall. From a distance he saw an old lady and an old man walking hurriedly towards him. The old man could hardly keep up with the old lady. As they approached, he saw it was Señor and Señora Chávez. Señor Chávez was shuffling, looking down at his steps as he was trying to keep up with his wife.

"Ay, Señor Rodriguez, you are up and awake."

"Yes, Señora Chávez. I prefer it if you call me Chico, as do all my familia and friends. Lydia and Rosa are getting dressed. I have found a padre down the street who will marry us today," Chico stated as he pointed to the small iglesia two blocks up the street.

"Ay, Chico, no! You do not want to get married in that small iglesia. I think, since this is a special day for you and the muchacha, you should be married in the biggest iglesia in town. The iglesia you found is for the very poor people, and certainly you are not a poor man and neither is your beautiful muchacha. I know what I am talking about."

Chico did not know what to say. He did not want to wait. He wanted be married right away. At the same time he wanted what was best for Lydia.

"I hope you do not mind, but I talked to the padre. I woke him up and asked him if he could marry the two of you around noon. He agreed. But if this is not good, then we can change it."

Chico thought, "Noon will be fine, and being married in the biggest iglesia in Tuxla will make Lydia happy. Even if the doctor comes, it will not be until evening."

"That is very nice of you, Doña Chávez. You are a very kind person," Chico declared as Señora Chávez stepped by him and entered the house.

"I found Lydia a beautiful dress. I know you will love her even more when you see her in it." Her voice faded away as she kept walking.

On the porch there were three chairs and a small table. The old man, Señor Chávez, sat in one of them. He seemed to be very exhausted. Chico thought to himself, "What makes this viejo strong and keeps him in shape are his efforts to keep up with his vieja (old lady)!"

Señor Chávez took off his hat and started to fan himself with it. Without looking at Chico and as he kept fanning himself, he asked, "Are you sure you want to get married, muchacho?"

"Oh yes, Don Chávez. I love Lydia very much. Nothing could change my mind about marrying her."

"That is good. As long as you are sure. As you know, once you do it, you cannot undo it," the old man stated as he turned to look into the house. He wanted to make sure his wife was not close by.

"Yes, you are right. You have been married for many years to Doña Chávez. How has it been, Don Chávez?" Chico asked, trying to strike up a conversation.

"When I fell in love with her, my familia did not want me to marry her. They had a young Spanish muchacha picked out for me, and my vieja had too much Indian blood for my familia. But she has been a good wife through all the years, and my familia has grown to love her very much."

"Do you have much familia here in Tuxla?"

"I have my two daughters and their children. You will meet them later. Antonia invited them over for the big fiesta later. A lot of my familia are gone now. Many of them grew old and died. Of course I do have some familia here: cousins, nephews, nieces and their children."

"Tell me, muchacho, how much money do you think you have? Well, I mean after you marry the muchacha," the old man asked, now looking at Chico to see his expression.

Chico thought, "This viejo is not that shy after all. He should know better than to ask me how much money I have. What does he mean, after I marry Lydia? Maybe he thinks Lydia will spend all my money. That is really funny!"

Chico replied, "Well, I have enough to start us off with a little rancho. I will write my father and acquire a small loan from him to buy a few more steers. I only have enough funds to purchase a few but not enough to really get us started.

"No, I do not mean your money. I mean the muchacha's," Señor Chávez appeared puzzled, wondering why Chico did not understand him the first time.

"What money? Lydia did not bring any money. When we left her home, she had to bring as little as possible. I know the doctor will not give her any now. As a matter of fact, I would not accept any of his money, even if he wanted to give us some. After all that has happened, I might accept his apology; but that is all," Chico replied. He felt his disposition change, thinking of the doctor and Señora Gonzales' relationship with his children and Lydia. It was not a pleasant thought.

Señor Chávez was now convinced the young muchacho did not know what he really had. When he and his wife went to find a dress and speak to the priest, as they were conversing, they learned Lydia possessed an inheritance. According to the priest, she had enough money to buy all of Tuxla Gutierrez and San Bartolomé de los Llanos with all their contents.

"I see," Señor Chávez uttered. He continued, "Has Lydia ever told you how she came to be with the doctor?"

"Yes, she told me all about her father who was a padre. He had to leave Spain and brought her here to live with the doctor. She said her father never returned to see her or anything," Chico answered, wondering why Señor Chávez was asking. He suspected he knew more than he admitted the night before when they were talking in the kitchen with Señora Chávez.

"Why, Don Chávez? Do you know of Lydia's father?"

"No. I do not know him, only of him; and I have heard of Lydia. If she did not tell you, then I really do not think it is my place to tell you anything."

"Tell me what?" Chico questioned as he looked into the old man's eyes, wondering what he knew that he did not want to say.

"Well, señor, you have to ask Lydia," the old man stated. Señor Chávez knew he had said too much.

"With all due respect, Don, you are the one who brought it up. If I am going to marry Lydia and there is something I should know, I will be in debt to you if you are the one who tells me."

The old man looked at Chico and thought with his imperfect thoughts of greed, "He will be in debt to me? He will owe me?" Then the old man replied, "Lydia's father left his daughter her portion of the familia's inheritance. This morning we talked to the padre, and it is no small sum. It is enough to buy all the land from here to San Bartolomé de los Llanos! You are going to be a very wealthy man, Señor Rodriguez! Now, señor, tell an old man the truth. Did you know this?"

Chico did not say anything for the first few moments. He was in shock. Not because of the money, he really did not care about that. Chico was in shock because his true love did not trust him enough to tell him she had so much money.

Thoughts were racing through his mind regarding all the conversations he and Lydia had shared. He recalled that in their conversations they had discussed how they were going to build their house and work hard to give their children all they could to make their lives comfortable. Chico was planning on spending many hours a day on the range, working hard for his new family. "She even wanted to go out and ride a horse alongside me as long as she could before our first child arrived." Chico felt disappointed that Lydia did not tell him of this. He believed they had no secrets. He remembered her saying, "And we will...."

"Señor Rodriguez! Señor, are you all right?" the old man asked as he shook Chico's arm.

"I am sorry, Don Chávez," Chico said as he came out of his trance.

"Are you all right, muchacho? Maybe I should not have told you what I know."

Chico rubbed his cheeks with his palms and pushed his hat over to the back of his head in disappointment. "I just feel bad that Lydia did not tell me. The money is not important, but the trust is." Chico tried to express his feelings to the old man.

Señor Chávez now knew why the young man was so distressed. "Ay, muchacho, do you know why she did not tell you?"

Chico looked up at the man again and waited for his explanation.

He wanted to hear something, a reason, so he would not feel so badly toward his dear one.

"Because she felt as you do! The money was not important. Why should she tell you if it did not matter? Listen to an old, wise man, muchacho! The best thing to do is not tell Lydia you know. That is if it is not important to you, as it is not to her. She may never tell you. Let it go, and continue to love her! You go on with your plans, taking care of her and your children to come. If she tells you, then that is just an added plus for you. If not, do not worry about it. After today she will be your wife for the rest of your life."

Señor Chávez was now lecturing, which he loved to do whenever he was given the opportunity. Chico's eyes were fixed on the old man, knowing he was receiving some very helpful wisdom from someone who had seen a lot and who had been around since the beginning of time, as far as Chico was concerned.

The old man continued, "I think the reason Lydia did not tell you is because she did not want you to fall in love with her money more than with her. You know, muchacho, most men would have. She was just making sure you loved her and not her money. Just think if she would have told you from the very start. What could have happened?" he asked. Raising and shaking his finger at Chico, he exclaimed, "Do not answer! I will tell you! We are all greedy. It is in us. You were born with it. It is something we fight with all of our lives!"

"If you had known of her fortune, you might have loved the money and not the muchacha. Count it as a blessing that she gave you the opportunity to love her first. Are you listening, muchacho?" the old man asked, hoping Chico was not in one of his trances again.

"Yes, Don Chávez, I am."

"Good, then the best thing is to leave it alone. If she tells you, bíen (good). If not, bíen also!" Señor Chávez stated, raising his voice at the end his lecture.

Chico sat on the chair, looking at the old man and not knowing what to think. "The viejo is right. I do not think I would have loved the money more than I love Lydia, but one never knows," he thought.

"Yes, Don Chávez, I will try what you said; and I will see what happens. To answer your question, no. I had no idea Lydia had any money. She never told me. I wonder if the doctor wants to keep the money for himself. Maybe that is why he is trying to prevent me from marrying

Lydia. Then again, maybe he thinks I want to marry Lydia for the money."

"Who knows?" Señor Chávez replied. "I do not understand why the doctor is making such a big fuss if the muchacha is not his. The padre said the muchacha's father paid the doctor to take care of her. So the doctor did not do anything out of the goodness of his heart."

"Paid him? Is that true?" Chico asked, thinking the doctor must be really greedy.

"I do not know. That is what Padre Salazar said this morning. He said the muchacha's father left the doctor a great deal of money, and all he had to do was take care of her."

Señora Chávez approached the front door. "Daniel, I need for you to go and get some meat for the fiesta!" she demanded.

The old man was out of his chair and ready to go as soon as his wife's words were out of her mouth. Chico thought, "Señor Chávez sounds powerful when he is lecturing me; but as soon as his wife speaks, he is a small man again."

"Muchacho, do you want to go with me to see Señor Rivera, so he can deliver some meat for this afternoon?" Señor Chávez asked Chico.

Chico reasoned that if he left and for some reason the doctor arrived, which he did not think could happen so quickly, then all he had done would be for nothing. "Why take chances? The doctor could take Lydia and go back to San Bartolomé de los Llanos," he thought. He remembered Roberto's words, "Do not take any chances!" Chico answered, "No, Don Chávez. I think it will be best if I remain here with Lydia."

"¡Ay, caramba! That is the way it is when one is in love!" the old man said as he shuffled away.

Chico was nervous and knew it was close to noon. The sun had a little ways to go before the shadows marked midday. Chico stepped into the parlor and sat on a chair, not knowing what to do with himself. "This has been the longest two hours I have ever had to wait!"

Chico's thoughts now reflected back to what the old man told him. If it was true that Lydia had all the money he said she did, then that would change everything he had planned. "How could I spend someone else's money? I did not work for it. I think I will tell Lydia to save it, and maybe later in life we will think of something to do with it."

"Chico, how do I look?"

Chico turned when he heard Lydia's voice. She looked as beautiful as ever. She was wearing a nice, big, fluffy dress. Her lips were red, and she wore a little makeup. Chico thought his true love looked gorgeous all the time, but she seemed to be radiating with beauty more so now. No matter what she had done to herself, Chico believed at that moment his true love looked prettier than any other woman on the earth.

"Lydia, you look so nice, I...." Chico did not know how to put his thoughts into words. He stood up and extended both his hands to hold hers at the same time. Chico recalled that just a few minutes earlier he was very upset with Lydia about the money. Now, as he looked at her beauty and her lovely smile, he felt he could never be angry with her again.

"Well, Chico, do I look all right for our wedding?"

"Yes, my love, you look beautiful. But then again, you have always looked beautiful!"

"Chico, I want to talk to you for a few minutes before we leave to the iglesia. May we sit here," Lydia asked as she looked at the chairs in the parlor.

"Yes, Lydia, let us sit in there," Chico answered, letting go of one of her hands. He took a few steps into the house and sat on a chair. Lydia sat next to him.

She started the conversation. "Chico, I have something to tell you before you marry me. I know I can tell you afterwards, but I would rather say it now. It really does not make a difference to me, and I believe it does not make a difference to you either."

"Yes, go ahead," Chico answered, hoping it was about the money. It was not that Chico wanted the money as he had told the old man, but he wanted for Lydia to clear the air on the subject.

"Well, remember I told you about my father bringing me to Chiapas from Spain and leaving me with the doctor?"

"Yes," Chico answered without taking his eyes from her.

"Well, remember I told you my father's familia was rich; and they were of royal descent?"

Chico remembered many conversations he had with Lydia about her family in Spain. "Yes, go on."

"When my father brought me to Miguel and Lupe's house, he also left me a lot of money in México City. It is safely put away for me. Miguel has all the papers on it."

"How much money are we talking about, Lydia?" Chico asked, wanting to know if Señor Chávez was telling the truth.

"I really do not know. All I know is what Miguel and Lupe told me in the past. I think it is a great deal of money. They told me I will be able to do whatever I want when I grow up. I will be able to go anywhere and buy anything. I have been thinking about telling you this for such a long time and have always wanted to do so. I remember when I shared the story about my father the first time we went for our walk to the Calvario. I wanted to tell you then, but I thought it was best not to. So there, it is done. Now you know. I do not have to worry about it anymore."

"What do you want to do with the money, Lydia?"

"Whatever you want me to, Chico. When we are married, it will be ours. I know you love me, and it is not for my money."

"How do you know I did not know about the money in the past and wanted to marry you only for your wealth?"

"Ay, Chico! I know! I know because of the way you look at me, the way you talk to me. What is more, you were willing to get shot for me; and look at the beating you took for me."

"Yes, Lydia, that is right. I love you. I am marrying you, not the money. Let's not worry about the money now. Let us get married, and for now we can worry and deal with the doctor. Then we can start our lives together. Once that is done, we can see what we will do with the money."

Lydia smiled at Chico without saying a word, showing that she felt Chico always had good ideas.

Just at that moment several young adults stepped into the house. Behind them were two older, large women. The young adults stood at the entrance to the parlor. One of the young ladies, who was in her mid-twenties, said, "Hola, my name is Martha. This is my sister Rebecca, my sister Susana, and my brother Daniel." All the people offered a greeting as they were introduced.

"Hola, señorita y señor. My name is Mildred; and this is mi hija Gloria y mi hijo Daniel, another Daniel. And, of course, my hermana (sister) Carmen. She is the mother of Martha, Rebecca, Susana, and the other Daniel," Mildred said as she pointed to the other older woman standing next to her.

Chico and Lydia were now standing. She said, "My name is Lydia.

This is my fiancé, Francisco Rodriguez."

"Yes, señorita, we know who you are. Hola, Señor Rodriguez."

The rest of the party all smiled and greeted Chico. She continued, "My mother came to my home this morning and invited us to your wedding. I hope it is all right with you. Is it?" Carmen asked, knowing this young muchacha was one of the wealthiest persons in the state of Chiapas.

Señora Chávez heard the conversation coming from the front parlor and entered, "Oh, how good! You have met my familia. Good!" Señora Chávez declared as she looked at her daughter. She said, "Did I not tell you she is a very beautiful muchacha? What about her young man? Is he not as handsome as I told you? Did you introduce the familia to them, Carmen?"

"Yes, Mamá, I did."

"Well, everybody," Señora Chávez declared, "let's go. The padre will be waiting."

Chico looked at Lydia and smiled, knowing this was it. He felt he had butterflies circling in his stomach. Lydia reached for Chico's hand; she had let go of it when the crowd came into the house.

"Where is Daniel?" Señora Chávez inquired as everyone made their way out the front door.

Chico answered Señora Chávez, "He never returned from going to get the meat for the fiesta."

"Ay, that viejo! I hope Señor Rivera did not give my viejo any vino (wine)!"

Chico stood before the altar with his true love next to him. Rosa was standing by Lydia's side. In the iglesia with them were Señora Chávez and her family. Señora Chávez wanted her family to be there. She knew the consequences of this marriage. She knew these young people would control the area one day with all of their money. She wanted her family to have special ties with them.

Señora Chávez did not know what happened to her husband. She was going to make sure he heard of her disappointment when he returned. She hoped he took care of his assignment before indulging in anything else. If not, she would take care of it herself as soon as they left the iglesia.

The priest looked down at Chico and Lydia and said something in

Latin that they did not understand. Then he said, "You are now Señor y Señora Francisco Rodriguez. I pronounce you man and wife."

Chico looked into Lydia's blue eyes and thought back to the time he met her on the street. He thought back, knowing then that Lydia was the girl he would marry. Now she was his. He did not know why, but he felt proud of himself for making this happen. He wanted their lives together to continue to the end of time; and he wanted them always to be happy, having a good relationship with each other all of their lives.

Lydia looked at Chico and smiled at him as if she were saying, "I am the happiest muchacha in all the world!" Chico was now going to kiss her. He wanted to kiss her rosy lips so many times in the past, but he always felt it was not appropriate. He remembered back to their first walk to the Calvario and his desire to kiss her. The urge was there so many times. Now he could kiss his beautiful wife in front of all these people, and it would be proper.

As his lips touched hers, he saw Lydia's blue eyes close. "This is the moment I have been waiting for. I will take care of my princess for the rest of my life and always remain faithful to her," Chico thought.

He hoped he would be able to fulfill what he had just vowed. He knew it was the nature of the men in his family to have other women on the side. Chico thought of his father and mother. It was a well-known fact his father often went to town with his friends and met other women. He was sure his mother knew of the affairs, but she never mentioned it to his father or anyone else. He never understood why his father looked elsewhere for women when he had such a good wife at home who took such good care of him. Chico felt he loved Lydia so much that he would never be able to indulge in affairs with other women, no matter how tempting it might be.

Chico's thoughts moved to years ahead when he and Lydia would have children, still happy and in love. He visualized Lydia as an older woman and still as beautiful as now. He envisioned his handsome children as they grew up, and he saw his gorgeous grandchildren.

As Chico pulled his lips away from her, he realized where he was. For an instant he had traveled into the past and the future. Lydia, at this point, was crying; tears of joy fell from her blue eyes. Chico again pulled her to him and embraced her in his arms tightly. "Lydia, I love you," he whispered in her ear.

"I love you too, Chico. I will always be good to you, and nothing will ever come between us. I promise I will always be a good wife to you." Lydia did not whisper but said these words in a low voice, not concerned if anyone heard her.

They turned and viewed all of Señora Chávez's family smiling at them. Lydia wished it were her family standing there. She thought it was nice for them to come to her wedding to support her even though they did not know her. She knew she would never forget them. "I will somehow return this good to them in the future," Lydia thought.

Before leaving the iglesia, Chico stepped up to the priest and said, "I want to thank you, Padre, for the ceremony. I will return and take care of whatever I owe you tomorrow morning, if that is all right with you?"

"That will be fine, Francisco."

The priest continued, "I would like to warn you that there is trouble brewing."

"What do you mean, Padre?"

"I heard from someone who came to the iglesia this morning that a very good friend of Dr. Gonzales saw you and the muchachas enter the pueblo last evening. They heard from someone that you and your muchacha were here to be married. The person left to inform the doctor of the situation."

"Do you know when he left?"

"I understand it was sometime during the night; however, I am not sure."

Chico thought, "If he left during the night and traveled hard and fast part of the night and all day, then the doctor could be returning tomorrow if he also travels hard and fast."

"I see, Padre. Thank you very much for the information," Chico responded as he extended his hand to the priest.

"Be careful, mi hijo (my son)."

As Chico approached the front doors of the iglesia to join Lydia, she looked at him and asked, "What was the padre saying, Chico? I noticed the serious expressions both of you had."

"He told me you were recognized by someone when we entered the pueblo last night, and they sent someone to inform the doctor."

Lydia looked at Chico with a stern expression, one Chico had never observed before. "What can he do now? I am your wife and have nothing to do with him anymore. I am not from his blood that he should put so much effort into stopping us from being married. I think Miguel and Lupe have other intentions," she said as she looked back at the people who came to join them. As her head turned, the smile of delight returned to her face.

Chapter Nine

The Director

The wedding party was returning to Señora Chávez's house. Chico noticed Señor Chávez was asleep, sitting on the porch. Chico and Lydia disembarked from the wagon they had ridden to and from the iglesia. The crowd of Señora Chávez's family followed closely behind on foot. Señora Chávez yelled at her viejo, "Where have you been, viejo? Did you get what I sent you for?"

Señor Chávez woke up, looked at his wife, and said, "Yes, yes, I did. It is all in the house."

Everyone was now approaching the porch and talking when they heard a commotion. Chico, Lydia, and Rosa turned and saw a horse racing toward them from down the street. The approaching horse had a man mounted on it. Chico noticed the horse was kicking up a lot of dust because of the speed it was traveling, and the man on the horse was slumped over as if he were hurt or did not want to be seen.

Chico stepped out into the street, thinking the horse was out of control. He put his hands up, waving, trying to bring the horse to a stop. The rider pulled on the reins and halted the horse as Chico secured the reins from his vantage point.

Rosa yelled out, "Papá! Papá!" Rosa ran to the horse to help her dear father. She was in tears, not knowing what had happened to him.

Roberto was in a daze and needed help dismounting. Chico reached for his arm to help him down. He noticed Roberto had dried blood all over his shirt. His face was also badly beaten.

"Roberto, what happened to you?" Chico asked as they brought him down.

"Papá! Papí! We will take care of you now!" Rosa declared, trying to stop crying.

Roberto looked up at Chico and said, "I rode all night! I had to warn you! I had to come so nothing would happen to mi hija, Lydia, and you, Chico!"

"That is all right, Roberto. You do not have to talk right now. You can tell us in a little bit." Chico looked at Rosa and Señora Chávez and said, "Let us take him inside where we can see how badly he is hurt."

"I am all right. I have no broken bones. I am just beaten up and tired from the journey," Roberto uttered.

Chico and Rosa helped him into the parlor. Roberto used his own power to walk. As he had expressed, he was not in really bad condition. Once inside, Roberto started to relate what happened to him.

"Chico, when I arrived back in San Bartolomé de los Llanos, I went to my house. Blanca told me a stranger had been there and asked for me. I bathed and got dressed. Then there was a knock at the door. Blanca informed me there was a man who wanted to speak to me. I was tired and did not know what it was about."

Chico interrupted, "Who was the man, Roberto? Did you know him?"

"No, I do not remember seeing him, ever. He turned out to be one of the doctor's friends. Blanca told me the doctor had people visiting him from out of town. Then when I went out, there were four men outside. They jumped me and knocked me to the ground. They gave me my first beating right there in front of my own house. Blanca did not know and did not see what happened. In fact, that was the last time I saw Blanca."

"Then they took me to the doctor's house, and the doctor asked me where Lydia went. I told him I did not know what he was talking about or why he would think I knew where Lydia was. He said he did not want to talk to me anymore. When he went back into his house, the men who beat me pushed me around the corner and beat me again. The doctor came out and pretended to be on my side and told the men to leave me alone. He told them I was his good neighbor and baker. He asked me again where you took Lydia, Chico.

"Agusto Bara, the señor we met on the road, approached from around the corner. Señor Bara stated he had seen a young muchacha and muchacho take cover in the foliage when he first spotted us from a distance. He told the doctor that when he spoke to Rosa and me he knew he was being watched by the two who took cover. He said he pretended he left. Once we left with you and Lydia, he turned his horse and followed us until we made our way to the highway leading to Tuxla.

That is when he returned to tell the doctor where we went."

"As I lay on the street from my beating, the señor told me he knew I was traveling with the muchacho Rodriguez. He asked who else would hide in the jungle."

Roberto was talking fast; he wanted to get to the most important part. Everyone standing around him was quiet, with their eyes wide open and fixed on him, waiting to see what Roberto was going to say about the doctor and his intentions.

"Go on, papá; then what happened?" Rosa asked, holding her father's hand.

"The doctor was waiting for some of his familia to arrive before coming here to get Lydia. Once they were done with me, I made my way back to the stables and rode here without stopping. My poor Blanca, she has no idea what happened to me!" Roberto exclaimed, appearing downcast.

"Roberto," Chico stated downheartedly, "I am really sorry this happened to you on my account. Now, what can I do to make it up to you? You have done so much for Lydia and me. Now this terrible thing has happened to you, and I am very sorry."

Chico was distressed. He knew he had to do something in return for the misdeed to which the doctor had subjected Roberto. "All Roberto wanted to do was protect his daughter," Chico thought.

Roberto, still on the chair, grabbed Chico's arm, "Chico, you do not owe me anything. I am the one who wanted to go along. The men who helped the doctor will pay for this. Do not worry; they will pay!" Roberto started to get up.

"Stay sitting down, Papá! You cannot get up right now," Rosa said as she tried to push her father back into the chair.

"Ay, Rosa, leave me alone. Do you not know how bad the situation is? Besides, as I told you, I am all right. The doctor is on his way here right now. He is behind me with all of his help and will be here in a matter of hours. I need to go and get the familia here in Tuxla together and see how many friends they can round up."

Chico stood up next to the chair behind Rosa and asked, "How far behind you do you think they are, Roberto?"

"Just a few hours, maybe two, three, I suppose," he replied as he sat up straight.

Chico gave thought to what he might do. He did not want to run.

He felt he needed to take a stand and fight, but he knew he would never be able to hold down the doctor and all the men he was bringing with him. Chico went into deep thought, "Even if Roberto is able to fight, we still will not have a chance. We will be outnumbered."

At that moment Señor Daniel Chávez, holding a gun in his hand, spoke up and said, "Well, we need to get ready for a fight! I have not had a good fight for twenty years! I am ready, muchacho! Tell me what you want to do."

Chico thought, "Well, I know Señor Chávez is small next to his wife; however, when it comes to things like this, I know he is a brave man."

Lydia stood next to Chico, looking down at Roberto, and said, "Chico, what are we going to do? I do not want Miguel to kidnap me!"

"Rosa, can you go and tell your familia what has happened to Roberto?"

Señor Chávez had an idea and said, "My cousin is in town right now. Maybe he can help."

"Does he have people with him?" Chico asked.

Señor Chávez laughed, "Does he have people?" He looked at his wife and continued, "He asked if he has people, vieja?" Señor Chávez started to laugh.

Señora Chávez looked at Chico and said, "Yes, Chico, his cousin is director of public affairs here in Chiapas. He has the whole army at his disposal."

"I know your cousin, Señor Chávez. I met him in San Bartolomé de los Llanos. He told me he would help me in any way he could. I might as well take advantage of his offer. I will go and see him to see if he is still willing."

"That will be good, Chico," Señora Chávez said. "You can tell him his cousin Daniel needs his help too."

"Ay, vieja, I do not see that man very often. I never liked him, and I never will. Do not ask me to ask him for any favors," Señor Chávez stressed.

"How well do you know him, Señor Chávez?" Chico asked.

"He is much younger than I, maybe twenty years. I never cared for him because his familia treated him as if he were a little king. He always got what he wanted and was able to do whatever he wanted. I guess that is the reason he is as he is today, greedy, always thinking of how he can get more money."

Roberto braced himself on Rosa's shoulder and stood up. "I will go with Rosa and see what we might be able to do with my familia. Maybe we can act fast enough and get help before the doctor arrives with his company of men."

"Who does the doctor think he is?" old Señora Chávez asked. "We will get the guns ready while you are gone. When you return, we will be ready here. We will show the doctor it is unlawful to take another man's wife!"

Holding hands, Chico and Lydia walked several blocks to see Señor Chávez of public affairs. Chico related his strategy to Lydia. "Lydia, we can make a deal with Señor Chávez. He is a señor who is always thinking about what he can do to get a good mordida (bribe). We could offer him some money and pay him as soon as you receive your inheritance."

"Do you think he will help us, Chico?"

"With my experience, money talks. This is how it works. Whoever is the one offering the most money is who Señor Chávez will side with. Once he agrees to help us to receive the money from your inheritance, we will present the situation we are encountering right now. We will see what he will do to protect his interests. If anything is to happen to us after he knows he is going to receive a good sum of money, he will be more inclined to defend us. Remember, he is an individual with a lot of power."

"Ay, Chico, how do you think up these things? You are so smart!"

"I am not that smart. Look at all the problems I have had with the doctor so far. I do not know if this will work, but you heard the viejo. He said the director was a greedy man. If that is true, it will work in our favor." Chico paused; he did not want to be presumptuous.

Chico slowed his pace, stopped, and turned to face Lydia. He asked, "Now is it true what you told me before we were married, Lydia?"

"What are you talking about, Chico? I never lied to you about anything."

"About the money belonging to the two of us once we are married? If so, I am now going to deal with a little of your inheritance."

"As I told you then, Chico, whatever you want to do is fine with me. As far as I am concerned, the money belongs to both of us," Lydia expressed, gripping Chico's hand tighter.

With Lydia at his side, Chico asked a servant at the door, "I would like to see Señor Chávez."

"I will see if he is available. Who may I ask is calling?" the servant inquired.

"Francisco Rodriguez. You can tell him I spoke with him a few months ago in San Bartolomé de los Llanos about buying land."

The man left Chico and Lydia standing at the door. "Lydia, do you recall you said I can do whatever I want with the money?" Chico knew what Lydia had said but still felt uneasy about spending her money only hours after they were married.

Lydia looked up at him and wondered why he was asking again. "Yes, whatever you want to do, my love. It will always be that way."

"Yes, he will see you," the servant said as he opened the door. "Please follow me."

They entered the house, following the servant. The home was very large. From the street it seemed to be designed the same as all the other homes, with flat walls lining the street. But inside the dwelling was magnificent with all the newest items of the period. The floors had colorful tile imported from Spain. The furnishings were plush and of the best quality, the finest Chico had seen in all his life. Chico was now sure Señor Chávez and his family appreciated fine things and needed money to purchase them. He thought, "If he appreciates fine things, then he will appreciate the money I am going to offer him."

The servant asked them to sit in the parlor and wait a few minutes.

Chico and Lydia sat and waited patiently but nervously. Chico spoke in a low voice, "I am not sure how much money I should offer the director. He is a rich man already, so I cannot offer him too small a sum."

"Whatever you think is right; that is fine with me, Chico. As I already expressed to you, my love, whatever you want to do, I am behind you. The money is yours as well as mine," Lydia maintained, looking at Chico, showing her love for him and wanting to build his confidence. She gazed at him, thinking she would rather be somewhere else with him on their wedding day.

"Señor Rodriguez," Señor Chávez greeted them as he entered the room. He was dressed well for lounging. "It is nice to see you in Tuxla.

Will you be here long?"

Chico looked up at Señor Chávez. He started to stand when he heard his voice. Chico extended his hand to shake the director's hand.

Señor Chávez saw his face and continued, "¡Ay, dios! What happened to you? Your eye! Have you seen a doctor for that?"

Chico was embarrassed. He thought, "A doctor is the one who did it." He answered, "I had a problem with another man, but I am fine."

"Well, I sure hope he looks worse than you do," Señor Chávez said jokingly. He continued, "What are you doing in Tuxla, and how long are you going to be here?"

"I will be in town only a few days, Señor Chávez. We are staying at an inn with an Antonia and Daniel Chávez. I believe they are of some relation to you."

"Daniel? Yes, that viejo does not want to die. I have not seen him for some time, but they tell me he is as strong as a bull. You know he was a tough man in his day. He was a man who, if there was any kind of trouble, you wanted him on your side. Make sure you give him and his familia my regards. Tell them to come and see me. I would really enjoy that. Daniel tells me stories about my father that I do not hear from anyone else."

"Señor Chávez, I would like to introduce you to my wife, Lydia," Chico said as Lydia stood, extending her hand to Señor Chávez.

"It is a pleasure to meet you, dear," Señor Chávez responded as he smiled at her. He was consumed in thought, believing he knew the muchacha with the beautiful blue eyes; however, he just could not place her. "So, how long have you two been married? If I recall correctly, I do not think you were married the last time we met."

"Actually, we were married here today in Tuxla by Padre Salazar. My wife Lydia wanted to come with me to speak to you of our situation," Chico answered.

Señor Chávez studied the two and knew there was some kind of trouble. He was waiting for Chico to tell him what it was. "And what is it I can do for you?"

"I do not know if you recognize my wife, Señor Chávez; but she was Lydia Fuentes and lived with Dr. Gonzales. Her father was a duke and a padre in Spain. He left Lydia with the doctor and also left a large inheritance in her name."

Señor Chávez's eyebrows rose when he remembered the situation. He had heard of the large sum of money that was left in the muchacha's name and wondered through the years what was going to become of all the inheritance. He hoped the large sum of money was going to be put to good use in the state of Chiapas. He had thought it would be a shame if the money was spent in other places, especially because the muchacha was raised in the state of Chiapas.

Señor Chávez was all ears at this point. "Go on; I am listening," he said.

"We want to live and raise our familia here in Chiapas. We want to build our home in San Bartolomé de los Llanos, but we have a slight problem."

"A problem? This is why people come to me when they need help, señor. That is what I told you the last time we met. If your familia is going to come, I want to help. But go on, tell me your problem."

"Well, first of all, we want to present you with a gift of 1,000 pesos and give it to you once my wife secures her inheritance," Chico expressed. The director seemed pleased, since 1,000 pesos was a lot of money. In those days a laborer made only a few pesos a week.

Chico continued, "We more than likely will not have any problems securing my wife's money. But if need be, we want to be able to mention your name. If we continue to have problems dealing with the matter, we would like to be able to call on you for assistance, if that becomes necessary." Chico knew the director would be willing to help, especially if it meant money for him.

Chico thought, "These people are all the same. Money talks with them. If Señor Chávez is not willing, I will increase the figure."

Señor Chávez thought it was admirable of Chico and Lydia to want to give him a gift. "Ay, Señor y Señorita Rodriguez, that is very noble of you two. Whatever I can do to help, it will be my pleasure to do what I can for you. It makes me happy to see such young and beautiful people as yourselves get a good start in such a difficult world. I will start working on your behalf right away."

Chico felt he had accomplished more than he wanted. He had not asked the director for specific assistance but merely to be able to use his name.

"And, Señor Chávez," Chico declared, "if there are any unforeseen problems in regards to anything you are handling for us and it seems to be taking more of your time than you thought, we will want to compensate you with a larger gift."

Now the director was beaming. This is the way Señor Chávez liked talking, frankly, up front. "Ay, gracias, señor, you are very generous! If there is anything else I can do for you, just let me know. Did you know I will be trying to secure the governorship for the state of Chiapas?" Señor Chávez asked, attempting to see if he could count on the young couple to help him with his campaign.

"Is that right? Well, we will surely want to help you, Señor Chávez. Once we have everything in order, we will discuss this to see how much we can assist you with your mission," Chico asserted, knowing he was winning over the director. Chico knew other men had the existing governor in their hands. He wanted to see if he could have the next governor working for him.

During this entire time Lydia did not say a word. She sat in her chair and listened to her new husband speak, saw how he handled himself with the director, and admired him for it. She would not know what to say to a man of the director's position.

"Oh, there is one more small thing, Señor Chávez."

"And what might that be? I would like to help you out in any manner I can."

"Dr. Gonzales did not want us to be married and tried to prevent our marriage. Now Lydia is my wife, and Dr. Gonzales no longer has any rights in regards to Lydia's welfare. I understand he is on his way here to Tuxla Gutierrez to try to kidnap my wife. Would it not be kidnapping, Señor Chávez? After all, we were married by Padre Salazar; and our marriage is legal."

"You are right, Señor Rodriguez. When do you expect him here?" Señor Chávez was thinking back to when he went to San Bartolomé de los Llanos to interrogate the young man. He remembered the doctor's request to the governor to obtain information. The director gave thought to helping this young man as much as he could, knowing he would be rich in a matter of days.

"In a few hours, from what I understand, Señor Chávez," Chico responded, hoping he would intervene. Señor Chávez had at his disposal the federal police and the few soldiers who were stationed in Tuxla.

"I will see what I can do, Señor Rodriguez," Señor Chávez replied. He now started to stand, indicating the conversation was over.

HIRED BANDITS

C hico and Lydia stood and thanked Señor Chávez for agreeing to help them retrieve her money.

Arriving at the street where the inn was located, Chico was very cautious. He looked for any signs of trouble. He also took note of any horses that were not there when they left. Once everything checked out, they walked up to the house and stepped onto the porch. Old Señor Chávez exited the house with a gun in his hand. "Francisco, what did my cousin say?"

"Well, first of all he asked for you and wanted to know how your familia was," Chico answered, wanting to see Señor Chávez's expression. "I think Señor Chávez likes you very much and does not feel the same as you do."

"He is all right with my familia and me. It is just that I do not know him well. I am much older than he is. The problem I have with him is that he always thought he was better than others. Well, what did he say? Is he ready to help?"

"He did not give me an answer. He just wanted to know when the doctor was arriving here in Tuxla. Have Roberto and Rosa returned?"

"Not yet, muchacho. I sure hope he returns soon. It is late, and we are going to need every gun we can get."

Chico, Lydia, and Señor Chávez were now in the kitchen and sat down around the table.

Lydia was seated and started to cry quietly. Chico and Señor Chávez looked at her, wondering why she was in tears. Chico asked, "What is it, Lydia? What is wrong?"

Chico stood from his chair and took a few steps to where his wife was seated. Lydia expressed, "This is our wedding day, and look what a mess it is! All I want is to be happy. I do not want a dead husband! I want a live husband and everybody to be happy; that is all!"

"Ay, ay, ay," Chico said as he took a seat next to his wife and embraced her. "Everything is going to be all right, my love. Do not worry. We will have a happy life together. One thing you have to remember is that we did not create this. All we wanted to do was to be in love and have a happy life together. The doctor and his wife are the ones who are making things happen this way by attempting to prevent you from marrying me. Not liking me is one thing, but you are my wife now. When they arrive, they need to understand that."

Lydia loved to hear Chico's comforting words. Each time he reasoned with her, he always sounded so convincing. She knew he was right, and the situation was not their doing.

Lydia looked up at Chico and said, "Lupe and Miguel did not like you from the start because you are a ranch hand. If you had been a wealthy man, it would not have mattered how old you are. You would have had their blessing. I know the way they think."

Chico knew as Lydia was speaking that it was now all beside the point. He let Lydia talk in order for her to clear her thoughts. He sat next to her and admired her beauty as she continued speaking about Miguel and Lupe.

Chico and Lydia did not notice that Señor Chávez stepped out of the room.

In a short while they heard someone entering the front door, "Hola, hola, where is everybody?" Roberto called out.

"We are in the kitchen, Roberto!" Chico answered.

Chico and Lydia did not see Señora Chávez when they returned. They thought perhaps she was taking a nap.

Roberto entered the room, still not appearing well from the beating he had received. He had two young boys with him. They both appeared about fourteen years old. One was very short and dark. He was holding a rifle. The other boy was a little taller and had black, straight, long hair that almost covered his eyes. His rifle looked as if it were too big for such a small, young boy.

"Chico, the only two I could find home right now are my two brave nephews. They said they are willing to help us. These are tough muchachos! Right, muchachos?" Roberto said as he looked at the boys and padded one on the back.

"Sí, Tío (Uncle)," the shorter boy answered, looking at Chico and wondering why he was staring at him the way he was.

Chico and Lydia glanced at each other to see the other's expression, wondering if they were thinking the same thing. They did not want to have young boys help them fight a man's battle. Chico knew the doctor was arriving with men, not boys. He pondered as he looked at them. Chico thought, "It would be a shame if one of these boys had a bullet hole in his chest after it was all over." He imagined the dark one lying on the cobblestone street covered with blood and with his mother crying over him.

Roberto was feeling good for recruiting the boys. "Now we will show them who they are messing with! Right, muchachos?" Roberto expressed as he gently tapped the long-haired boy on the side of the head. The young man looked as if he was proud of himself. He seemed to be enjoying his uncle's praise for the valiant act he was about to face.

"Ay, Roberto, do you think these boys are old enough to die?" Chico asked, trying to make Roberto re-think his choice of fighters.

The boys looked up at Chico with frightened expressions. He did not want to be kind about the danger they were about to face. He wanted the boys to know what it meant to help their uncle.

Roberto looked at the boys and also noticed the frightened expressions. "What do you mean, die? They are not going to die! Ay, Chico, you are scaring them!"

Lydia looked at Chico and knew what he was doing. She again admired him for saying the right thing at the right time.

"Roberto, just having the guns in their hands when the doctor arrives will mean they are willing to fight. Those men who are going to be with the doctor will have no mercy on someone pointing a gun at them. I know this, I have experience with the doctor and his friends," Chico said as he paused and gazed at Roberto and the boys. He continued, "And if the muchachos fire one round, that means they will more than likely die. The men will use them as target practice, and I am sure those men are good shots. Do you boys know how to kill men?" Chico asked, wanting the frightened boys to answer.

Roberto looked over at them, waiting for an answer. He now realized what Chico was saying and in his heart acknowledged he was right. He thought to himself, "My beloved nephews. How will my sisters feel if I return their sons home dead?"

"Well, I have shot a coyote, señor," the darker boy replied.

Roberto now spoke for Chico. "Did the coyote shoot back? Did he have a gun and make you take cover and hide? Did you feel like crying because you were going to die also? No, no, muchachos, Chico is right. I should have never asked you for help. He is right about dying. The men who are coming are tough men. I know. See how I look! Do you think the two of you can overpower me? Well, those men are strong and grew up around guns; and they will not hesitate to put bullets into your small bodies."

Chico felt good that Roberto saw things his way. He knew he would. Roberto was just desperate to receive help.

"All right, muchachos," Roberto told the boys, "go home. We are going to let you live the rest of your lives!"

"All right, Tío," the taller boy said, not arguing with his uncle.

As the boys stepped out of the room, Roberto looked at Chico and said, "Gracias, muchacho!" Roberto walked outside to see the boys off.

"What are we going to do, Chico? We cannot fight Miguel all by ourselves. We can leave and go somewhere else," Lydia expressed, concerned for all involved.

Just as Chico was going to reply, Señora Chávez's grandsons — Juan, another Juan, and another young man — entered the kitchen. The Juans were cousins to each other.

"This is my sister Mildred's husband, Chava. Chava, this is Francisco Rodriguez and his wife Lydia," one of the Juans introduced.

The three young men were both wearing guns in their holsters. They were about Chico's age. Chico and Lydia felt relieved that Señora Chávez's family was going to help them. Chico now felt better that he had men helping him, not just boys.

"My brother-in-law told me you and your wife had a very nice wedding today. I am sorry it is turning out the way it is," Chava said as he reached for Chico's hand to shake it. He also looked at Lydia and smiled.

One of the Juans interrupted, "Francisco, we came to support you. If anything happens, we want to be on your side. Besides, you are here in our grandparent's house; and we do not want anything to happen to them either."

"Gracias, we can use all the help we can get; but are you sure you want to help? We might be outnumbered. We do not know how many men are coming. For that matter, we do not know if they will come at all. But we want to be ready!"

Señora Chávez's strong voice could be heard from behind the young men. "I am so proud of you, muchachos. Your mother raised you right. You are not cowards but are brave men. You are willing to put your lives on the line for your old grandparents who do not have much time left to live. You also put your lives down for someone you do not know very well." Señora Chávez reached out and hugged her two grandsons. She also embraced her granddaughter's husband Chava who was always well liked by the family.

At that moment Rosa ran into the house yelling at the top of her voice, "Papá, Chico, they are here! They are here!" Rosa ran into the kitchen, looking for her father. Roberto stormed into the kitchen from the parlor as he heard his daughter screaming.

Chico stood up and so did Lydia. Roberto grabbed Rosa by the shoulders and said in a loud voice, "Calm down, Rosa, calm down, hija! Tell us slowly, what you are trying to say?" Roberto paused and looked at Rosa, still holding her by the shoulders. "Are you ready? Are you calmed down?"

"Yes, I think so, Papí," Rosa conveyed, trying to catch her breath. "They are here," she said, trying to talk calmly and in a low voice as her eyes moved all around the room. Rosa was very excited. "I saw them ride into town. There were about 20 men on horses. They looked angry, Papá. They all had guns and were riding fast. I was coming out of my tía's house, and I heard the roar of the horses' hoofs hitting the street. But, Papí, they were not heading in this direction. They were going the other way!"

Chico asked, "Are you sure it was the doctor with his band, or could it have been some other men?"

"No! I saw the doctor. He was in front of all of them. I am scared, Chico! They did not look as if they wanted to talk to you. They had expressions as if they want to kill!"

"All right," Roberto declared, wanting to keep everybody calm. Roberto looked around at everyone. By this time Señor Chávez, his wife, and the other men who had just arrived were in the kitchen listening to Rosa's story. They also wanted to know what their plan was going to be. "Are you muchachos here to help?" Roberto asked the Juans and Chava. Roberto was not in the kitchen when they arrived.

"Roberto, these are Señora Chávez's grandsons, Juan and his cousin Juan. Also her granddaughter's husband Chava. And yes, they did come to support us. This is Roberto, Rosa's father," Chico introduced them. They all nodded their heads as they greeted Roberto.

"All right, we are glad we have others who are willing to die with us," Roberto stated as Chava and the Juans looked at each other, wondering why Roberto was being negative.

One of the Juans said, "Excuse me, señor, but we are not planning on dying. We came to fight and not to die." The other Juan and Chava nodded their heads in agreement.

"Good! That is what we want to hear. A positive attitude!" Roberto exclaimed. "We need a plan. Chico, do you mind if I say what I would like to do?" Roberto now seemed to have fully recovered from his low-spirited self and recuperated from the beating he had experienced only hours earlier.

"Go ahead, Roberto. As of right now we do not have a plan. Yours will be the best one," Chico expressed, waiting to see how Roberto wanted to do things.

"Well, I think the doctor and the other men went the other way because they do not know where you and Lydia are. They need to ask someone and find out. Once they find out, I think they will be here shortly. So we need to move fast and be ready. Chico, I think you should stay in the house. Lydia and Rosa, you need to go to your tía's home and stay there. We do not want anything to happen to you muchachas."

"Wait, Roberto!" Lydia interrupted, "I do not want to go and leave Chico here without me. I can fight too. I can shoot a gun also! I might miss, but I can still pull a trigger. I will not leave Chico!" Lydia demanded.

"What do you think, Chico?" Roberto asked.

"Papí, I will not leave either. I know you are my father, but this is life or death. I will make my own choice if I will live or die."

Roberto had an expression as if he did not really want to argue about the subject. They did not have enough time before the men and the doctor arrived.

Chico spoke up, "Well, if the muchachas want to stay and die with us, then let them. It is something they want to do."

"As Juan said, we will not die; but we will fight!" Lydia declared.

Roberto paused a moment, looking at Rosa and thinking about the situation that he and his lovely daughter were facing. It would be a sad thing if he had to see his hija die. The thought flashed through his mind, "Is all of this worth it?" He thought of throwing Rosa on a horse and leaving with her. Then he spoke up, "All right, we do not have time to argue about it. We have to fight with the troublemakers. All right! I think we should do the following. Chico, Señor and Señora Chávez, Rosa and Lydia, you can stay in the house with your guns ready, pointing them out of the windows. You muchachos can go with me out in the street. We will spread out and find hiding spots on the street. When the shooting starts, they will think we are many. They might start to run. Chico, I think if the doctor tries to talk to you, go ahead and try to speak to him. But do not show yourself. I would not put it past the doctor to shoot you in cold blood. Who knows, he might come to his senses before it is too late. I will take care of my revenge later. Right now, there are too many of them. What does everybody think about my plan?"

Señor Chávez spoke up first, "That sounds like a plan to me! I am ready! What do you muchachos say?"

The Juans and Chava were nodding their heads as if they thought the plan was good.

"I cannot think of a better idea right now. Let's do it your way, Roberto," Chico said, as he turned and headed for the parlor, holding Lydia's hand.

One of the Juans said, "¡Vamonos (Let's go)!" The Juans and Chava stepped outside, taking out their guns and checking them as they walked out of the door.

"Do you muchachos have enough cartridges?" Señor Chávez called out as they were leaving.

"Sí, Abuelito (Grandfather), we do. We have what is in our guns and belts. We also have our pockets full," one of the Juans replied.

Roberto gave his darling daughter a big hug and told her to try to keep her head down. "We will keep them back from outside. If they make it into the house, I want you to promise you will lie on the floor and act as if you are dead. Is that a promise?"

"All right, Papí. I will try. Be careful yourself, Papí! I do not want Mamá to be unhappy for the rest of her life," she said as she embraced her father tightly. Roberto stepped out of the door and onto the street.

Chico and Lydia looked at each other and both thought, "This is it." They went to the windows, turned two chairs around, sat on them, and looked out into the street. Chico stuck his head out of the window and looked both ways. It was clear all the way to the other avenue that crossed the street. "No sign of them yet," he said.

Rosa sat on another chair in the parlor, not knowing what to do.

Señor and Señora Chávez had a few guns in the house. Señor Chávez stacked them against the wall in the parlor. He put a bucket of cartridges next to all the guns.

"Lydia, do you know how to load guns?" Chico asked, hoping she knew.

"I think so. I think all you do is stick the bullets in the little holes on the side of the gun, right? That is what I see men do."

Chico thought she was not going to be much help. Señora Chávez heard Lydia and said, "Muchachas, both of you, come here. I will show you." Lydia and Rosa stepped to the other side of the room where Señora Chávez moved the bucket of bullets. "Look! Pay attention. When the shooting starts, you are going to be doing this fast. We will not have time to learn again. I know because I went through this many times when I was young. Daniel liked to go and gamble. Then we had to have gun battles with men who were loco because my viejo got mad fast and wanted to fight."

Señor Chávez sat next to Chico. "Muchacho, are you ready?" he asked.

"Yes, I am ready. Don Chávez, you are really a good friend. I think of you and your wife as my familia. I do not know why you are doing this. You only met us last night; and here you are giving us so much help, actually your lives. I do not know how to thank you."

"Well, muchacho, I am old; and I have been wanting one more good fight. I miss these kind of fights with guns. When they are over, I have something to tell my friends."

"Well, Don Chávez, I think you are going to get what you want."

"I wanted to ask you," Senor Chávez spoke in a low voice, "what else did you do to make the doctor so angry with you? You had to do something to anger him into bringing all those men here to get you."

"I do not know. The only thing I can think of is the money," Chico explained, looking out the window.

Chico saw Roberto down the street. He was hiding behind a watering tub for horses. He also saw Chava down the street, standing up against the wall. The doctor and the other men did not know him and would not know what he was doing anyway. Chico could not see the

Juans but knew they were out there somewhere.

"Do you really think it is the money?" Señor Chávez asked, trying to make conversation.

Chico looked at Señor Chávez. Even though he was asking questions, he was ready, holding his finger on the trigger of his rifle, ready to take care of business. Chico thought of the viejo who was seventy-nine years old. He was not scared and did not appear frail. "That is what the director said, that the man is as strong as a bull," Chico thought.

Señor Chávez kept speaking to Chico, asking him who his father was and how he was raised. "The viejo is trying to kill time," Chico thought.

"How are you doing, Lydia? Are you learning how to load guns?"

"We are almost done. But it is as I said; all one has to do is to put the bullets in the little hole on the side."

"Muchacho," Señor Chávez said, "if the doctor and his men do not come in the next few minutes, it will be my turn to give you a plan."

"And what will be your plan, Don Chávez?"

"My plan is that we go and look for them and run them out of our pueblo. If we go after them and they see they are in for a good fight, they will be scared and leave."

"I do not think they will run, Don Chávez."

"I think...." Señor Chávez stopped talking as he adjusted his head to the side. It appeared he could hear something.

Chico thought if Señor Chávez could hear better than he, he probably was better at everything else too, even shooting. Just as Chico thought this, he heard a roar coming from a lot of horses.

Chico turned and looked at Señor Chávez and then turned and looked at Señora Chávez, Lydia, and Rosa. He asked, "¿Listos (Ready)?"

Lydia and Rosa did not say anything. They were scared quiet. Señora Chávez looked at Chico and grabbed a gun. She was moving over to where her husband and Chico were sitting, ready for a fight. She looked back at Lydia and Rosa and said, "All right, niñas (young girls), I showed you how to load guns. Now if we empty them, you fill them."

Señora Chávez moved close to her husband and said, "Move over, viejo! Make room for a vieja (old lady) who knows how to shoot!"

They could see all the horses moving toward them. In the lead was the doctor, just as Rosa had said.

The men behind the doctor had tough faces. Some seemed to be wealthy with their high-priced clothing. Others seemed as if they were hired bandits. They appeared dirty with their gun belts hanging around their chests and serapes thrown over their shoulders. All the men wore sombreros (big hats).

As they approached the house, they slowed down. The doctor was looking at the house as they neared it. He raised his hand, indicating to all the men behind him to stop. The doctor did not say anything for a moment. He then drew his gun and shouted, "Lydia! ¡Muchacha! Come outside!"

Neither Lydia nor Chico answered. Chico hid behind the drapes that hung from the window. He could see the doctor, but the doctor could not see him. As far as the doctor was concerned, no one seemed to be home.

"Lydia, are you there, hija? Come out! Señor Rodriguez, if you are holding my daughter against her will, you will pay for it! Let her go!" the doctor yelled.

Lydia never heard the doctor refer to her as his daughter. She wondered why he was doing so at this time. Señor Chávez spoke up, "¿Qué quieres, señor (What do you want, señor)? We do not know you! Go home!"

They all waited for the doctor's reply. Chico had his pistol in his hand, waiting for the shooting to start. Señor Chávez had his rifle ready to shoot if the doctor or any of his men tried to invade his home.

"Look, señor, I do not have a problem with you. If you want to come out, you can. If there is anyone else with you, they may come out. We will not hurt them or you. We do not want to hurt anyone if we do not have to!" the doctor shouted, now aware there were people in the house.

"Oh yes, how nice you are, Doctor!"

Señor Chávez had the urge to let the first bullet go. He thought it was wrong that the doctor beat up Francisco and had all of his friends helping him. He also did not like the way he beat up Rosa's father. Therefore, he was lying when he said he did not want anyone else to get hurt.

Chico thought of the other Señor Chávez. He hoped he would help before it was too late. He knew the doctor could not get his friend, the governor, to stop the director, because the governor was at home in San Cristóbal de Las Casas, the capital of the state.

The doctor was now convinced Chico was in the house. How else would this man know who he was. "Señor Rodriguez, are you there? Come out and talk like a man!" the doctor yelled, trying to convince Chico to step outside. If he did, the doctor would have it easy. All he had to do was put a bullet in him. Because of his past experience, Chico knew better. He was not about to make himself an easy target.

"Doctor, I am here. What is it you want? Do you want to talk?"

"Yes, come out so we can talk!" the doctor answered, thinking the muchacho was stupid enough to do it. Talking with him is what Chico wanted from the very beginning.

"Sure, I will come out and talk. But first, you send all your men away!"

"Muchacho, I will give you a chance to live! All you have to do is send Lydia out, and I will leave here with her. You will be able to do whatever you want with the rest of your life!"

Chico listened to the doctor. He knew how he spoke in double meanings. He also knew he might depart, but he would leave his fighters to do the dirty work and kill him. "Doctor, I do not know if you have heard; but Lydia is now my wife! She is not yours anymore."

"Muchacho! Listen to what I have to say. Do you really think I am going to let you keep Lydia? I will have the cardinal annul the marriage. That will not be a problem! Look out here, and see how many men I have with me! Do you really think you can keep Lydia from me and live?"

"Doctor, right now I have guns pointed at you. If you try to come in, we will make sure you receive one of the first bullets!" Chico answered truthfully.

The doctor became nervous. He sat up on his horse and looked around. As far as he could tell, the muchacho was bluffing. He did not see anyone with guns. He saw one man down the street who was wearing a holster with a gun in it; but the man was observing the situation, as were other people who were watching.

"Last chance, muchacho! Let Lydia go!" the doctor demanded as he turned and looked at one of his men.

Chico did not say anything. He knew there was no point in talking. "The doctor did not come all this way to turn around with a few small words," Chico thought.

The doctor nodded his head at the man next to him. A man who was dressed like a hired bandit dismounted, along with another man. They both drew their guns and started towards the house. Señor Chávez did not like what he saw. "¡Alto (Stop)!"

The men stopped when they heard Señor Chávez's harsh, strong voice. The doctor called out, "What is it, señor? Have you changed your mind?"

"No," Señor Chávez answered. "I just want to give your men a chance to reconsider, to avoid ending their lives!"

"Go," the doctor said to the men as they turned to look at him, undecided on what action to take. The men looked at each other, turned, and continued in the direction of the house.

Señor Chávez took aim and fired his rifle. The bullet went over the doctor's head. Señor Chávez wanted to scare him into reconsidering his options. The doctor drew his gun and fired a shot into the house, hoping he did not hit Lydia. He was, however, willing to take a chance.

The bullet hit one of the targets for which it was intended. Chico ducked as the gun went off. He saw Señor Chávez fall over while holding his shoulder.

"¡Ay, Viejo!" Señora Chávez screamed in panic, seeing her life-long husband take a bullet.

Chico looked back in the direction of the street and noticed the men were ready to fire their weapons toward the house. He took aim and was going to take his first shot. Aiming his gun at the doctor, he thought about all the bad things he had done to Lydia and him.

At that moment the doctor and his men froze as if they saw a ghost. He heard many shots being fired. Chico knew it could not be from Roberto and the young men who were outside. There were too many guns being discharged at once.

Chico held his fire. Lydia was at Señor Chávez's side. She looked up to see what was going to happen next, or who was going to be killed first. When she saw them, she yelled, "¡La polecia!"

The police and the soldiers outnumbered the doctor's men three to one. As the soldiers approached the doctor's men, their horses scuffled, not knowing what to do. The soldiers and the police wore neat and clean military attire.

One of the police shouted, "¡Arriba (Up)!" The doctor and his men elevated their arms with their guns in hand.

As the police and soldiers approached the doctor and his men, one of the officers said, "Señores, you are all under arrest!"

"Do you know who you are talking to? I am Dr. Miguel Gonzales! The man you want is in the house, señor! His name is Francisco Rodriguez!" the doctor voiced loudly.

Chico listened to see what the police were going to say. He thought maybe he was mistaken and that the soldiers really came to assist the doctor.

"No, Doctor, it is you who is breaking the law. You are being charged with attempting to kidnap and causing a problem in the streets of Tuxla Gutierrez! The orders are from the director of public affairs!"

"Señor! You go and tell the director that if he intervenes the governor is surely going to hear about this. I want my daughter. She is in that house!" the doctor yelled, pointing to the house. "She is being held by a man who goes by the name of Rodriguez."

The doctor wanted the police to help him. He did not remember a time in the past when he did not have his way with the authorities, since he always paid his share of mordidas (bribes).

At that point Chico and Lydia stepped out of the house. Chico spoke first. "This muchacha is my wife. We were married today by Padre Salazar. I am not holding her against her will. As I told you earlier, Doctor...." In the last phrase he turned and looked at him.

The doctor seemed to want to lower his gun to shoot Chico. Now Lydia spoke, "Miguel! You have shot an innocent man. He is lying on the floor in the house dying from your bullet! Señor Chávez is a good man!"

The police officer who was speaking to the doctor while sitting on his horse gazed at Lydia with utter surprise. He said, "Tío? My tío has been shot?" He dismounted and walked hurriedly into the house.

One of the other police told the doctor and his men, "Drop all your arms on the ground and dismount! Listen, men. If any one of them tries anything, shoot him!"

As the doctor dismounted along with the others, the head police officer stepped out of the house. He had examined his tío Daniel and did not appear happy. "Who fired the bullet that hit Señor Chávez?" he asked, as if he already knew who it was. He looked at the doctor for an answer.

"The only reason I fired was because my life was in danger!"

"You will be held responsible, Doctor! You came into our pueblo as if you own it. Do you think because you are friends with the governor you own everything? I have seen you here in Tuxla many times; and I have never liked you, Doctor. Now if my tío dies, I will see to it personally that you are hung here in Tuxla!"

"The governor will not like it if you hold me against my will!" the doctor shouted, hoping the police would let him return to his pueblo of San Bartolomé de los Llanos.

"I do not think my father, who is the director, will want you to be released after you shot his cousin, Doctor!" The police officer now looked at his subordinate and said, "Take them to headquarters!"

"¡Andalé! Leave your horses and arms! Start walking! And keep your hands up, so we can see them!" one of the police demanded.

Lydia was standing next to her true love, weeping. She did not want things to be this way. "If only Miguel had left things alone. What is Lupe going to say now that Miguel is in this terrible trouble?" she thought.

"I am sorry, Señor Rodriguez, for all that has happened on this special day. My father told me about your visit to him, and we came as soon as we could get all of our men together," Señor Chávez, Jr. said as he extended his hand to Chico. "Unfortunately, we arrived a little too late."

Señor Chávez stepped out of the house. He was holding his arm with his other hand. "I will be all right. It is just a flesh wound. The bullet came out the other side. It will heal."

Chico and Lydia looked at Señor Chávez and felt relieved. Neither one of them wanted the doctor to be hung.

"I am so glad to hear that, Tío! My father was right about you. He told me many times as I was growing up what kind of man you are. I should have known a simple bullet cannot stop you."

At this point Roberto, the Juans, and Chava were all standing on the porch. All were relieved no one was killed, as Roberto had said.

The Juans and Chava knew some of the police and soldiers. Some were also related to them.

"¿Qué pasa aquí (What happened here)?" a man with a black bag asked as he approached with his eyes fixed on the older Señor Chávez. "Ay, Daniel, what happened to you? I was told you were in another gun battle! I could not believe it. It has been a long time since you had this kind of fun!" the doctor exclaimed. He reached out and turned Señor Chávez around to lead him back into the house for an examination.

"Señor Rodriguez, because my tío is going to be all right, we will not have to hang the doctor," Junior Chávez said. Lydia was relieved. He continued, "We will do as you wish, as long as it is all right with my tío because he is the one who has been shot. We can hold him for the night and release him in the morning, or we can prosecute him to the fullest extent of the law. Whatever you prefer."

Chico looked down at Lydia, "What do want to do, my love?"

Lydia had a sparkle in her blue eyes. She felt happy, knowing things were not going to be as bad as she thought. She replied, "Can you hold him for the night without telling him much? In the morning we can try to reason with him. Then you can release him."

"That will be fine. I will speak with my tío about it."

"Listen, everybody!" Señora Chávez announced as she stepped out of the house. "The doctor said my viejo is going to be all right. The doctor just informed me that Daniel should be able to dance. We are going to have a fiesta tonight, and you are all invited. It is a fiesta for a wedding!" She really knew her husband would probably be too sore to dance, but she was making sure everyone knew he was going to be all right.

Lydia thought to herself that things were going to turn out the way she wanted them to be. She looked up at Chico and smiled. She knew it was going to be a wonderful evening and also knew it was going to be a wonderful night.

That evening in Tuxla Gutierrez, in 1868, they had one of the biggest wedding fiestas the town could remember. The word went out that everybody was invited. The fiesta went on all night even though Chico and Lydia retired early to be alone on their wedding night.

Lydia was so overwhelmed with all the people and with being alone with Chico for the first time that she did not have much time to think about Miguel's sitting in jail. She felt he deserved at least one night in jail for all he had done.

The following morning Lydia talked to the doctor. She told him she no longer wanted anything to do with him. She knew the love he had for her was not sincere but was an interest based on greed. As far as Chico was concerned, he did not care for the doctor and also did not want anything to do with him or the family. However, he did not mind if Lydia continued to have a relationship with them, knowing she had deep feelings for the family.

The doctor finally accepted that Lydia was not his anymore. He had always had selfish feelings regarding her inheritance and had always hoped it would benefit his own children.

CHAPTER ELEVEN

ROMULO AND LUZITA

As the years went by, the love between Chico and Lydia continued to intensify. Señor Chávez, the director, was able to help secure her inheritance and transfer the money into her name without any problems. Chico, in turn, did what he said he would do and paid the director for his help. Chico and Lydia thought it would be best to help the director to secure the governorship, thinking it would be to their advantage. After all, they had so much money that they could not spend it in a lifetime.

Chico and Lydia had a house built in their town of San Bartolomé de los Llanos, a big house compared to all the other homes in the area, but not a mansion. Lydia was content with life and felt she did not need more. Chico, on the other hand, wanted his dream rancho. He worked the next few years, purchasing, negotiating, and organizing everything he was going to buy and add to their estate.

Chico negotiated with his old employer, Don Rios. Don Rios wanted to retire and travel and not to have to deal with his rancho.

Chico named his new rancho "U-Chem," an Indian term meaning, "Land of the Monkeys." In that area of the jungle where the rancho was being established, there were many, many monkeys.

Chico and Lydia did not forget the people who showed them kindness during those troubled times when the doctor was opposing them. Even the orange man, Pepe, was set up with a small store of his own by Chico.

The Chávez family became very close friends with Chico and Lydia over the years. Chico and Lydia always recalled the goodness that was shown to them, even though they had not known them well. Señor Daniel Chávez lived five years after the wedding and died; his wife Antonia died shortly thereafter. Chico and Lydia helped the family in whatever way they could. Whatever their family trade was, the

Rodriguez's had business sent their way. Rosa and her family were treated as close relatives by the Rodriguezes. And as Chico and Lydia told her, their children called her tía.

Shortly after their marriage, Chico went out to the jungle and cut down trees that exhibited and retained different colors. Chico took the wood home and worked with it, wishing to create something special. He created a box and carved beautiful monkeys on the top and the sides. He prepared it so it was airtight. In this box Chico and Lydia stored items related to their heritage, the old documents Lydia received from her father, which Miguel Gonzales had returned to her. From this point on the box was always referred to as "The Monkey Box." They wanted the precious documents to remain in the family for generations to come.

In 1873 just a few short years after they were married, Lydia told Chico the good news he had been anticipating. As he entered their home after a long day at the rancho, Lydia said, "My love, I have something to tell you. Sit down."

"What is it, Lydia?" Chico asked, knowing it was something serious because of her expression.

"I am with child!" Lydia declared.

Chico sat down. He had wanted to hear these words for some time. He felt a great satisfaction knowing the day had finally arrived. He and Lydia wanted a child right away, but things did not work out in that manner. "How far along are you, Lydia? Have you seen the doctor? Who told you?"

"Ay, Chico, we women know these things! I thought I was expecting, and now I am sure. I saw Dr. Escobar."

During this time another doctor arrived in town. Even though Lydia kept a limited relationship with Miguel and Lupe, she would not see Miguel as her doctor.

"I will have our baby in about six months, Chico. Are you happy?"

Chico looked into Lydia's eyes and saw the love she had for him was stronger than ever before. Chico loved her very much. He would be happy with or without a child.

After six years of marriage, Chico was not like his father, who had relationships with other women. Each time Chico saw an attractive woman and had a desire to be with her, he would think to himself, "Would I be willing to trade or lose my Lydia for her?" He always came up with the same answer.

"Lydia, you know I am happy! I will always be happy and will always love you. You will forever be my mujer (woman)," he declared as he stood up and took her into his arms.

In 1874 Lydia had her first child on schedule. They had a boy and named him Romulo Rodriguez de Fuentes. Romulo was a very easy child to rear. He was light complected and had his mother's blue eyes. He always tried to do things right and did whatever his parents asked of him, even during his early years. He was a child who always tried to impress his parents by showing them his intelligence.

In the years that followed, Chico and Lydia had five more children, all daughters. Romulo was the only male, and he was the eldest. He would be the one to carry on the family's name in this part of México.

Chico, in the meantime, continued to work on his dream rancho. He purchased enough land to have the rancho he always wanted. The amount of land he acquired was so large that it was said one would have to ride eight days on horseback to circle the entire property of U-Chem.

Schools during this time were for the privileged. Most of the indigents did not go to school at all because it cost money. The children were either taught the basics by their parents or were taught by a tutor. To obtain a real education once they were done with their basic learning, they had to go to a boarding school in San Cristóbal de Las Casas and then to the university in México City.

After young Romulo became of age to attend school, Chico and Lydia sent him to San Cristóbal de Las Casas. Romulo not only wanted to be a doctor but also to be a lawyer. As Romulo matured, he became a well-liked young man.

When Romulo attended school, he really liked the beautiful muchachas. At twenty-one years of age, he met a particularly lovely girl, Seneida, whom he started to see. Romulo had plans for his future and had no intentions of getting married at such a young age. His mother and father would have never approved of his having a girlfriend on a steady basis, and Romulo knew it. Chico and Lydia wanted the best for their son and did not send him to school merely to be married at such a young age.

Romulo had not been dating Seneida long before one thing led to another. One day Romulo was called to the office in his school and was told there was a señor who wanted to see him.

The school was small. It was contemporary for the time. Things could be kept looking nice because it was the best and most expensive school in Chiapas.

As Romulo walked into the waiting area in the office, he saw a man sitting with his worn and dirty hat on his lap, showing respect to those around him. He seemed to be very nervous. Romulo could tell the señor was a peasant by the way he dressed. His trousers were unclean, and his soiled feet were visible through his dirty and worn sandals. It appeared the señor had not shaved for a day or two.

"Señor, I was told you want to see me. My name is Romulo Rodriguez," Romulo stated. He wondered what this señor, whom he had never seen before, could possibly want.

"So, you are Señor Rodriguez. I have seen your father in San Cristóbal de Las Casas a few times, but I did not know he had a son here," the man said sarcastically.

Romulo, still standing, asked, "What can I do for you, señor?" At times different people approached Romulo for money, knowing his family was wealthy. Romulo was the sort of young man who, if he were able and if he were carrying enough funds, would give a helping hand.

"I am the father of Seneida," the señor said.

Romulo sat down. He hoped this was not going to be serious. "Yes, is Seneida all right?"

"As a matter of fact, no, she is not!"

"I am sorry to hear that. What is wrong with her, señor?" Romulo asked, not knowing what to call the señor. He did not tell Romulo his name, and Romulo did not remember Senida's last name.

"She is embarasada (pregnant)!" the señor said unpleasantly.

"Embarasada," Romulo uttered in a low voice, wondering why he was speaking to him about this. Romulo did have relations with her, but he knew the baby could not possibly be his. "Besides it was only once," Romulo thought.

"Yes, Señor Rodriguez. And Seneida says you are the father. I came to find out what you intend to do about this situation," the señor explained, hoping Romulo would admit to it and avoid problems. He also hoped Romulo was willing to marry her.

"No, señor, there must be some mistake. The baby is not mine." Romulo saw his future falling apart before his eyes. He stood up, not wishing to carry on the conversation any longer. He continued, "I am sorry if that is what Seneida told you, but I cannot go along with her story. There is no basis for me to say this is true." Romulo took a few steps back, turned, and walked away.

Seneida's father stood up and called out to Romulo, "Señor Rodriguez, I will contact your father and advise him of the situation. If Seneida said you are the father, then you are the father!" Romulo did not like the loud remark since it attracted the attention of those who worked in the office.

During the next few months, Romulo refused to take responsibly for what happened, feeling the unborn child was not his. He knew Seneida had a reputation for having different male friends, and Romulo felt the child could be any one of theirs.

Romulo told his father he did not think the child was his. Chico knew how things could occur and wanted to see what was going to happen once the child was born.

In a few months as Romulo continued to attend school, Seneida had her baby. She continued to insist that Romulo was the father. Seneida gave the baby Romulo's name; the child did resemble him.

She went to Romulo's father, Chico, to ask for help in raising the youngster. Chico knew if he agreed to this, it would be an acknowledgment the child belonged to his son. Because the child did have Romulo's features, he made an agreement with the young lady. Chico told her he would help support the child if she kept it to herself. Seneida agreed.

After he completed his school in San Cristóbal de Las Casas, Romulo continued to learn on his own by studying and reading all the literature he could obtain. He started to treat people who suffered from their sicknesses, always referring to a big, thick book he carried. The people of his town were putting trust in his medical assistance.

Romulo also helped people with their legal papers and business, becoming a self-taught lawyer. He had grown to be a very intelligent young man, even mastering various trades, such as a tanner of leather, tailoring, and others. He had a mind that was always thirsting for knowledge, and he always pushed himself to master something new.

As time passed, he became a well-liked doctor in his community, caring for the poor as well as the rich. Romulo loved people and always did what he could for them. This is why he loved his work more than anything else. Making money was not important to him. At times, outside his small office, people lined up down the street to see him. Some brought chickens, eggs, or livestock to pay for their medical care.

Romulo knew the people who were very poor; he would tell them they could pay him in another life. "For now, God pays me with a good life," he would state. If Romulo wanted anything, his parents took care of it. He felt that with all the money his parents had they would never be able to cure the sick. However, he could.

From time to time Seneida came to see if Romulo would be a father to her child. Romulo did not care for her and did not want any part of her life or of the child's. He found out she went to his father and said the child was his, although he was convinced the youngster was not. He had calculated when the baby was born and when he was with Seneida; he concluded it was impossible for the child to be his.

In later years a rich man by the name of Ramirez went to San Cristóbal de Las Casas and married Seneida. He took the child and adopted him, changing his name. They had other sons. When the sons grew up, they became world renown for playing marimba instruments, famous in Central America.

During the early part of his life, Romulo did not marry. His life was complete, and there was no room for a wife. He was too busy with his own obsessions, in particular, beautiful women. He also felt there was not enough time to raise a family.

He enjoyed life and knew the tragedies of it. Seeing firsthand the joy life brings, he had observed the happiness of parents when they received their newborns as a gift from God. He also saw the sorrow of life and understood the hurt that death and sickness brought. He told himself that one day he was going to invent a medicine to cure all sickness. If he did not, then his offspring would.

Even though Romulo was a good doctor, he enjoyed drinking. He enjoyed having a drink or two or three at least once a day but did not get drunk daily. Every six months to a year, he would overindulge; and all would know it. Romulo's other vice was gambling, but it was never to the point of being out of control.

Chico wanted to see his son take over his rancho, but he also wanted Romulo to continue to care for people as a doctor. Romulo did not have the same love for Rancho U-Chem as his father did.

Chico had many men working for him. They cleared the land, harvested corn, and started a sugar plantation. U-Chem became big business. Chico achieved what he had always wanted, more cattle than one could count.

When Dr. Romulo Rodriguez had time, he would accompany his father and ride out to U-Chem. He was given the grand tour and was told it would soon be all his. The rancho was rich with money, supporting itself and all who worked on it.

The year was 1904. Romulo rode into town after visiting a sick person who lived a day's ride on horseback from his community. As he rode his horse into town, a man ran out to meet him. Approaching the doctor, he reached for the reins and walked alongside Romulo and the horse. He said with a sad and worried expression, "Doctor, your father is very ill."

"What is wrong with my father?" Romulo asked anxiously as he brought his horse to a halt, knowing it was time for his father to pass on. The years were moving along, and Chico was now very old and appeared frail.

"We do not know. He refuses to let any other doctor see him. He has been waiting for you. Ay, Doctor, he looks very bad. I did not think he would make it until you arrived," his friend said, trying to hold back the tears. He knew how much Romulo loved his father, as everybody else did.

Chico was loved by all. He felt God blessed him with such a good life that he wanted to share it with everybody. Having reached his seventieth birthday, he had lived a happy life.

Lydia was as vigorous as ever. Only sixty years old, she felt strong and healthy.

Romulo rushed home to tend to his father's needs. His mother and sisters greeted him. They were standing by the front door and had already received word that Romulo was in town.

"¡Ay, Mamá! What happened to Papí?"

"We are not sure, Hijo. He was fine. Then he felt a pain in his chest and fell over. We put him in bed, and that is where he has been for the last two days. Hijo, he does not look well at all. Ay, Romulo, if anything happens to your father, I do not want to live anymore!" Lydia started to cry. Her five daughters came to her side. At this point Romulo greeted his sisters, kissing them all. He also greeted all who were there to support his family through this difficult time. As Romulo started for his father's room, his sisters tried to comfort their mother.

Romulo's sisters were all married and knew the family's inheritance was designated for their brother Romulo, since he was the oldest and the only male in the family. That was the custom of the people in the state of Chiapas as well as in most other places in México.

Romulo entered the room where his father lie. Chico opened his eyes. Catching sight of his only son whom he loved so much, he was comforted by his arrival. Chico showed it in his expression.

"Ay, Papí, what happened to you?" Romulo asked as he reached for his father's hand. First, he checked his pulse. He lifted his eyelids.

"Hijo, how are you?" Chico asked, not trying to start a conversation with his son but drawing attention away from himself.

"I am fine, Papí; but it is you we are concerned with," Romulo uttered, as he scanned his father's frail body to see if he saw any other signs or symptoms of what might be wrong. "How do you feel, Papí? What hurts? What do you think is wrong with you?" Romulo asked, now looking into his father's big, tired, brown eyes.

"Romulo, I want you to take care of your mother," Chico whispered as he reached for Romulo's hand.

Romulo wanted to tell his father he could take care of Lydia himself. He wanted to say he was going to be around a long time, but Romulo acknowledged in his heart that this was not true.

"Ay, Papí, you need not worry about that. My mother will be fine. It is you we are concerned about," he repeated, trying to draw attention away from the request.

Chico's eyes closed as if he did not have the strength to keep them open. His breathing was shallow. Romulo opened his father's shirt and rested his head on his chest to listen to his heart. He did not like what he heard. "A weak, faint, irregular heartbeat. My father is dying," he thought. He remembered as a young boy how big and strong his father was. Back in those days his father's heart had such vigor. He recalled when he slept with his father and his mother in their bed; the whole bed would thump with his father's strong heartbeat.

"This is going to be a sad day," he thought.

Romulo stepped out of the room and looked at his sisters with a worried expression. "Hermanas (Sisters) y Mamá, I think you should go in and stay with Papá for the rest of the evening."

His mother as well as his sisters knew what this meant. If Romulo had said they should let him rest, it would have indicated Chico would be recuperating. To spend the rest of the evening with him only meant it was not good news.

Romulo walked into the parlor as his mother and sisters went in with his father. He sat on a chair with friends around him and cried, remembering all the things he and his father had done together as he was growing up. He thought of the stories his father had told him about meeting his mother. Now in a matter of hours, it would be all over.

Romulo re-entered his father's room. His mother made room for him to sit next to her by the top of the bed. Romulo put his hand on his father's forehead and brushed his hair back gently. Chico's eyes opened slightly, and a smile moved across his face. Within a minute or two, his breathing stopped. Chico's body jerked and twitched; his life had ended.

Their friends in the parlor heard wailing coming from the room where the family had gathered to be with Chico in his last moments of life. Big Chico Rodriguez from Sonora had died, the man who loved Lydia.

At the time of his father's death, Romulo was thirty years old.

Shortly after Chico's death, Lydia had a family meeting and told everyone she was turning the estate over to her oldest son. Romulo's sisters did not contend with her decision, knowing it was what their father wanted. They knew and loved their brother Romulo and knew he was not going to forget about them. They knew their brother was not a materialistic man.

Immediately following the meeting and when everything was put in his name, Romulo bought or built all of his sisters their own beautiful houses. As an attorney Romulo took care of all the legal work himself. He established bank accounts for his sisters. If something were to happen to him, they would have their own estates.

Even though Romulo loved helping people, he had his difficulties with the temptations of life. People wondered when Dr. Rodriguez was going to be married and settle down.

One evening, when Romulo was forty-one years old, there was a wedding celebration of a wealthy landholder's daughter. Many were invited. Twenty-five-year-old María de La Luz Ordoñez was present as a close friend of the bride. The Ordoñezes were not a wealthy family, but they were happy and lived comfortably.

The wedding was held in the iglesia, and the fiesta was held in the

Town Square. Decorations with beautiful, colorful tablecloths were set out. A large gazebo was to be used for the music and dancing. The Town Square was covered with greenery, such as banana and coconut trees, typical to a tropical climate. In the late afternoon a few people started to gather. Romulo was one of the first to arrive. The guests were looking forward to a long night of festivities and to the sound of their beautiful marimba music.

Marimba musical groups have five- to eight-playing members. The marimba is officially a member of the xylophone family. The instrument has full length, hollow chambers or cavities with dimensions chosen to permit internal strong and deep tones and to swing back and forth with a steady, uninterrupted rhythm or acoustical waves of specific frequencies. On top-of-the-line instruments, the hollow chamber, or cavity, is made of aluminum or some other metal. The instrument is carefully tuned to bring out the fundamental note of each bar. The marimba is played by striking the bars with mallets that come in a wide variety of shapes, coverings, weights, and sizes. Each imparts the instrument with a different tone, as does, of course, the player's technique. Some mallet heads are simply made of rubber or other synthetics graduated in firmness from soft to hard. Other mallet heads consist of a core covered with yarn, cord, or rubber. By controlling the core and winding it, a large variety of timbres are possible.

As people gathered, Romulo made his rounds, greeting friends and socializing with important individuals from different parts of the region. As he was conversing, he saw María de La Luz stop and begin a conversation with a captain of the military who was sitting at one of the tables nearby. The captain was new in the area. María de La Luz Ordoñez was her proper name, but she was called Luzita by family and friends. Luzita was a very beautiful, young lady. She always desired to find a husband and marry, but as of yet, she had not found the man of her dreams. At twenty-five she was beginning to wonder if she ever would.

Romulo knew the Ordoñezes and knew Luzita, but he had never really taken note of her. Romulo was standing, having a conversation with someone regarding politics. He observed Luzita's mannerisms as she spoke from across the way. This was the first time Romulo saw her beauty; he was stunned. He stopped speaking to the individual. As Luzita spoke, she presented a lovely smile. She tossed her long, black hair back over her shoulder. Romulo noted her gorgeous, big, brown eyes and how they shined as she spoke. Luzita was prieta (dark complected); her family was of Indian descent.

Whatever the captain was saying, it kept a smile on her gorgeous face. Romulo was so fascinated that he had to take a seat and watch her. Once he sat down and gazed in admiration, he knew Luzita was the woman of his longings. He believed and told others that there was such a thing as love at first sight. And the way his heart was pounding, he knew this was it.

Luzita was done with her conversation and picked up the glassware from the captain's table. She then started walking toward the doctor. Even the way she walked excited Romulo. Never in his life had Romulo felt the way he did at this instant. Ten feet away she stopped and smiled at a male friend. Ay, how Romulo wanted that smile to be for him. He knew positively that he would have it, since he was an important man in the area.

Just as Luzita approached, he heard a voice from behind him. "Romulo! There you are, mi hijo! We were looking for you," Lydia, his mother, said as she approached. She was accompanied by two of her daughters, Martha and Marina, and their husbands, Ricardo and Jésus.

Lydia was still a beautiful woman, even though she was an older lady of sixty-four years in 1915. She still had her charm, accompanied by her big, enchanting, blue eyes. Everyone was dressed in their best clothing.

Romulo stood. "Mamá, hermanas y muchachos, how are you?" Romulo asked as he embraced them and shook the men's hands.

"We are fine. Did you not bring a señorita to accompany you, Romulo?" Martha asked, thinking it strange her brother was sitting alone.

"No, Martha. Tonight I will enjoy the evening with all the women. I will have a little tequila and dance the evening away," Romulo declared, although he thought of Luzita and knew secretly he had found the woman of his heart.

"Do you know if my other hermanas (sisters) are coming?" Romulo asked. He had not talked to them because he had been very busy tending to the sick.

"We believe they are; but, Romulo, it is still early," Martha stated.

Just as the words came out of her mouth, Romulo's thoughts went back to the young woman he was observing when they approached. Romulo looked around for Luzita; she was nowhere in sight. "She must have gone back to the wagon that carried the food and articles for the fiesta," he thought to himself. He wanted to converse with her and receive that adorable smile he had seen her give to the captain.

As the evening progressed, he saw her a few times but was unable to get her attention. At one point as she entered the area, Romulo observed the captain get up and motion Luzita over to his table. He did not know if some kind of romance was going on between her and the captain. It seemed to him that Luzita purposely avoided looking in the captain's direction.

Marina asked Romulo why he was not dancing. They found it unusual that their brother was sitting out every dance. Romulo had a bottle of tequila in front of him and was enjoying the dancing from where he was. The marimba and the dancers were in full swing. All he did was sit and look for his new, secret love, Luzita. Finally he saw her walking toward him.

She approached their table and asked, "Is there anything I can get you, Doña Rodriguez?"

"No, I am fine, gracias."

"And you, Doctor, do you need anything?" Luzita asked, not smiling, not realizing the doctor had been waiting for a smile all evening.

Romulo stood and looked at Luzita. Lydia glanced at Romulo and wondered why he rose. Marina and Martha knew their brother and knew why he stood up. They both smiled at Luzita and then smiled at each other. Romulo could not find any words. He spoke low and was very nervous. He did not know if he could find the proper words and was not even sure what he wanted to say.

"Luzita, I... I wanted to know if you might dance with me as soon as you have time?" Romulo asked. He felt his voice shaking from within, even sounding hoarse. He did not know if Luzita was able to discern his nervousness.

Martha and Marina knew exactly what was going on, knowing their brother so well. They sat and enjoyed those few seconds, sensing it could change things forever for Romulo. Lydia looked up at her son. Because of the hoarseness in his voice, she thought Romulo was starting to become ill. She also wondered why he was asking Luzita to dance when she was helping her friend with the fiesta. There were many beautiful, wealthy women from miles around with whom to dance.

Luzita smiled at Romulo. She thought it was kind of him to want to dance with a common girl like her when there were so many lovely and prestigious women present. "That would be nice, Doctor. It will be in a little while. I will inform you, and you may pick the piece we will dance to. Thank you very much."

"Thank you, Luzita," Romulo said with a shaky voice.

Luzita left the table. Romulo sat in a daze, thinking of her and wondering what it was that was making him so nervous. He had much experience with women. He had been with and courted the most beautiful women from all the area. But now his heart was pounding. He realized he had found the woman of his dreams. He knew he would not have a problem in getting his way with Luzita. Women who Romulo saw always hoped to marry him, but he never found one with whom he wished to spend the rest of his life.

As the evening progressed, all the tables were occupied; there was standing room only. Nervously, Luzita appeared, attending to the guests. Each time she passed the captain's table, the captain smiled at her and asked her to sit with him. He told her he had some nice words for her. He was already intoxicated. Luzita tended to the necessities of the table and left. As she walked away, the other officers sitting with the captain laughed. Romulo sat at his table and did not like this at all; he was a little intoxicated himself. He felt his insides boil. Romulo was not a fighting man; but if he had to defend himself, he was no pushover.

Well into the evening, Luzita came out and sat at a table with two of her girlfriends. She looked over at Romulo to let him know she was ready to dance. The floor on the large gazebo was full of people having a good time. The bridegroom and family members were dancing. Just as Romulo stood up, the captain rose from his chair. The captain patted one of his fellow officers on the back and headed toward Luzita. Luzita looked at Romulo and anticipated dancing with the well-known doctor. She wondered why he had suddenly taken an interest in her. All three girls saw Romulo making his way towards them; however, the captain approached the table first where the girls were seated.

"Muchacha, I would like to dance with you!" the captain demanded. He knew Luzita would have to dance with him. If she did not, it could mean trouble for her father. During this time the Mexican revolution had begun, and the military was overbearing with the people.

All three girls looked at the captain with fearful expressions. Luzita looked over at Romulo as he was making his way towards them. "I am sorry, Capitán; but I have this dance promised to someone else."

"What do you mean, you have this dance promised to someone else? You come and dance with me!" the captain demanded as he grabbed her upper arm and started to drag her to her feet. Luzita did not know what to do. She felt as if she was being assaulted by this man. Marina and Martha saw what was happening and rose to their feet.

Luzita was trying desperately to pull away from the captain. "¡Dejamé (Leave me alone)!" Luzita declared, pushing him at the same time. The captain's friends were observing him, wondering if he was going to succeed in dancing with Luzita.

"Hey! Hey! What do you think you are doing?" Romulo's voice was no longer shaking. "Señor, what do you think you are doing?"

"Doctor, you stay out of this! If you do not, you will regret it!" the captain shouted. He was still trying to pull Luzita to her feet.

In that instance Romulo's feelings for Luzita welled up in his heart. He recalled how he felt about her, how his heart was pounding with her presence. He was not going to let the captain do what he wanted with the woman who had his attention and made him feel as he had never felt before.

"Capitán!" Romulo called as he grabbed the captain's shoulder. As he did this, the other soldiers stood up, knowing there was going to be trouble. They had no idea who the doctor and his mother were. Nor did they know they had close ties with their superior, the general, and also the governor.

The captain released Luzita. At the same time he pushed her with such force that she went tumbling back over the chair and onto the ground. Romulo reached back and swung as hard as he could. His punch hit its mark, and the captain went flying back. Romulo felt the pain in his hand as the punch connected. All at once the soldiers raced to the doctor and were ready to defend the captain, thinking they were going to make the doctor pay for what he had done. At the moment they approached, Ricardo and Jésus were on their feet and fighting with the soldiers. Within those few seconds there was chaos.

Romulo squatted down at Luzita's side and asked if she was all right. She did not know what to say. She could not believe what was happening around her and that people were fighting because of her.

"Come on. You have to get out of here!" Romulo declared.

Romulo and Luzita stepped over to where his mother and sisters were standing. Lydia said anxiously, "Leave, Romulo. More soldiers are coming. I will see what I can do for Ricardo and Jésus as soon as it is over. They will want to kill you. Hurry! Go!"

"Martha, take Luzita and go home! Marina, go and get Luzita's familia and take them to Mamá's house. Hurry! They will be sending soldiers over there as soon as this is over. Mamá, see what you can do to get us out of jail!" Romulo shouted, as he looked back at his two brothers-in-law.

"Ay, but my Ricardo! I need to help him! What if they kill my husband!" Marina exclaimed as she looked over at the men fighting.

Luzita had a sad expression. She did not know where things were going. Everything was happening too fast. Romulo looked at Luzita and said, "Do not forget me. You still owe me a dance."

Romulo turned and headed back in the direction of the fight. He felt his hand in pain, but that was not going to stop him. The tequila he drank would help him get through what was coming.

Martha grabbed Luzita's hand and said, "¡Vamonos, muchacha (Let's go, girl)!" Both of them started to make their way out of the area to Martha's house. Martha thought of her husband but knew there was not much she could do. She would take Luzita to her house and return to see what she could do for Jésus.

It had only been seconds. It seemed as if the fight was winding down. People were trying to break it up. Some of the bride's family was holding the captain back and telling him to cool down. Others were holding the soldiers back. The captain drunkenly yelled from the top of his lungs for reinforcements.

Nobody was holding Ricardo and Jésus back. They had stopped fighting the first chance they had. They knew this whole affair would mean trouble for them. They had been married to the Rodriguez sisters for some time, but at that moment they had forgotten how much power and influence the family had.

Lydia stepped over in front of the captain and said, "Do you know with whom you are dealing? Do you know General Ochoa is going to hear what you have done?"

"And who are you, mujer (woman)? I will have you arrested as soon as my men arrive! I will have all of you who are holding me arrested! Let go!" he yelled, trying to shake loose from those who were restraining him. The families of the men who were holding him back also had influence; but if they had Doña Rodriguez on their side, they had nothing to worry about. Lydia, even after Chico had died, made her share of contributions to the politicians.

Just at that moment ten soldiers arrived, holding their rifles up and trying to see who the captain was going to order them to shoot.

"Those men, including the doctor, have them arrested! All of them!"

The soldiers pointed their rifles at Romulo, Ricardo, and Jésus. Romulo looked over at them and said, "Do as they say. It will be all right."

The captain wiped the blood off his lip and yelled, "Have these men arrested also!" He pointed at the men who had been holding him. The soldiers who were at his side were trying to straighten themselves up, thinking the fiesta was still going to continue. "Where is the desgraciada? I want her arrested! And find out who her familia is! I want them brought in to be interrogated! And you, mujer vieja (old lady)!" the captain said, pointing to Lydia, "One word out of you, and I do not care if you are a vieja, I will have you taken in too!"

Lydia knew he did not know what he was doing. She wanted to leave and get word to the general and to her friend, the governor, as soon as possible. She turned and looked at her son and gave him a smile, indicating everything was going to be all right. Quietly, she turned and walked away.

CHAPTER TWELVE

BRAVE AND COURAGEOUS

As soon as Lydia arrived home, she was met by friends. She sent two messengers to the general and two to the governor. In case something was to happen to one, the other would make it.

In the next few hours, the pueblo of San Bartolomé de los Llanos was in chaos. Soldiers were running around everywhere. It seemed as if the revolution had started there. They were searching for Luzita and her family, rounding up people who seemed not to cooperate with them. They were nowhere to be found.

In the meantime the captain began his interrogation of Romulo. "Who are you working for?" he asked.

"For you, Capitán. I am the people's doctor," was his answer.

"What did you say your name is, Doctor?"

"Romulo Rodriguez."

"Who are you working for?" he asked.

"For the people."

"Do not lie to me, señor."

In a little while the captain started to sober up and became more composed.

The interrogation went on in this manner for quite awhile, back and forth.

"What is your real name?" he asked, over and over.

"Romulo Rodriguez," he repeatedly answered.

Finally the captain looked at one of his subordinates and asked, "Do you know this familia, Rodriguez?" He was not slurring his words anymore.

"Yes, Capitán. They are one of the richest families in Chiapas."

The captain thought for a moment. He had not heard of a hacienda in the area owned by a family Rodriguez. His subordinate spoke again,

"They are the owners of Rancho U-Chem, Capitán."

Now the captain's brown face turned red. He knew with whom he was dealing. He had heard of the family long before arriving in Chiapas and knew the influence they had as well as the trouble he had created for himself. He shouted at one of his men, "Untie him! Who told you to tie him up?"

The soldier did as he was told. "Señor Rodriguez, I am sorry for the trouble. These men do not know what they are doing! And they will pay for it!" he vented. As he looked at the soldier, he said, "¡Desgraciado (miserable)!" He then looked at Romulo and said, "Maybe they do not know who you are, Señor Rodriguez."

Romulo was rubbing his wrists and stood up. The captain extended his hand so Romulo could shake it.

Romulo did not extend his hand but said, "It is not I you need to apologize to. It is my mother who you insulted at the wedding. And at the wedding, Capitán, those were important people there. Were you invited, or did you want to be there to police it? For your sake I hope you were invited."

"Señor Rodriguez, I heard the wedding was going to be unsupervised. I wanted to make sure things were going to be handled properly."

"Do not explain to me, Capitán. It is to the general and the governor to whom you will need to explain. May I go?"

"Yes, you may. As I said, I want to apologize for all that has taken place. My men who started the fight will be punished for their actions."

"And the muchachos, will you release them now?"

"Yes, by all means." He looked at the soldier and said, "Hurry, desgraciado, go and get them!"

"And another thing, Capitán Herrera, the young lady Luzita is my fiancé. I hope you know that."

Captain Herrera was lost for words. He knew the general was not going to like this one bit.

Upon arriving back at his mother's house, Romulo saw Luzita crying. "Luzita, everything is going to be all right," he said. He was saddened to see this young, pretty muchacha shedding tears.

"I am sorry I caused all this trouble. I did not mean to do any of this. I cannot believe this happened on such a beautiful evening. And Rebecca, her wedding is ruined for life on my account!"

Romulo put his hand on her shoulder and said, "It was not your fault. The capitán is the one who assaulted you. You did not do anything you were not supposed to do, Luzita. I will see to it that this man is punished for this!"

"I do not want you to do anything to make things worse for my familia. They will suffer for this as it is."

Romulo looked at her. She appeared beautiful even though she was upset. He wondered why he had never taken note of her beauty in the past. "Maybe God has hidden it from me until this day," he thought.

During the next few days, things settled down in San Bartolomé de los Llanos. The governor sent his people from San Cristóbal de Las Casas to investigate the situation. The general disciplined the captain and sent him to another locality, a more remote area.

Romulo called on Luzita a few evenings later. The Ordoñezes did not live far from his office. The Ordoñez family lived a few doors down from the Cabrillo's home; they were also good friends of Romulo. Romulo went to the Cabrillos front door and called, "Hola, Is anyone home?" The door was open.

Wiping her hands on a cloth, Señora Cabrillo came to the door and answered, "¿Bueno? What can I do for you? Ay, Doctor, it is you! What brought you to our home? Gabriel will be happy to see you. Come in. Come in." She stepped to the side, allowing Romulo to enter.

Romulo entered and took off his hat. "Actually, I came to see the Ordoñezes. But I wanted to give my regards to you and your husband first."

"That is nice of you, Doctor. The Ordoñezes, hum? How is your mother?" she asked, still wiping her hands.

"My mother is fine. She is still recuperating from the wedding. She continues to be troubled with the capitán and wanted him to be disciplined more than he was."

"Yes, that is what the talk is in the street. But you know, Doctor, the revolution is taking its toll. They say the new governor has orders from the President that he needs to seek out any who are in opposition to the government. And I understand General Ochoa will be leaving to México City soon. We do not know who will be taking his place. Gabriel said he heard it will be a harsh general who is presently in the city of Vera Cruz."

"Who is it you want to see of the Ordoñezes? Don Ordoñez?"

Señora Cabrillo asked, really believing it was Luzita he came to visit. The whole town knew what happened at the wedding, but she wanted to hear it from the doctor himself. She would then have something more to tell her friends.

"Well, actually, it is Luzita to whom I wanted to speak. I hope she is in."

"I am sure she is. I saw her walk by a little while ago. She could have left, but I do not think so. Would you like me to go for her?" she asked, knowing if the doctor and Luzita had their conversation in her house, she would be able to overhear and would have more details to tell her friends about the romance.

"No, that will not be necessary. Thank you anyway."

"Doctor!" Señor Cabrillo greeted him as he stepped into the parlor. "I thought I heard a different voice here."

Romulo turned. Before he could speak, Señora Cabrillo interrupted, "He came to see Luzita, Gabriel."

"Yes, I did. But I wanted to come to visit you also, since I was coming by your home."

"It is our honor to have you here anytime. The pueblo has been talking about what a brave and courageous man you were to step in and defend Luzita the other evening. That capitán! He ought to have been shot! They really should have shot him! You know, no one at the wedding and in all of San Bartolomé de los Llanos liked the way he treated Luzita, you, your brothers-in-law, and even Doña Rodriguez," he said as his smile disappeared and a frown appeared.

"Well, that was nothing. I was just doing my duty as a man in the community," Romulo stated. He felt he was getting too much praise about the incident. He also felt he might as well enjoy all the attention.

"I will go and get Luzita for you, Doctor. You have a seat," Señor Cabrillo said as he put his hand on Romulo's shoulder, trying to move him back to where he was seated.

"No! No, Señor Cabrillo. I will go to her door. I want to greet her familia also."

Romulo stayed and talked. In a few minutes he stood and said, "It was nice to see both of you. Come to my office and see me once in awhile. We just do not visit as much as we should."

"Yes, that is true, Doctor. I was just thinking of when we were boys, all the fun we had."

Romulo smiled and said, "Yes, that is true. So much fun." With that he said good-bye and left to Luzita's house.

Romulo stepped up to the door and called out, "Bueno, is anyone home? Don Ordoñez, are you home?"

Señora Ordoñez stepped to the front entrance and said, "Doctor. What can I do for you?" Señora Ordoñez thought the doctor arrived at her home because he was bringing bad news about someone, an accident or illness.

"Doña Ordoñez, how are you?"

"I am fine, Doctor. What is it? Did you come to inform me of something?" she asked as she gripped both of her hands tightly, hoping it was not serious.

"I came to visit Luzita, but I would like to ask Don Ordoñez if that is possible. I would like to have his approval."

"Ay, Doctor, Señor Ordoñez is not in at the moment," she answered, feeling relieved. "Come in, Doctor. Please, sit down. Sit. Let us get you something to drink."

Romulo entered her home, sat on a nice chair in the parlor, and said, "Thank you, Doña Ordoñez. That would be refreshing on this warm day."

She turned and called to her servant, "Carmen, get the doctor a refreshment." She turned back to Romulo and said, "Doctor, if you want to speak to Luzita, that will be fine. I will go and get her. By the way, Doctor, that was a very brave thing you did for our niña (little girl) the other night. Señor Ordoñez and I appreciate it very much. More men should stand up to them!" she declared, meaning the military.

"Oh, Doña Ordoñez, I only did what I should have done; but all the same, you are most welcome," Romulo answered, feeling proud of himself.

"Excuse me, Doctor, I will go and get her."

As Romulo waited for a few seconds, he looked around the parlor. He also could see the back yard. It was very pleasant, and the garden was green with many plants. He also saw banana, coconut, and mango trees. Under the large mango tree, there was a long bench with tropical plants all around it. "That spot will be nice to sit and visit with Luzita," he thought.

"Doctor, is there anything wrong?" Luzita asked as she rubbed her eyes, awakening from a deep sleep.

"No, Luzita. I wanted to come and see how you are and to visit with you for a few minutes. Do you have a little time?"

"Yes, of course."

"May we sit on the bench," Romulo asked, pointing toward the mango tree.

"That will be fine, Doctor," she answered, stepping out of the house and to the back yard. The house had no back wall, as most of the other homes, because the weather was warm all year around.

As they sat, Romulo looked at Luzita. He could not get over how he had never noticed her beauty. "Luzita, how are you? Has anyone given you any trouble, any of the soldiers?"

"No. It seems as if the incident never occurred. The capitán went away, and that was it. What about you, Doctor, has anyone called on you to give you trouble?"

"Luzita, I would like you to call me Romulo. I feel very close to you."

Luzita did not know what to say and did not know why the doctor felt this way. She had not really talked to him before the wedding, although she and her family had been in to see him many times throughout the years. Her father and mother always spoke very highly of him, but that was it.

They both sat and chatted for a few minutes. Romulo reached for Luzita's hand. He always did this, and his girlfriends always enjoyed it. Just as he held her hand inside both of his, she pulled it away. She was embarrassed; Romulo also became embarrassed. He could not remember a woman withdrawing her hand from him, ever.

"Doctor, you should not do that," Luzita said as she glanced at the house to see if her mother was watching. At that instant Romulo realized what a foolish thing he had done. He thought, "What if her mother observed my trying to hold her hand?"

"Luzita, I am sorry. I will be more careful."

Luzita knew what kind of man Romulo was, especially since that evening at the wedding. People were talking about him, saying both good and bad things. The bad things were about his having many girlfriends. Some even said he had children in San Bartolomé de los Llanos and San Cristóbal de Las Casas. Luzita did not really think much of it at the time since she did not have a relationship with him. However, now as Romulo sat next to her, she recalled all that was said of him.

"Luzita, my mother is having a dinner out at Rancho U-Chem. I would like to ask if you will accompany me?"

"Ay, Doctor, that is very nice of you. But I do not think I will be able to attend. Thank you very much for the invitation."

Romulo was lost for words. He was not expecting to be turned down. He was rarely turned down unless it was for a good reason.

"Is there a problem, Luzita? Are you sure? I will really be honored if you can attend."

The servant approached with a tray of pineapple juice. Luzita took her drink and sipped it. Romulo took his glass. He smiled at her.

Luzita thought to herself, "I regularly attended the iglesia, and I know Romulo is not one who goes to the iglesia often. Even though I feel he believes in God and wants to do his will, he is not one who is as devoted as I am."

As the servant girl walked away, Luzita knew she still had to answer the doctor's question. She raised her cup and took another drink of her juice. It would give her a few more seconds to think of her answer. Romulo, not drinking but waiting to see what she was going to say, was curious as to why she was refusing him.

"Well, Doctor, I do not think it will be a good idea. That is all. I really do not know you, and you do not know me. It will be inappropriate for me to accompany you to your mother's rancho if we are not well acquainted," Luzita said, trying her best to be kind, speaking in a persuasive way, and not wanting to hurt his feelings.

"Also, Doctor, I mean, Romulo, I want to thank you again for coming to my defense the other night. I know I already thanked you, but I would like to thank you again," she said, trying to change the subject. Luzita felt the only time it would be appropriate to go with him to his parent's place for the evening would be if they were courting and had plans to marry.

Romulo knew how he felt. He had the same feelings for her that he had the night of the wedding. He felt overwhelmed with pleasure as he sat next to Luzita. He also felt his stomach give way to pain with her refusal. Romulo understood how she must feel and knew they had the rest of their lives to get to know each other. There were going to be many other dinners at his mother's rancho.

"Bueno, Luzita, I understand," Romulo said as he took a drink of his juice. "May I come and see you again?"

Luzita looked down at the ground. She did not want to see Romulo's expression of hurt when she gave him her answer; Romulo was not for her. He loved medicine and loved caring for people. She knew he would never be devoted to her and to her God. She also felt he would never be able to restrain himself from other women. He was too old and set in his ways to change.

"I do not think that will be a good idea, Doctor. I mean, Romulo. Because, well, I appreciate what you did the other night. But I do not feel I have to repay you in any way since I did not ask for help. You did it on your own."

"Oh no, Luzita! You do not have to pay for anything. I want to visit you because I want to, not because you owe me," Romulo answered worriedly.

"I think it is better if you go, Doctor," she said, trying not to sound rude.

Romulo stood, put his glass back on the tray, and replied, "I see. Well, you know I really would like to see you and...."

"Doctor!" Señor Ordoñez called, Walking toward them, while taking off his hat. "Thank you very much for what you did for my hija the other night. I have been meaning to go to your office to thank you, but they tell me you have been very busy." Señor Ordoñez's clothes were dirty; he had just returned from the small rancho he owned.

Señor Cabrillo also entered the garden with Señor Ordoñez. Romulo extended his hand to Señor Ordoñez. "Don Ordoñez, it is good to see you. You look very healthy. I have not seen you for some time. You need to come by my office. I can examine you to make sure you are as healthy as you look," Romulo said, knowing busy people never went to his office just to be examined.

"I have been meaning to come in. I have had this pain in my side that will not go away," he said as he reached back and pulled his shirt up. The doctor looked and felt the tissue on his back; he told him he needed to go in to be examined properly. Luzita was embarrassed that her father pulled up his shirt and took advantage of the doctor's presence. Romulo was accustomed to having people show him their injuries or ailments, no matter where they were.

Señor and Señora Cabrillo approached and Señor Cabrillo asked, "Doctor, we were talking in the house. We would like you to join us for supper on Saturday."

Luzita looked at Romulo and knew his mother was also having a supper.

"This Saturday?"

"Yes. I am also inviting Luzita and her familia," Señora Cabrillo said, knowing Romulo had an interest in Luzita.

"Will you be present, Luzita?" Romulo asked, looking at her.

"Oh yes! Of course she will," her father declared.

Luzita did not say anything. She could not because her father had spoken. She loved him so much and had always been respectful to him.

"Yes, I will accept. I just told Luzita my mother is also having a supper, but I am with her all the time. She will not mind if I do not attend. I would really enjoy spending the evening with all of you."

"Very well, we will expect you at five."

The following Saturday night went very well. Romulo, the big talker, kept everyone entertained and laughing. He won over Luzita's family and had a lot of fun with the Cabrillo family.

As time passed, Romulo tried to convince Luzita to see more of him; however, she felt the same as she did from the very beginning. She liked Romulo and knew it would not be difficult to fall in love with him. Luzita knew Romulo's life and really did not want any part of it.

Every few days Romulo stopped and visited Luzita and her family. Eight months after that Saturday-night supper date, with persistence, Romulo won Luzita over. He was madly in love with her and even stopped seeing other women at this time.

Luzita saw how much Romulo cared for her. She was building strong feelings for him also; she could see his sincerity from the way he treated her; and she finally fell in love with Romulo.

One day Romulo went to Luzita's home and asked her father for her hand in marriage.

Señor Ordoñez was happy and agreed. As long as Romulo's proposal was accepted by Luzita, it would be all right with him, he said.

Romulo asked if he could take Luzita on a walk to the Calvario. He informed Señor Ordoñez he would take his sister Marina's daughter, Gina, as a chaperon.

Walking up the ancient volcano to the Calvario, Romulo asked Luzita what she wanted out of life. Gina was following not far behind as Romulo had instructed; he wanted to speak with Luzita privately.

"I want a husband who will take care of me and make me happy.

You know, Romulo, many men have wanted to court me. I have been waiting for someone special, and I will wait until he comes along."

Romulo did not like her answer, hoping he was the one she awaited. Luzita was not good at choosing the right words. Even though she was in love with Romulo, she had to be careful. She knew that after forty-three years he had not married. She did not want to put herself in a presumptuous position.

"Luzita, do you realize I am in love with you?"

"Yes, Romulo."

Reaching the top of the old volcano at the Calvario, the same spot that Romulo's mother and father had walked to the first time they met, they stopped and looked down. Romulo wanted to hold Luzita's hand but thought it would be a bad idea. "There will be many opportunities in the future," he reasoned.

From their vantage point at the Calvario, they could see 50-60 kilometers away, a beautiful scene. Everything on the jungle floor was a gorgeous green. Adding to the beauty were the rolling, small hills. In the distance they could see a thick, black cloud with rays of lightning flashing under it. Romulo and Luzita loved their land and knew they would never tire of such beauty in all of their lives.

"Look," Romulo said, pointing out past the town a few kilometers. "There, my mother's rancho."

Luzita had a good feeling about Romulo, and she felt a joy in her heart anticipating where the relationship was leading. She had not heard wild stories about Romulo since she had been keeping company with him. Her family and friends told her Romulo was in love with her, and she was a very fortunate woman.

"Yes, I see it," she said, as she looked down. She turned and stared at him. Romulo saw her peer deep into his eyes. He could see her love for him as she stared. He felt his heart beating fast. Throughout the last eight months, he wondered if he would ever see that expression of love on her pretty face.

"What about you, Romulo, what do you want out of life?"

Romulo looked deep into Luzita's eyes and had no doubt what he wanted for his life. The only thing that was missing was Luzita and the children she was going to bear him.

"Luzita, I want something that no other man can have. I want to have the most treasured life with the most beautiful familia one can experience. And I want the woman with the most gracious heart in the entire world. Luzita, I want you!"

As he spoke his romantic words, Luzita looked just as deeply into his eyes as he looked into hers. He continued, "I want to wake up every morning and have your presence in my life. I want your heart in the palms of my hands, and I never want it to leave me. As you know, my darling, from the first day I saw you, that very evening at the wedding, I have not given up in trying to win you over. I fell in love with you that very night. I know I will never be happy with any other woman. Luzita, I want to ask for your hand in marriage. Before you answer, if you feel you are unsure, then I want you to think it over. I want you to know right now, my darling, that if your feelings toward me are in anyway negative, I will work on that for as long as it takes. I will never, ever, for the rest of my life, never give up trying to win you over," Romulo expressed, taking a deep breath.

Luzita faced Romulo in deep thought and with so much joy in her heart that it felt as if the joy wanted to explode. She knew she had to control herself. She understood she had to be very careful. Even though she knew what she wanted and recognized at that moment that she really loved Romulo, she had to take her time. Luzita was a very strong-minded woman. She took Romulo's hand and replied, "Thank you, Romulo, for being who you are. I know I do care for you. I will have to speak to my father first and see how he feels about this."

"I have asked your father already if I may ask you for your hand in marriage. He said it all depended on the way you feel, Luzita."

"I knew my father would tell you that, Romulo. However, it does not matter. He is my father, and I have the deepest respect for him. I have to consult him first. If I did not do that, I might hurt him; and I would never want to do that. May I give you my answer in a few days?" She knew her answer was going to be yes.

"Yes, that will be fine, Luzita," Romulo replied, feeling disappointed in not receiving an answer at that moment. However, he felt good that his proposal was not declined. He wanted to take her into his arms at that instant; but knowing the kind of woman she was, it would be unwise. Luzita, on the other hand, stood there wishing Romulo would take her into his arms and hold her tightly. She was in no way going to stop him if he did embrace her.

From this point on she longed for his sweet words and his tenderness.

Luzita went home and talked to her father. Both of her parents were happy for their hija, not because Romulo was wealthy but because he was a kind-hearted man. They knew he would treat her well.

Following the proposal and her affirmative answer, the wedding was planned and arrangements were made. Romulo even arranged for many of the common people to be invited.

THE BOX

During this time there were more clashes between the government troops and the revolutionary party. Many of the peasants were joining the revolutionaries in fighting against the government. The federal army continued mistreating the common people, causing more of them to join the struggle. As it was said months before, the present general was replaced with a general who was tougher with the people, a strict military man. His only concern was in winning the conflict against those who opposed the government.

The year was 1916. Many wondered if Romulo and Luzita's wedding was going to proceed since there was so much fighting. Romulo tried to keep neutral in his discussions of the revolution, knowing his duty to humanity was to save lives. Even though, his heart was with the people.

There was talk the government was not going to authorize any large gatherings, and Romulo was not going to be an exception. With all the plans and preparations he had made for the wedding, he did not want this to happen. Romulo readied his things and was on his way to San Cristóbal de Las Casas to visit the governor and the new general. He was going to see if they could make an exception for his wedding.

Romulo was told by his family and Luzita's family not to go, since the roads were much too dangerous. People were found dead and missing during these last few months. With all the traveling he had done in the past and as brave a man as Romulo was, talk of people dying would not stop him.

A good friend of Romulo, who he knew and loved since childhood, insisted he needed to accompany the doctor on his journey, just in case something was to happen on the road. Daniel Gómez loved Romulo as a brother. When they were young men, they were always together. Romulo was not a fighter, but his friend Daniel was. Whenever there was trouble, he would step in and defend Romulo. Daniel was a big man, six-feet tall, and well built. He had a round face and always had a smile, except when he was angry. At times through life Romulo found himself fighting alongside Daniel. As they grew older, Romulo restrained himself.

Daniel married at a young age and had four children. At this time they were older. His wife Monica loved him with all her heart. She always worried about her husband, knowing the kind of man he was, especially during this time of war. When he told Monica he was going to accompany his best friend Romulo, she feared for them both because of all the reports she had heard. She knew there was nothing she could do to persuade him not to go.

Daniel took along two guns and a rifle. He hoped he would not have to use them; however, he did not want to take any chances.

After six hours on the road, they decided to stop for the night. They had a late start. The sun was on its way down. Just as they stopped, a burst of heavy rain poured down, followed by uncountable flashes of lightning. Romulo and Daniel enjoyed it, even though in those parts it was an everyday occurrence. To them it was as if God was having his say.

Once Romulo's and Daniel's canvases were draped over the foliage, they lined the ground with deerskin to keep out the wetness. Daniel took out provisions and was about to serve Romulo his portion. All of a sudden they heard many horses approaching. Quickly Daniel went for his rifle and tried to hand Romulo one of his guns. "Hurry, Romulo! Take it before they get here!"

"No, I do not need a gun, Daniel. I am a doctor! If I have a gun, then I will be defeating my purpose," Romulo vented, not knowing why he was telling this to Daniel. He had spent many occasions lecturing Daniel on his philosophies.

"Romulo, you are not in town now. We do not know who these men are. We may be killed here as many others have been. Take it!" Daniel ordered, with his hand stretched out to Romulo and the handle of the gun facing him. Romulo stood and threw his sarape over his shoulder to show he was unarmed. The rain had now subsided, and the plants were dripping out their moisture. At the same time there was a stillness in the air. Daniel stood and told Romulo to take cover behind a large tree that was to his side.

"I have no reason to hide. We are on a friendly journey, and there is no reason why anyone should give us any trouble."

"Doctor, this is a war! They will shoot us just to say they shot two people from the other side. You know that as well as I do. Take cover, and I will see who they are."

Romulo did not move. He was a proud man and was not going to be hiding from anyone. Just as Romulo's words were out of his mouth, they saw many men riding towards them. Dark had not yet fallen, and one could still see a distance. On this night there was a tropical moon; it lit up the night. It was big and bright, as if one could reach out and touch it.

The riders were not expecting to see anyone next to the road. When they approached Romulo and Daniel, they pulled back on their reigns. They were moving fast, and their sarapes were flapping behind them. Some were wearing sombreros, and some were not. Their horses galloped to a stop with uneasiness. All the men in this group looked tired and worn. All were holding rifles. Their bullet belts crossed their chests.

The rider who took the lead had a big mustache. He lifted his arm, indicating to his men to come to a complete stop. A small smile crossed his face as if he thought he was about to have fun.

The men on the horses came to a stop. As the horses moved around with uneasiness, the man with the big mustache said, "Buenas noches, señores. Who are you, and what are you doing so far from your homes?"

Four men behind him had their rifles pointed at Romulo and Daniel.

Daniel had his rifle pointed down to his side, and his other hand was on his gun in his belt. He knew he needed to be very careful. The way these men looked, they were not going to put up with anything or anyone and would not hesitate to shoot him and the doctor in a second.

"We are on our way to San Cristóbal de Las Casas on business, señor," Romulo answered.

"What kind of business, señor?" the man asked, not smiling anymore.

"I am Dr. Romulo Rodriguez, and this is my assistant."

"Ay, a doctor," he declared, thinking and rubbing his jaw. "I am very sorry to inform you, Doctor, but your services are being called on by the people. We need for you to come with us." The revolutionist was thinking he would like to have a doctor riding with him. They were needed; and if he had one with him, it would make him look good.

Daniel knew Romulo would never go willingly. He hoped he would move as fast as he could in the next few seconds.

"Ay, señor, be reasonable! We are not bothering anyone here. Please, you go and let us be. We do not want any trouble," Daniel said. He knew the "please" was for himself as well. He understood that it meant if the man did not agree perhaps Romulo and he could be shot and killed.

"Muchachos," the man said, looking behind at the others. "Put the doctor on a horse and see what they are carrying!" He turned his head in the direction of Romulo and Daniel and continued, "Do not give my men any trouble; or you will be shot, Doctor!" The man looked at Daniel and started to raise his rifle.

Daniel knew they did not want him. He felt he was going to be named in another report in the following days as one more man found dead on the road. He was going to be shot, and Romulo was going to be taken along and perhaps shot for not cooperating. It was necessary to act fast, and there was no time to think it over. He just wished Romulo were carrying a gun to help him with this suicide.

"Look, señor, let me say this one thing...." Daniel brought his rifle up with his finger already on the trigger. As his rifle was raised and as he took aim dead center on the man in charge, he pulled the trigger without hesitation. The man's chest burst open with the force of the bullet. At that instant four bullets were heading toward Daniel's chest. Romulo knew what he had to do. He wished he had listened to his good friend whom he loved. As he saw Daniel's body falling back, he knew he would never be able to grab his gun without receiving the next bullet.

Romulo turned and dashed behind a large tree and then into the foliage. He heard shots and knew they were intended for him, but in his head the shots seemed as if they were far away. Continuing deeper into the jungle, he heard more shots and men yelling as if they were getting closer. He found a place under a number of fallen trees and hid under them, lying very still and knowing he would not be found if he did not move.

Romulo lay under the tree, trying to breathe quietly. He heard men moving around the area and getting closer. In a short time it seemed as if the soldiers were moving away. He was not sure if they went deeper into the jungle or went back to where the shooting occurred.

As he waited, he thought of Daniel, his beloved friend. How he had loved him throughout the years. He remembered back to when he was young. In school in San Cristóbal de Las Casas, he thought his life was doomed because of the affair with Seneida. His friend Daniel encouraged him and helped him get over his anxiety.

Romulo heard a shot ring out. He put his head down and cried quietly, wondering if the shot hit Daniel's head. "At least one of the men responsible for it was dead or going to die," he thought. If Romulo was found, he would be shot rather than attend to the man who killed his best friend.

Romulo stayed under the trees, not moving as the stillness of the night approached. He wondered if the men had left or if they had decided to spend the night in his camp. "These are the men who the general and governor are afraid of. And as the reports are coming in, they seem to be winning the war," he thought.

Romulo knew there were bad men on both sides of the conflict. He just wished he had not met the bad ones.

Romulo heard noises. He could not imagine the revolutionary soldiers still looking for him in the jungle. "It must be the jungle noises," he thought as he cried for his friend.

Many thoughts crossed his mind. He thought back to his father being pursued by the guardian of his mother. He thought of his grandfather, the priest, and wondered whatever happened to him. He wondered if his grandfather Fuentes started a new life with a new family. "Maybe I have familia in other parts of México." He also thought of his future wife Luzita and what she would do if he were to die out here in the jungle. "What if I am killed out here in this lonely place, never to be found by anyone?"

He then thought of Daniel's wife, how she was going to miss her good man. Romulo recalled many occasions when she said that if anything was to ever happen to her beloved husband she would never marry again. Daniel would tease her. He would tell her that if she found another person who was a charm of a man then she would marry him in a minute. She would slap his back and tell him he was loco. "Ay, ay, ay, she is going to miss him! I am going to miss him. My friend," he uttered to himself.

Romulo could not hear anymore noises. He rose from where he was lying. He thought at first it might be better to stay in the same location all night and leave in the morning. He reasoned that, if he stayed and the soldiers were to return, they would find him for sure in the morning. He did not want this to happen.

Romulo tried to be as quiet as possible just in case the soldiers were waiting for him to make his move. It had been two hours since the last time he heard them. Romulo envisioned Daniel trying to hand him the gun. He knew it would not have made a difference then; however, it would now when he was defenseless and walking through the jungle towards the soldiers. It was the only way out. If he went deeper into the jungle, he might find himself lost. If he could catch one of them, he might be able to overpower him and take his gun as well as a horse.

Romulo stopped when he heard voices. He knew now they had not left. In a distance he could make out a campfire. He squatted down low and looked around, making sure he was not being watched. He analyzed the situation and decided to see how he was going to proceed. If it was possible, he would bypass the soldiers, make his way to the road, and make his getaway on foot. "I will save myself for my Luzita," he thought.

Then the picture of Daniel and Daniel's family appeared in his mind. He wondered if Daniel was still alive. After all, he did not see him and had to make sure he was dead before leaving, even if it meant risking his life. He could not go back home and tell Daniel's wife he thought her husband was dead; he had to know for certain.

Staying low and moving very slowly, Romulo proceeded. In a few steps the campfire was visible, and he was out of the dense jungle where he could see with the moonlight. He knew he had to be careful. If he could see the soldiers, then that meant they could surely see him. He moved along the foliage, quietly listening to the men talking. He could not make out the words, but they were not laughing and by their tone sounded as if they were angry. It seemed to him there were only two or three men by the campfire. He wondered what happened to the rest of the soldiers. When he was close enough, he realized they were there. The ground was covered with sleeping bodies. The men he heard were not too far from the horses. He looked around for Daniel, but he was nowhere to be seen. Sleeping men now covered the spot where he was shot. Romulo thought it would be best to keep his position for a few hours to see what would develop; maybe he would find an opportunity to make his move.

An hour later one of the men sitting by the campfire rose and walked toward the horses. Once away from the other men, he relieved himself. In the process he looked to his side and said, so the other men could hear, "This menso (dummy) made a big mistake. He deserved to die for killing the capitán. Now he will not have a decent burial as men do. Instead the bugs will eat him! And that doctor, we need to find him. When we do, he will be next to his friend!"

The soldier fixed his pants. As he turned, he asked the other soldier, "What was the doctor's name? Did you hear?"

"I am not sure. If the capitán were here, he would know," one of the other men said as he sat by the fire.

"Muchacho, el capitán is dead. We need to find out who killed him. We are going to be asked questions. If we do not have answers, there will be trouble. I am the capitán now; and if I do not have answers, it will not go well for me."

The other soldier said, "Look, this is what we can do. Let us make a name up if we do not find him. I think he said Romulo something. I could not hear."

The soldier sat back down by the fire. Romulo could no longer make out what they were saying. At least he knew where Daniel was. He started to make his way through the green undergrowth. He wanted to get to the other side where the horses were tied.

As he moved slowly through the foliage, a branch caught on his leg. He stopped, but it was too late. As it released from his leg, it swung around. The noise captured the attention of the soldiers. All three men rose, each looking in Romulo's direction. Romulo lay flat on his stomach and did not move a muscle. It was dark where he was. He knew if they came close, they would not be able to see him.

"Who is there?" one of the soldiers called out. He approached with his rifle pointed in front of him. "I said, who is there?"

The two other men stood nearby, wondering if it was noise they heard or their imagination. "Maybe it was a chango (monkey)," one of them said.

They went back and sat down but still felt nervous about the noise they heard.

Romulo slowed his pace. He did not want to rush and get himself killed. He knew he had all night to accomplish what he had to do; therefore, he stayed where he was and did not move for an hour.

Very slowly he made his way around the sleeping soldiers and the campfire. The men by the fire were a lot quieter. "Probably getting tired," Romulo thought. "Likely guarding the horses," he reasoned. He knew he was close to Daniel's position when he approached the horses. He moved on his hands and knees and at times inched his way on his stomach.

One of the horses turned his head and looked at Romulo as if he were wondering what he was doing. Romulo put his hand on its leg to keep him calm. He did not want a horse to give away his position.

As he moved closer to where his friend lay, he saw Daniel's boots. He hoped there was still some sign of life in him. He wanted the boot to move. He moved closer to him but could not see because of the darkness. Once he was next to him, he turned Daniel's head toward him. An ugly face stared at him, a head with a big, ugly mustache. The eyes seemed as if they were staring right at him with a blank stare. Romulo's heart jumped from fright. The dead man did not scare him. It was the surprise of seeing the dead soldier who Daniel shot instead of his friend.

Romulo looked around to see if Daniel was nearby. He lifted his head and saw Daniel's boots on the other side of the dead soldier. He had to make his way to him and get closer to the fire. Romulo felt he could do it without disturbing the men by the fire. He quietly rolled over the dead man, not worrying about getting blood on himself. He thought he felt it move. Once over, he turned and looked at its stillness and thought it must have been his imagination.

Just a few feet over, Daniel was lying on his stomach, face down. Romulo slid next to him. Once he was at his side, he reached and turned Daniel's face toward him. Daniel's head eased over; his eyes were closed. Daniel had an expression as if he were resting peacefully. He did not appear as the other dead man had. Romulo looked at Daniel's chest. It looked as if it had exploded with the bullet shots. He knew his friend had died with almost no pain.

As Romulo lay on the ground looking at his friend, his thoughts went back to a conversation he had with Daniel just a few weeks before. They were having a drink. Daniel said when it was his time to go, he only wished it would happen fast and with no pain. He felt he was a tough man, but he hated pain. He would rather die fast than to live longer and suffer. Romulo looked at his dear friend and knew he received his wish.

He put his hand on Daniel's cheek and patted it, showing his affection for the last time. He wanted to take Daniel with him but knew it would be out of the question. For one thing, there was Daniel's weight; it would take two or three men to carry him. He also knew he would never make it out alive trying to carry him alone. He had to leave and return for him later. Romulo hoped he would be able to return without getting himself killed.

Without speaking but feeling the words in his heart, Romulo told Daniel he would tell his family he had died a brave man, trying to save both of their lives. Romulo also told him he would be in his thoughts for the rest of his life. He said adios.

Romulo moved back in the direction he had approached. He was past the dead soldier and about to lift himself up when another soldier stood and turned his way. Romulo did not move. If he did, the soldier would be able to see him. This man wanted to relieve himself as the other soldier did earlier.

The man stopped 15 feet from where Romulo lay and about 30 feet from his friends. Romulo saw a large rock next to him the size of a coconut. He put his hand around it. Once he had a grip on the rock, he did not move. Romulo had big hands for a doctor. People did not know how at times he could perform procedures with such large hands. Now that he held the coconut-size rock in his hand and waited, he appreciated his large hands.

When the soldier was done relieving himself, he looked in Romulo's direction. His eyes stopped, not understanding what he saw. He looked over at Romulo and then at the other two dead men, wondering where the third dead man came from. As he stood there in deep thought, he tried to get his facts together. He did not say anything to his friends but took off his hat and scratched his head. In a matter of seconds, he was going to call out to the other soldiers. Romulo knew he had to act and act fast. He held the rock tight in his hand, knowing he only had one chance to hit his mark. He had to throw the rock as hard as he could.

Romulo stood up, reached back, brought his arm forward as hard as he could, and let the rock go. The soldier did not know what was happening. He froze with fright, thinking the dead man rose and was haunting him for not burying him quickly. Before he realized what was really happening, the rock was in the air and zipping toward him. Romulo saw the soldier's mouth open as the rock approached. When it hit, he heard a thump; the man fell back without making much of a sound.

Romulo thought it was too good to be true. He looked toward the campfire and was hoping the other men did not take note of what happened. As his eyes moved in the campfire's direction, he heard commotion and at the same time posed his body, ready to respond to the worst situation.

The other two men were on their feet, bringing their rifles up to shoot. Romulo was headed toward the horses, knowing the men would not shoot their rifles with the horses in the background. Shooting a horse was worse than murdering a man. Horses were badly needed.

Romulo continued running behind the horses. The soldiers were in pursuit, yelling and waking everybody.

"¡El doctor! Wake up! El doctor, do not let him get away!"

Romulo grabbed the last horse and ran with it, not mounting it just yet. He wanted the horse to move rapidly, so the soldiers would not have a target that was standing still.

Romulo was on the road moving quickly beside his horse. He heard a lot of yelling behind him but did not turn to see how far behind the soldiers were. He heard a shot from a rifle. As Romulo pulled himself up to mount the horse, he heard another shot ring out. The bullet buzzed over his head. This shot was a close call. Once he mounted the horse, he had a better chance of escaping.

Just as he gained his balance on top of the horse and thought he was off, he heard two more shots ring out. Another shot rang out. He felt a pain as if someone had slugged his thigh with a club. The shock of the pain was almost overwhelming. He realized he had to keep moving as fast as he could. If he did not, he would suffer much more pain than the one bullet caused.

Two more shots rang out. He heard bullets buzzing over his head and hoped none would hit their mark. Romulo needed to gain just a little more distance between himself and the soldiers, and then he would be around a bend in the road and be clear of the oncoming bullets.

Finally, Romulo knew he was in the clear. He continued moving at a fast speed, knowing the revolutionary soldiers would be right behind him. They needed to mount their horses, giving him time to gain more ground. He did not know how long he was going to be able to continue without looking at his leg.

As he was riding, he recalled the many times he had traveled this road. He knew it well. There was a clearing in the direction he was going. Once past the clearing, there was a small road that led to three little ranchos. In five minutes of hard riding, he approached the clearing. Following the clearing, he reached the small road. Romulo turned, stopped, and dismounted. With his horse in tow, he limped into the trees and kept moving into the jungle. He felt the pain in his leg. It was difficult to put pressure on it. If it had been another time, he would not stand on it. But he knew if he did not move fast, he would lose his life in just a few short seconds.

With the moonlight that was penetrating through the trees, Romulo sat on a rock and examined his wound. It was not as bad as he imagined. The bullet had not entered his leg but grazed it and took some flesh. The pain had subsided somewhat. He knew he needed to take care of it with ointments and clean bandages or an infection was going to set in. He would then be in really big trouble.

He waited for the soldiers to race by in pursuit. As he sat on the rock, he thought they should be stampeding by at anytime. He wondered if they were going to go straight or take the road to the ranchos.

Romulo planned out what he was going to do. If the soldiers were to go straight, he would go to the ranchos and stay. He would have one of the family members go to town to seek help for him. He knew most of the people in the area through his visits to the sick throughout the years. If the soldiers were to take the small road, he would be on his way home.

For ten minutes Romulo sat on the rock waiting, but the soldiers did not ride past him. Another downpour of rain started, accompanied by lightening flashes. Romulo picked a big piece of banana leaf and put it over his wound to keep out the water. As soon as the rain stopped, things dried out quickly because of the warm air. Romulo sat, trying to listen for noises on the road. He thought, "Maybe they are not coming. I must not be that important for them to follow me. Good!"

He wanted to lie down and rest but felt it would be best for him to start on his way back to San Bartolomé de los Llanos. If he rode at a steady pace, he would arrive in town in the late morning.

As he led his horse back out to the road, he was very careful and quiet, hoping there was no one waiting for him. If 20 men did not come after him, they could have sent just two or three men to kill him. He reasoned, "Why would they waste time with me? I am a doctor and am not fighting a war with them." He hoped the soldiers thought as he did.

On the journey home Romulo was in a lot of distress over the death of his friend Daniel. He was also in pain over his wound and hoped it would not develop an infection. At each small rancho he was tempted to stop to seek help but did not because he was anxious to return to town.

Eight miles outside of town, a small rancher met him with a wagon. He was headed in the opposite direction.

"Hola, Doctor," he called as soon as he saw it was Dr. Rodriguez.

"Señor Caballero! I am glad to see a friendly face," Romulo answered with a pleased expression.

"Doctor, what happened to you?" Señor Caballero asked, as he stopped his wagon and disembarked. He walked over to Romulo and looked at the ugly wound on his thigh. "Doctor, let me help you," he said as he reached for Romulo, helping him off the horse. He walked him to the back of the wagon. Romulo did not resist but let Señor Caballero help all he wanted. Romulo was worried he might not finish his ride to town; he was feeling very ill. In meeting Señor Caballero, he knew he was safe and would soon be home. As the wagon moved down the road, exhaustion overcame Romulo; he drifted into a deep sleep.

As he arrived in town, word spread quickly that Romulo was shot and had arrived at his office. He did not want to tell anyone about Daniel until he saw Monica. Romulo had to be sure he was the one to tell her the terrible news.

Dr. Contreras was called to attend to Romulo's wound. As the doctor was working on him, Luzita rushed in. "Ay, Romulo, what happened? What is this?" she asked, looking down at his gunshot wound.

"I was shot, Luzita; but it will be all right. It is only a flesh wound. It will heal fine."

"And Daniel? Did he go on to San Cristóbal de Las Casas?"

"Well, I...."

Monica burst into the room with one of her sons and one of her daughters following behind her. "Romulo! Where is my Daniel? Where is he?" she screamed with terror written all over her face.

Romulo asked the doctor to stop what he was doing. Sitting up, he reached out for Monica, wanting to embrace her. He wanted to comfort her when he told her what she already imagined was coming. As a wife and someone who had such deep love for her husband, she knew something had happened to Daniel when she heard Romulo returned alone. She moved close to Romulo, wanting to be held and cry when she was told. "Ay, Doctor," Monica blurted out, starting to weep, "¿Qué paso (What happened)?"

"Monica, Monica. I am so sorry," Romulo said, beginning to cry himself.

"Tell me, Doctor! No! No! Please do not tell me! Tell me he is coming! Please, Doctor, please!" she exclaimed, weeping even louder.

"Your husband died a brave man. I am so sorry," Romulo replied with tears running down his eyes.

Monica let out a wail and did not stop crying. Her son and daughter were behind her, holding their mother and crying along with everyone else in the room. Daniel was loved by all.

Daniel's sons and their friends went out and recovered his body. The next morning they had a burial for him.

The wedding was postponed for two months until the shock of Daniel's death had worn down. Romulo and Luzita felt it would not be a happy occasion if they were to hold the wedding at this time.

When the wedding was finally held, conditions were getting worse day-by-day. It was not a big fiesta, as they originally had wanted. Nevertheless, it turned out to be a happy occasion.

Romulo and Luzita lived in the house that Luzita's father had given them when they were married.

One day a few months after Romulo and Luzita's marriage, his mother Lydia asked Romulo to come to her bedroom. She wanted to speak to him about something very important.

"Yes, Mamá, you wanted to speak with me?" Romulo asked as he entered the bedroom, wondering what she wanted to discuss.

Lydia was lying on her bed. She had been feeling very tired during the last few weeks. "Sí, Hijo, I want to speak to you. I am getting grande (aged) now. I have been wanting to turn something over to you for some time now, before it is too late and I die."

"Ay, Mamá, don't speak like that. You are still in good health!" he said, knowing his mother was looking older and more frail during the last few weeks. "What is it you want to talk about, Mamá?" Romulo knew it could not be about money because this matter was taken care of when his father died.

"See that box on top of my dresser? Please bring it over to me, Romulo."

Romulo stepped over to the dresser and picked up the beautifully carved Monkey Box. He remembered always wanting the box. The beautifully carved monkeys had fascinated him when he was a young boy. But it was always off limits to him. In time, he did not even see it anymore; it became part of the dresser in his eyes. The Monkey Box appeared as beautiful as it did the day Romulo's father made it; fine wood was used to construct it. Romulo never knew or questioned what was in it.

He handed it to his mother as she sat up on her bed. "Sit down, Hijo," she said as she opened the locking device that helped keep it airtight.

Romulo sat on the bed next to his mother. "What is it, Mamá? I always wondered what was in the Monkey Box and always had the urge to ask," he said a little untruthfully, realizing he had forgotten about it all those years.

"And why didn't you, Romulo?" Lydia asked. She stopped opening the box and looked at her son, sitting in wonderment as if he were still a small boy.

"Well, Mamá, I always thought you had something in there you did not want me to see. If you had wanted me to know, you would have told me. I remember on more than one occasion when I was young, I started to get the Monkey Box. You always stopped me in my tracks and scolded me. So I never went into it again or asked about it," he explained as he stared at the Monkey Box. He realized that after all these years this was going to be the day he would see and know what was in it.

She smiled, lifted the top of the Monkey Box, and looked inside. "Papers, Romulo. Papers. That is what it is. They are going to be your papers to hand down to your children."

Romulo did not understand what she was talking about but waited for his mother to continue what she was saying. "Romulo, as your father and I told you, our familia is a special familia. Our blood is special blood. Our familia comes from a line of royalty," Lydia said as she looked deep into her son's eyes.

This was not new to Romulo; he had heard the story many times. He looked at her and wondered where she was leading. "Yes, Mamá, I know that."

Lydia started to take the papers out of the box. She handed them to Romulo and said, "These papers show our familia line. These prove who we are and where we come from." Lydia pulled out another very old document and handed it to him.

Romulo took the paper. His eyes scanned the writing on it. "This is very old, Mamá. Very old."

"Yes, hundreds of years old. That is why this Monkey Box was so special and why you were never allowed to go near it. It should not be opened often. The documents will not last if they are exposed to the air. However, this is a special occasion because I am turning them over to you, to show you who you are and where you came from."

Lydia handed the entire box to Romulo. He took it and placed it next to him, examining all its contents, never realizing such papers existed. He sat there and appreciated what he was holding and knew his future children would also.

Romulo went to the kitchen where Luzita was working. She was going to start supper. He showed his wife what he had. She glanced at the Monkey Box with the documents but did not really understand the importance of what she was seeing. She thought it was no big deal. "Ay, mi amor, we are all people and are made of the same material. It does not matter where you came from. God made everybody the same with the same blood."

"No, Luzita. We, my familia, have blue blood. We are a special people! Remember that! These papers prove who we are and our lineage. Look, Luzita," Romulo said enthusiastically as he raised his arm in an effort to show her. He pointed with his other hand at the vein in his arm. "In this vein I have blue blood! And my children will carry the same blue blood to their families," he explained, looking at his wife.

Luzita looked at him. As she moved things around to cut up a chicken, she said, "Ay, Romulo, I think you are loco if that is what you think. There is no such thing as some people having different blood than others. You are a doctor and should know that. As I said, God did not make some people better than others."

"What about us and the Indians, Luzita? Can you not see we are more intelligent than they are?" Romulo asked, trying to reason with her.

Luzita did not like this reasoning because her family had a lot of Indian blood. "Romulo, I do not want to talk about it. If we do, I am going to get angry with you. Then you will leave to who knows where for a day or two to visit a sick person!" she vented, upset and moving her cookware roughly.

"Ay, ay, ay, Luzita, do not get upset just because I have blue blood and you do not. One good thing to remember is that you are now my wife. You will have children with blue blood, and you will have a part in it."

Luzita did not like this comment at all and was ready to throw one of her clay pots at him. Romulo had never seen this angry expression in her eyes and thought perhaps it would be a good time to drop the subject and continue it another day. Romulo stood up and walked out.

CHAPTER FOURTEEN

THE MAÍZ

In just a few months, Lydia's health worsened. Romulo was at her side most of the time and did what he could for her. He realized his mother was an elderly woman and had lived a happy and full life.

One day Romulo was in his office when a boy burst in and said, "Doctor, you should go home at once!"

"What is it, muchacho? What has happened?"

"It is your mother. I think you need to go and find out for yourself, Doctor."

Not saying anymore, he knew what this meant. When he left his mother in the morning, he sat with her and kissed her. She was so weak that she did not respond. His sisters were with her all the time during the last few weeks, taking care of all her needs. Romulo recalled how he had left her, sleeping and very frail. He recalled when he was just a boy, how beautiful and vibrant his mother was, always doing things and keeping busy.

Romulo left his office immediately. He hurried down the street and turned the corner to return home. He looked in the direction of Señor Díaz's house and saw a crowd of people at his front door. One of the men turned and saw Romulo walking toward them and said, "Here comes the doctor. Make room for him, everybody.

As Romulo approached the people, one of the older women who was crying grabbed Romulo's arm and said, "I am so sorry, Doctor! Your mother and father were so good to us. They loved all the people, no matter who they were."

Romulo knew from these few words that his mother had died. He entered his home and saw two of his sisters sitting in the parlor consoling each other, crying. "Hermanas, ¿qué pasa? (Sisters, what happened?)" Romulo asked.

"Romulo, Mamá has gone with Papí. She did not wake up this morning." Saying this, she released a wail.

Romulo held them; they cried together. Then he turned to the room where his mother lie, the same room his parents had slept in ever since he could remember, the same room in which his father had died. As he stepped into the bedroom, he saw his other sisters around Lydia, weeping over her. They turned, saw him, and made room for him to sit next to his mother. Romulo took Lydia's hand and held it tight. He thought of how much they and his father loved her. His mind went back to his father's stories about their courtship. Lydia and Chico's love story would live on; Romulo just knew it. Her story and her big, blue eyes would be passed on to generation after generation. Beautiful Lydia Fuentes Rodriguez was dead.

Arrangements were made for Lydia's burial. Many people attended the ceremony. Lydia and Chico had established a reputation of caring very much for others.

In the following months the revolution became worse. Soldiers from both sides would pass through town and confiscate supplies. Sometimes they would bring in wounded men for Romulo to treat.

Because Romulo's time was occupied to a great extent by his work in caring for the people of the town, he did not have time to attend to the work of overseeing Rancho U-Chem. Consequently, those duties fell to his wife Luzita.

Luzita was a woman who took charge and did not let anything get by her. Since she had always helped her father with his small rancho, she knew where all the money went and how much she needed to cover her expenses.

During their first year of marriage, Luzita bore her first daughter, Marina. The following year she bore Jorge. Soon she was embarasada (pregnant) with Pancho.

One day the foreman Antonio was out in the fields with a crew of campesinos (country peasants) watering the maíz (corn).

"Pablo, go and stop the drainage on the other side," Antonio yelled and pointed west. While pointing, he saw many riders traveling his way, leaving a trail of dust behind them. He wondered who they were and hoped they were not going to give them any trouble. He had seen soldiers ride through the rancho many times in the past, but they never stopped and talked to him.

"These men are riding straight for us," he whispered to himself. "Hey," Antonio called to his campesinos (labors), not wanting any of them to be hurt by the approaching men. "Come over here. Get behind me when these men approach."

All the campesinos looked to see what Antonio was talking about. When they saw the soldiers, they dropped what they were doing and ran to where he was standing. They did not want any trouble. They were campesinos, not fighters.

As the men on horseback neared, Antonio saw they were from the revolutionary side. The federal army always wore uniforms, and the soldiers of the revolution wore whatever they had but always wore their bullet belts around their chests.

They came to a stop. The big man riding in the lead asked, "Señores, who is in charge here?"

"I am, señor," Antonio answered. "We do not want any trouble. We are working the field; that is all. We do not have any arms."

Some of the men behind him raised their hands and opened them to show they did not have any weapons.

"I know you are not fighters. We did not come here to fight with you. We just want to talk to you. That is all. We represent the people. We are fighting this war for your rights, campesinos. Do you understand that, muchachos?" he asked as he dismounted.

"Yes, señor. We know there is a big war going on, and we know many people are being killed for no reason. That is why we do not want any problems."

The big man approached Antonio and asked, "What is your name, señor?"

"Antonio, señor."

"Good. I am Capitán Alfonso. I represent the revolution. Who told you we are fighting for nothing, and people are being killed for nothing?"

"That is just what I have heard. That is what is being said by some."

"Señor Antonio, I will tell you right now. This is not true. We are fighting for a very good reason."

"I see, Capitán," Antonio answered, wishing to hear about the war but thinking this was not a good time to know. "What is it I can do for you?" Antonio asked, hoping the man would not be too difficult to satisfy.

"Well, first you can answer my questions. I first wish to know who are the owners of this land and the maíz?"

"This is Rancho U-Chem, Capitán. The owners are Dr. Rodriguez and his wife Luzita."

The captain thought for a moment and wondered where he had heard the name. "Dr. Rodriguez? Huh. Where is the doctor's hacienda?"

"Capitán, he does not live in a hacienda. He is the town doctor of San Bartolomé de los Llanos, and he is a very good man. He does not come out here. It is his wife, Doña Luzita Rodriguez, who does all the business here at the rancho," he said, knowing the captain was not asking for a reason.

"I see. Well, I want you to deliver a message to the doctor, not his wife. I do not deal with women. Understand, Antonio?"

"Sí, Capitán, whatever you wish," he replied, not wanting to offend the captain in any way.

"I want you to tell the doctor the people of the revolution are asking for the crop, the maíz. We are not going to sell it, but we will use it for our soldiers. Our army needs his help. If he complies, he will be remembered once the war is over. Do you understand, Antonio, what I want you to tell him?" he asked. He waited for Antonio to reply.

"Sí, Capitán. I think I understand."

"Tell me what you're going to tell the doctor, Antonio."

"Not to harvest the maíz because you are going to come for it," he answered in a frightened tone.

"No, no, no, Antonio! I did not say that. I do want the doctor to harvest the maíz. But once it is done, we will come for it. Do you understand now? I want you to get it right. I do not want you to be the one responsible for any misunderstandings, Antonio."

"Yes, Capitán. I do understand. You want me to tell the doctor to harvest the crop, and you will return for it."

"Yes, that is right. Now make sure you tell the doctor exactly what I am telling you. His life is at stake. Do you understand?"

"Sí, Capitán."

"Good. My next question is where are the cattle located on the rancho?"

Antonio did not want to tell the captain. He wanted to tell the captain a lie; but if he lied to him, he might return and take his life. The cattle were not his, and he was not going to give his life for them. "They are to the east side of the rancho, about 10 kilometers from here. There is good grazing grass there, Capitán."

"Good, Antonio. Now for my final question. How long until the maíz is harvested?" he asked. He liked the way Antonio was responding to all of his questions.

"Capitán, the way it looks today, in two weeks, give or take a day."

"Good! We will return in three weeks for the maíz. Tell the doctor we will not take all of it. We will leave him enough to take care of you campesinos. We are on your side, Antonio, and all of your men," he said as he looked over at the men standing behind Antonio. He continued, "We are fighting for your rights as I told you. Remember that!" He turned and mounted his horse.

Before leaving, he raised his hand to all the campesinos and told them he wished them well. He repeated that he and his men were fighting for them and added, "Soon this land will be yours. When the war is over, we will divide it up for all the campesinos. You will not have to work for others. We are fighting so the rich will not control everything, and you the people will prosper as the rich have done for so many years!"

All the campesinos stood astounded at what he said. They stared at the captain, not really understanding what he meant. They were always preoccupied with their work; they never grasped the reason for all the fighting. For them to own their own land was beyond them. They were in a state of shock at hearing the explanation of the war. Some even turned their heads and looked at their fellow workers, wondering if they understood what was being said.

"Adios, muchachos!" the captain shouted as he pulled the reigns of the horse and rode away with his men following. All the campesinos waved, still thinking of what they were told.

Antonio wanted to leave right then and inform the doctor about what had taken place. He reasoned he would wait until the end of the day to ride into town and inform him.

Romulo was still at his office late into the evening. Luzita was home getting ready to start supper when Antonio knocked on the door. Luzita's servant answered the door. "Antonio, what are you doing here? Did something happen?" the servant asked. She rarely saw him in town because there was so much to be done on the rancho.

"Is the doctor in, Arlette? I need to speak to him. It is urgent!" he said anxiously. Arlette was a live-in maid who worked for the Rodriguezes since they married; she was very well liked by all the family. She came from a very poor family who lived on the outskirts of town.

From the parlor Luzita heard Antonio and stepped to the door. "Antonio! What are you doing here? Is there a problem?"

"Sí, Doña Rodriguez. I have a message for the doctor from the capitán of the people's army."

"Regarding?" she asked, wanting Antonio to tell her what it concerned.

"It is about the maíz and the harvest, Doña Rodriguez," he answered, not wanting Luzita to force him to tell her. He remembered the captain's expression and knew the man meant business.

"Ay, Antonio, you know I am in charge of the rancho. You can tell me if it concerns the rancho and the maíz."

"Doña Rodriguez, the capitán meant business; and he informed me not to tell you. He said he does not deal with women. So he instructed me to make sure to tell the doctor. And I wish to do that," he explained as he nervously played with his hat.

"Come in, Antonio, so we can talk," she said as he stepped in and took a seat in the parlor. He hoped she was going to call the doctor for the important news. Instead Luzita sat down next to him and waited for Antonio to become comfortable. "All right, Antonio, tell me what the capitán said. I am listening."

Luzita wondered what the news was. She did not want the soldiers to tell her how to run the rancho's business. It had been a lot of work for her to get things going at Rancho U-Chem during these last two years. With the harvest it seemed this was the year that would make up for the past few years when U-Chem did not do as well.

"Well, Doña Rodriguez, I will tell you. But please tell the doctor. The capitán said it meant his life. He said he wanted the doctor to harvest the crop, but he is going to return in three weeks for the maíz. He said he is not going to take all the maíz but is going to leave some for the campesinos."

"He what? He thinks we are going to pick the maíz for him? Is he loco? Did he seem loco to you, Antonio?"

Antonio did not know how to respond. He liked the captain. He thought and felt that he was considerate with him and the other campesinos. The captain even told them the land was going to be theirs; they would not have to work for others; and they would be able to plant their own crops.

"No, Doña Rodriguez. To me it seemed as if the capitán meant business. I think we should do as he says, Doña Rodriguez."

"No, no, no, Antonio. We have worked too hard for this. We are not going to just give it all away."

"But, Doña Rodriguez, I think the doctor should be the one to make that decision since it is his life we are talking about," Antonio said, trying very hard to sound respectful.

"I will tell my husband, Antonio. After I speak to him, I will ride out to the rancho. We will do what we need to do. Now, you return to the rancho; and I will see you in a couple of days," she said as she stood up.

"Doña Rodriguez, if the doctor is at his office, I would like to stop to see him on my way out."

"No, Antonio. I told you I will speak to him!" Luzita insisted, not wanting him to tell the doctor anything. She knew her husband and knew he would probably do as the soldiers told him to do. He did not care much about what happened to U-Chem. Now that she was married to Romulo, Luzita felt it was her duty to help him all she could. It was important to keep the rancho going to benefit the family and the community.

"All right, Doña Rodriguez. But I am not accountable for anything that takes place," he said, hoping he would not be held responsible for the results.

Antonio left as he was told and returned to the rancho. He knew if things did not work out the way the captain asked, he was not going to be around when he returned. Antonio did not want to be an enemy of the people's army. From all the reports, the revolutionary army was winning the war.

That evening Romulo came home late. He was tired and looked forward to a good night's sleep. He loved his work even though it took all of his time and was very exhausting.

"Romulo, how are you, mi amor (my love)," Luzita asked as she put both her arms around his neck and kissed him. She wished she could have more of his time but understood what she was facing when she married him.

"I am fine, Luzita. How are you?" he asked as he made his way to the parlor and sat down to give his beautiful wife some of his attention before retiring for the night.

"I had a busy day, mi armor. Tomorrow I would like you to come home, and I will have lunch with you. We can spend a little time together if that is all right."

"Ay, Luzita, I am sorry. I have to ride out to Señor Rios' rancho. Señora Rios is very ill, and I told them I would be out to see them first thing in the morning. On the way back I will stop and see the López familia."

"I see. Well, maybe the following day, Romulo."

"That should be fine, Luzita. I am sorry."

"I know." Luzita thought back to when she decided to marry the doctor; she knew how busy he was. "Romulo, Antonio came to town today to speak to you about the rancho."

"Ay, Luzita! I do not have time for U-Chem. I thought you were going to take care of everything out there."

"I am, but a capitán of the revolutionary army went out and told Antonio they wanted the maíz this year."

"They want the maíz? How much are they willing to pay for it?"

"I do not think they want to pay for it. I think they just want it. They want us to harvest it, and they want to take it."

"They want to take it? That does not sound right. Mi armor, you take care of it. I trust you can take care of any business the army may have."

"Yes I can. But Antonio said the capitán wanted you to know; the capitán said it meant your life."

"My life? What does that mean? They are going to come into the pueblo and kill me for the maíz? No, that does not sound right either. You take care of it, my Luzita. I have all the confidence in you," Romulo said as he stood. He turned and motioned to Luzita to follow him into their bedroom. He loved and trusted his wife very much and knew she would be able to handle anything that had to do with U-Chem. The family business of U-Chem did not interest him, and he really did not want anything to do with it.

Two days later Luzita went out to Rancho U-Chem to see what needed to be done with the soldiers. Upon arriving, she found all the campesinos in the fields getting ready for the harvest. She went to look for Antonio.

"Doña Luzita, it is good to see you. Did you come alone?" Antonio asked.

"No, I brought Arlette with me. I left her at the campo (camp). I came to see what needs to be done to protect our maíz."

"What do you mean, 'protect our maíz,' Doña Rodriguez? Did you not tell the doctor what the capitán said?" Antonio asked, staring at Luzita and wondering if she understood the seriousness of the situation.

"Yes, I did talk to him. My husband instructed me to oversee the rancho and do what I think is best. That is why I came out. Antonio, we cannot surrender the maíz just like that," she said, snapping her fingers. "We need that money to pay for next year's expenses. If we give it all away, we will have to let all of you campesinos go. We do not want to do that."

"But, Doña Rodriguez, with all due respect, these men mean business; and the doctor's life is at stake."

"No, Antonio, I do not think so. I think the doctor will be fine. What do you think they are going to do? Go into the pueblo and kill a doctor? The doctor who the people depend on? Why would they want to do such a thing? And besides, what about General Díaz? What do you think he will say about it? As you know, the general has always been good friends with Romulo."

General Victor Díaz and Romulo were good friends when they were younger. However, when Romulo took Carmelita as his girlfriend, Victor did not like it. He had always loved Carmelita; he ended up marrying her. Victor never really liked Romulo's taking her as his girlfriend; he stopped associating with Romulo for the sake of his wife Carmelita.

"Doña Rodriguez, if you had seen these men, you would be thinking differently."

"Look, Antonio, this is what I want to do. I want to dig a storage shed underground and hide the maíz until this crises passes. When they return and find nothing, they will leave. Everything will be fine. Then we can find a buyer for it."

"A storage shed underground? You want us to dig a storage shed, Doña Rodriguez?" Antonio asked, not believing her. He felt Señora Rodriguez was bold and did not care much for her husband's life.

"Yes, and I would like you to get started on it right away, Antonio."

Antonio thought for a minute. He looked at Luzita and said, "Doña

Rodriguez, if you are going to do this, once it is completed, I will have to leave the rancho. If the capitán returns, as he said he will, he will ask me about the maíz. I will have to tell him the truth. I am being honest with you, Doña Rodriguez. I will not put my life or any of the campesinos' lives in danger for the maíz."

Luzita stared at Antonio and appreciated his honesty. "That is fine, Antonio. Once the work is done and the maíz is harvested, I will pay what I owe you. You can go to town or leave the area, whatever you wish."

"Thank you, Doña Rodriguez. We will start on the work right away. Where would you like us to dig?"

"About a kilometer from the campo, next to the large mango trees. We can cover it with.... Well, I will show you. Let us ride to the campo and see what we will have to do," Luzita said, feeling confident. She really believed that if the soldiers returned and found no maíz they would leave and not bother them any more.

Luzita showed Antonio what she wanted and where she wanted the storage cellar dug. She wanted it to be of adequate size to store all the maíz.

Luzita told Antonio she would return before the harvest and make sure everything went well. On her return she would stay through the harvest.

Antonio was not to tell the other campesinos of her plan. As soon as the work was done and the maíz was safely stored, she would dismiss the campesinos and have them leave the rancho.

Once all was taken care of, Luzita returned to San Bartolomé de los Llanos. As she and Arlette were nearing the town, they saw many riders approaching. She stopped her wagon, worried it might be the soldiers to whom Antonio had spoken. As they approached, they did not stop but continued on, leaving a cloud of dust.

That evening Luzita told Romulo what had taken place at the rancho. As far as the maíz was concerned, Romulo questioned whether or not Luzita had made the right decision.

"Luzita, do you think it is wise to deceive the army? I mean, why not move the maíz out of the area before the army returns? If they find out you are hiding it just so they do not get their hands on it, it will not go well for you. I believe it would be best to take the maíz, put it on the wagons, and move it to another location as if it were harvested and sold," Romulo stated seriously.

"Romulo, you told me to take care of it; and that is what I am doing. This is the best and easiest way to do it. It will be all right. I will take care of it. Once all this passes, I will find a buyer for it."

"Yes, I know you will. However, I am just thinking, what are the soldiers going to do if they find out you hid the maíz? They might be so angry they will want your life," Romulo declared, worried about what could happen to her.

Luzita thought for a moment, recalling her conversation with Antonio. "Romulo is responsible," she thought. She then dismissed it from her mind.

"Romulo, it will be all right," Luzita insisted, not knowing anything about Romulo's past relationship with Carmelita and knowing he had so many girlfriends during that time. "We can even invite Señor Díaz and his wife for supper one evening next week..."

Romulo interrupted, "Luzita, what is wrong with you, mujer? Do you know what could happen to us if the governor found out we are entertaining Díaz? He will no longer be our friend. In fact, he will be our enemy!" Romulo exclaimed, raising his voice.

"Who cares, Romulo? What has the governor done for us? In the last few years, he has not done anything. All we are doing is sending money to him and receiving nothing in return. I think soon it will be this army who will be controlling the whole area. In fact, I think they will be the new government," Luzita stated, also with a strong voice.

"Ay, mi armor, I do not know. I think you are right. We are getting all these different reports about the war. Even the people who were once neutral are now on the side of the revolution. The people are developing a strong hatred for the government. We must remain neutral in all of this. I am a doctor; and my work is saving lives, not contributing to taking them."

"But, Romulo..." Luzita answered, still wanting to persuade him.

Romulo interrupted again. "No, Luzita! That is it! That is what I want to do. I do not want to discuss having them join us for supper any more. I will get angry with you, and I do not want to do that. Perhaps we can talk about it another time but not now." Romulo stood and walked to his room to prepare for supper.

One week later Luzita informed Romulo she was going to U-Chem for the harvest. She would return in a few days. She would also take

Arlette with her. This was fine with Romulo. He was used to Luzita visiting the rancho a few times during the year during the planting and harvesting season. Romulo did not mind it at all. This gave him time to himself. He would be able to overindulge in his drinking and to see his women friends without Luzita's knowing.

Chapter Fifteen

Treason

"Antonio, how are things going here?" Luzita inquired as she and Arlette rode into the campo. Antonio saw her and went to the road to meet them.

"I think everything is the way you want it, Doña Rodriguez," he answered as he held one of the horses, bringing it to a complete stop. "The underground storage shed was going to be difficult to dig. However, I remembered some old Mayan ruins not far from here. These ruins have underground compartments made of stone. They are ideal for storing the maíz. It will also be difficult for the soldiers to locate them."

"How far are these ruins?"

"I would say about one kilometer from here, Doña Rodriguez. In that direction," Antonio replied as he turned and pointed in the direction where she wanted the shed to be dug.

Antonio continued, "What is more, we do not have the time to dig the sheds because the maíz is ready to be harvested. I overestimated the time, and the maíz will be ready early. It is better this way, Doña Rodriguez. It is good because it will give us more time before the soldiers return."

"Very well, Antonio. As long as the ruins will work, it will be fine. I would like to see these old Mayan ruins right away," Luzita insisted, worried the ruins would not be sufficient. Luzita was tired from the ride to the rancho; nevertheless, she had to see it right away. She had dreamed they would not have enough room for the maíz.

"Sí, Doña Rodriguez. Let us go." Antonio walked alongside the wagon to the site.

As they arrived at the Mayan ruins, Antonio stopped the wagon by holding the horse again. Luzita discmbarked. Arlette stayed behind at the campo. She had no interest in seeing where they were going to hide the crop.

Luzita looked around. She saw large square stones, as large as her wagon. They were spread out in the vicinity where she stood. It looked as if it had been some sort of structure that had tumbled down and fallen in all directions. The stones had green foliage growing all around them and on top.

Antonio had built a nice, easy access ramp to step down into a cellar-type room.

As Luzita stepped down the ramp, she was amazed at the stone structure. Each stone seemed to be cut exactly to fit the next. As she entered, she felt the coolness of the stone floor. She could not see the end of the room-like cellar. It was dark.

"How far back does it go, Antonio?" Luzita asked, admiring what seemed to be a natural hiding place for the maíz.

"It goes back a few feet from where you can see."

"Antonio, do you think this will be large enough?" she questioned doubtfully, even though she thought the ruins were beautiful.

"Doña Rodriguez, I do not know. I think it should be big enough. If it is not large enough, there are many more like this all over the area. They are just hard to see from up there. They must have been some kind of storage facility for the Indians."

"More of them?" she answered, amazed that all of this was on her land. "How many more?"

"I am not sure, Doña Rodriguez, but many."

"I see," Luzita acknowledged. All of her life she had only heard stories of the ruins; however, she had never visited one nor knew where they were.

"I know when the soldiers come, they will never be able to find this," Antonio expressed, feeling relieved as he watched Doña Rodriguez. She seemed pleased with what she was seeing. Antonio worried that Doña Rodriguez would be unhappy they had not dug the storage shed as she had instructed.

Luzita thought a second as she peered into the cellar. She knew if the crop was going to be as plentiful as Antonio had indicated, there would not be enough room for all of it. Luzita said, "Well, when this is full, we will then use another cellar."

"Yes, we can do that. That will be no problem, Doña Rodriguez," Antonio agreed.

The following morning the work started on the harvest a week earlier than Antonio had indicated. He felt he could have left the maíz out in the field for two more days; however, because of the situation it was best to get it all inside. Antonio wanted to make sure everything was ready for the return visit of the soldiers.

Two days into the harvest, the Mayan storage cellar was almost full; and they still had half of the crop to pick. This was more than they had picked in the last two years combined. Antonio was right in anticipating it was going to be a good year. Luzita felt that if the market price was high they were going to earn a good profit. She knew from talking to different persons that it would be a high-priced market because of the war and the scarcity of food.

Two-thirds into the harvest, Antonio and Luzita sat at the rancho under a patio shaded by palm branches. They discussed their progress. Antonio informed her the first cellar was almost full. He was going to start putting the maíz into one of the others. Antonio felt he should next fill the Mayan cellar farthest from the one they had just used. In this way if the soldiers found one storage cellar, it would be difficult to find the other. "They will think they found all of it," Antonio expressed.

Antonio and Luzita both became silent, thinking they heard yelling from a distance. They both stood when it became apparent there was someone yelling and running in their direction.

"¡Don Antonio! ¡Don Antonio!" Carlos screamed.

As Carlos reached the porch where Luzita and Antonio were waiting for him, Antonio asked, "What is it, hombre (man)? What is wrong with you, Carlos?"

Carlos was out of breath and could not find words. They just would not come out.

"Take your time, Carlos. We are not going anywhere," Antonio stated.

"Don Antonio, the..." he said, taking a deep breath. "Don Antonio..."

"Carlos, calm down. Catch your breath and settle down, señor! I will wait until you are ready to tell me what you have to say," Antonio said, reaching down and putting his hand on Carlos' shoulder.

Luzita was standing next to Antonio, anticipating whatever Carlos had to say. She did not say anything; she knew that whatever Carlos had to say it was going to be important. She hoped no one was hurt in the field or, for that matter, killed.

"Don Antonio, the soldiers came back!" he declared, catching his breath.

"They came back?" Antonio repeated with a frightened expression. "Where are they, Carlos? Are they coming here?" Antonio felt his heart start to race. He did not know if he should hide or run.

"No, they left; but they wanted me to give you a message. It was the same Capitán Alfonso who came the last time."

Antonio looked anxiously past Carlos, making sure the soldiers were not following him. As his eyes watched the road, he asked, "What did they say about me, Carlos? Were they upset with me?" Antonio did not believe they could be angry with him, yet he was worried they might have found out about the plan for hiding the maíz. However, he thought, "How could they have found out?"

Luzita saw how frightened Antonio was and tried to comfort him. She said, "Antonio, it will be all right. They cannot do anything. I am the owner here, not them!"

Carlos stood there, not saying anything as Luzita expressed herself.

Antonio did not hear Luzita. He wanted to know what they told Carlos and wanted to know if his life was in danger. "What did they say, hombre? Tell me!"

By now Carlos was in control of himself and had caught his breath. "The capitán said to tell you he knows you got the message to the owners of the maíz. He wants you to know you are not responsible for anything; the owners are. He also said to remind you he would return in three days and pick up whatever we have harvested. He will be looking forward to seeing you then. He also wants you to tell the owners he means business. If the doctor wants his life, he needs to cooperate. To him it does not matter; he will get all the maíz if the doctor lives or dies," Carlos stated. He stopped talking to observe Antonio's expression.

Antonio did not know what to say. He remembered that the captain was really nice to him. He had told Antonio he was fighting for his rights to own the land. At the time he worked for the Rodriguezes, Antonio felt he had to be loyal to them. However, once the maíz was taken care of and he did not work for the Rodriguezes any longer, he might even join the revolution. Antonio looked at Luzita and said, "Doña Rodriguez, this is a dangerous situation. I advise you to give the maíz to the capitán. It is not worth your life or the doctor's life. Please, give it some consideration. Please, Doña Rodriguez!"

Luzita did not know what to say. She looked at Antonio and thought that perhaps he was correct. Then again, it was a lot of work and money to give up. She thought maybe it would be all right because no one would be left at the rancho when Captain Alfonso returned.

"Antonio, I do not think he will want to take our lives for the maíz. Also, remember what Carlos said. You are not responsible. We are! So we will proceed with our plan. Everything will be all right. Trust me," Luzita declared as she put her hand on Antonio's back, patting it.

Antonio did not agree with Doña Rodriguez. She should know the danger in which she was putting herself and her husband. However, he knew he was just a campesino and did not know how to handle business matters. He recalled how the rancho, at times, had big problems. Although certain things should have been done, the owners felt differently. Their decision always worked out for the best. Therefore, he reasoned Doña Rodriguez must know what she was doing.

He looked at Luzita and nodded his head in agreement. "Doña Rodriguez, I should go back out with the campesinos. They need all the help they can get if we are to finish on time," Antonio explained as he waited for her approval.

"Yes, Antonio, go. They do need you out in the field."

The following evening Antonio rode to the rancho looking for Luzita. "Oye (Hey), have you seen Doña Rodriguez?" he asked a woman.

"Yes, she went to the Mayan ruins."

Luzita was making sure the Mayan cellar was covered properly; if anyone rode by, they would not notice it. She wanted to be certain that when the soldiers arrived they would not find anything, not even a trace of the maíz.

"Doña Rodriguez, where are you?" Antonio called out.

"¡Aquí (here), Antonio! What is it?" Luzita hollered as she pulled a large branch from the foliage in the surrounding area. She had the cellar well covered at this point; it would be difficult for anyone to find it.

"Doña Rodriguez, we are done. The last wagon is on its way to the other cellar."

"I see, Antonio," Luzita said as she stopped and dropped the branch. She wiped her forehead and continued, "How does the other cellar look? How much do we have stored there?"

"Doña Rodriguez, it is almost full. In fact, the campesinos said they do not know if they are going to be able to fit the last two wagons in it. I told them to use the next cellar that is closest to that one."

"All right, Antonio. I want to settle all I owe you and the campesinos. Tell them they need to vacate the premises for one month. They are not to return any earlier. I do not want any of them here when the soldiers return."

"Ay, Doña Rodriguez. They are good men; and I do not think they will say anything, even if the soldiers return. Some have nowhere to go. What will they do?"

"Tell them they can take extra maíz with them. I will give them ten sacks each. They can sell it. That should carry them for a while," Luzita said, knowing that taking care of the campesinos was not a big sacrifice. She felt they earned it. "They can even trade some of their maíz for frijoles," she thought.

"See, Antonio, what I mean? What will they do if we give all of our maíz to the soldiers? Where will they go if there is no money or food here? Where will they go? Where will they work if there is no work here?"

"Si, Doña Rodriguez," Antonio answered out of respect while thinking the Rodriguezes still had a fortune from the doctor's mother.

"That should do it, Doña Rodriguez. Once we are completely done, I will inform the campesinos what we have planned," Antonio said as he turned and mounted his horse.

Everything seemed to go well as far as Luzita was concerned. The campesinos understood the situation and left the rancho. Luzita ended up feeling sorry for some of them, so she let them relocate to the other side of the rancho. When the soldiers returned, they would not have to talk to them. Luzita knew if it meant their lives they would tell everything.

Two days after arriving home, Luzita was preparing to leave to purchase food for their evening meal. Romulo was in his office attending to the usual line of people who stood outside waiting. They held their chickens, small sacks of frijoles, and queso (cheese) to pay the doctor. It was the only way they could compensate him.

All of a sudden from down the street, 15 men on horseback rode towards the doctor's office. The patients were surprised at the speed the horsemen were traveling. They watched with anticipation to see where they were going. As the riders approached the doctor's office, they came to a sudden stop. The soldiers dismounted and scanned the line of peasants, making sure things were safe. They wore ammunition belts across and around their chests and had big sombreros. Almost all wore big mustaches that reached from one side of their faces to the other.

From inside one of the rooms, Romulo heard the many horses. He wondered what was taking place outside and thought it was possibly the federales who came into town with their wounded. He did not like it when this happened because they made all the people leave while they took all of his time. They never paid for his services; however, they told him once the war was over they would make sure he received a commendation for his services during the war. Romulo never replied to the offer because he did not want any commendation from either side.

Romulo heard commotion coming from the front door of the building. People were yelling, demanding to know where the doctor was. "Excuse me, señorita, I will be right back. Let me see what is going on. Sit here and make yourself comfortable," Romulo said, not really knowing if he would return. He was anticipating the federales.

Just as he was going to open the door, it burst open. A large man stood at the entrance of the room and pointed his rifle at Romulo. The soldier stepped into the room with another soldier right behind him and asked, "Dr. Romulo Rodriguez?"

"Who are you, and what do you think you are doing?" Romulo questioned with a loud voice. He did not like these men barging into his office, demanding his services and taking over.

"Are you Dr. Rodriguez?" the big man asked again.

Romulo looked at him and was reminded of his friend Daniel. He knew if these were the same men who took Daniel's life, he had better be careful how he handled the situation. "Yes, I am Dr. Rodriguez."

"Dr. Rodriguez, you are under arrest! Come with us!" the big soldier demanded. He moved his rifle back and forth, indicating for Romulo to proceed out of the room. They would follow.

"What is this about? Who are you? Who do you think you are arresting me?" These men were not wearing uniforms. Romulo could not believe he was being arrested by men who did not represent the federal authorities or the local authority.

"We are here under the orders of Capitán Alfonso of the revolution army. Now come with us!" he demanded once again. He continued to move his rifle back and forth, directing the doctor to move.

Before moving, Romulo asked again, "Under arrest? For what? May I ask"

"Doctor, you are going to be hung for not surrendering the maíz as you were instructed. You are under arrest for treason! Now move, or you will be shot here! Those are my orders!" the man declared with a voice that suggested Romulo was going to receive a bullet if he did not comply.

Romulo did as he was told. He walked around all the people, not saying anything. An old woman waiting in line started to cry. Another old woman gave the sign of the cross and called out, "Ay, Doctor, we will pray for you! ¡Dios vaya contigo (God go with you), Doctor!"

Before Romulo mounted a horse that was brought to him by the revolutionaries, the soldier in charge told Romulo to stand still. He tied Romulo's hands together in front of him. Romulo felt the rope squeeze his wrists so tightly it felt as if his skin were burning with fire. He wondered if he was going to be able to ride in this condition. One of the soldiers helped Romulo mount his horse, almost throwing him over its side.

People stood shocked in the street as they rode away on the cobblestone avenue. As they departed, Romulo seemed as if he were going to fall off his horse.

Romulo did not know where they were taking him. After riding a few kilometers, he determined he was being taken to the rancho. As they were traveling, Romulo recalled his conversations with Luzita regarding the maíz. He knew Luzita hid the maíz, but he had no idea where. Rancho U-Chem spread over many thousands of acres. He was going to ask her exactly where she buried it, but he had never followed through with this question. He thought, "I should have taken charge of the situation. Ay, I hope we can fix things. I do not want to lose my life over this."

Most of the people at the doctor's office did not know what to do. Some ran to the federal building that consisted of a small office on the other side of town. It was guarded by two officers who would not leave the building unless there were other federal soldiers in town, fearing revolutionaries would ambush them.

The federal soldiers were sitting and sleeping in their chairs when several women burst into the office. They frightened the soldiers to their feet. Startled, one asked, "What? What is it? What happened?"

"Please, quick, you have to come. The doctor has been kidnapped and taken away on horseback. Soldiers from the revolution! You need to go after them!"

One of the soldiers glanced at the other and then looked back at the woman who was speaking. He said, "Why did they take him? What did he do?"

The woman was feeling frustrated because the soldiers were asking questions and not leaving, giving the kidnappers time to get away. "They said he is under arrest for treason! They said he will be hanged! You need to hurry and go after them before they get away!"

Trying to stall for time, the soldier asked, "How many are there?"

One older lady answered, "There are 10 or 15 men on horseback."

"Who do they think they are? They do not have authority to arrest anyone! Did you recognize any of them?" the soldier asked.

"No. You need to hurry! Every minute we stand here, they are getting farther away!" another woman exclaimed.

"They do not have authority to arrest anyone in Chiapas! Tomorrow we have troops coming into the pueblo. We will make sure we dispatch soldiers to look for the doctor," he stated, not wanting to go out and be killed. He knew the town was under the control of the revolutionaries. The soldiers recognized they could be killed at anytime. They did not know why it had not already happened.

Other women who were at the doctor's office ran to Luzita and Romulo's home. Upon arriving, they banged on the door and called out, "¡Doña Rodriguez! ¡Doña Rodriguez!" They repeated this several times.

"¿Qué pasa? What is all this about? What happened?" Arlette asked.

"We have to see Doña Rodriguez right away! Hurry, it is urgent!" one of the younger women demanded.

"She is not here. She went shopping at the market. What is it? What happened?" Arlette asked again, knowing it was urgent by the way the women were acting.

The women turned without saying a word and started to rush away. Arlette stepped out of the door, still not knowing what had taken place and what the emergency concerned. "¡Oíga! Before you go, you need to tell me what this is about in case Doña Rodriguez returns!"

At last one of the women in the group turned and yelled to Arlette, "The doctor has been kidnapped! The revolutionaries took him and said they were going to hang him! Something about the maíz. Tell Doña Rodriguez as soon as she returns. She will know what to do. We are going to the market to look for her." The lady turned and ran, holding her dress up to keep up with the others.

"Luzita, it is nice to see you. Come in. Come in," Señora Cabrillo said. She thought it was kind for Luzita to stop by to visit on occasion.

"How are you, Doña Cabrillo?"

"Oh, I am fine. How are your parents, Luzita? I hope they are fine," Señora Cabrillo asked as she motioned with her hand for Luzita to sit on a chair in the parlor. She turned her head and called out, "Yolanda! Yolanda! Come!" Yolanda was the housemaid.

Yolanda entered the parlor, "Si, Doña Cabrillo?"

"Please bring Luzita some hot chocolate."

"Right away, Doña," Yolanda replied as she turned and stepped toward the kitchen.

"Ay, no, Doña Cabrillo. It is all right. I am not staying long. I just wanted to stop and say hello for a few minutes," Luzita said, knowing it would take more than a few minutes for her to get a fire going and even longer to prepare the chocolate.

Luzita always enjoyed stopping and seeing the Cabrillo family. When she lived by the Cabrillos, they were always kind and considerate, more so with her parents. Luzita would never forget their kindness.

"No, no! The chocolate is already warm. You have to have a little bit with me before you go."

Yolanda stepped back into the parlor with a tray and two cups of chocolate. Just as Luzita reached for her cup, Señor Cabrillo entered the house and yelled out, "¡Oíga! Mujer, where are you?"

Señora Cabrillo and Luzita both stood, knowing by the tone of Señor Cabrillo's voice that it was something urgent. Señor Cabrillo entered the parlor and caught sight of Luzita. "Ay, Luzita. I am very sorry for the bad news. Anything we can do, you just name it," Señor Cabrillo said as he reached for Luzita to embrace her.

Luzita pulled back and looked at Señor Cabrillo with a bewildered expression. "What are you talking about? I do not know what you are talking about."

Señor Cabrillo still had his hands on Luzita's shoulders, "It is all over town what happened to Romulo, Luzita."

Luzita's heart began to race. She hoped he was mistaken and that nothing happened to her sweet love. "What happened to Romulo?" Luzita asked, staring into Señor Cabrillo's eyes. Señor Cabrillo saw the distress in her stare, anticipating something terrible had happened to her husband.

"You do not know? I am so sorry. I did not know you have not heard of it yet, Luzita."

Luzita could feel herself getting angry with Señor Cabrillo for not telling her immediately what was wrong. She could not wait any longer to be told what happened to the man she admired and loved so much. "Señor Cabrillo, tell me right now! What has happened to Romulo?"

"He has been kidnapped, Luzita. It was the soldiers from the revolution. Fifteen men rode into the pueblo and told Romulo he was under arrest for treason and that he was going to be hung! They tied his hands, mounted him on a horse, and took him away. They told him if he resisted in any manner, he was going to be shot right there on the spot! It had something to do with the maíz at U-Chem. I am not really sure what it is about."

Luzita felt her heart drop. Her stomach turned in pain. She had a blank stare and said in a low voice, "What have I done? Oh blessed Virgin, please help my poor husband." Luzita did not know if she should go to the church and pray or chase after her husband. She wanted to be with him and even trade places with him.

"Luzita, men are talking about getting together and going to rescue Romulo. I will join them," Señor Cabrillo said.

"No, Don Cabrillo. That is a very bad idea. You all might be killed or will be accused of taking sides with the federales. I do not want that. I know how you feel about the war, not wanting the federales to win. Besides, it will cause problems not only for you but also for your families. No, I will go and talk to Señor Díaz, the general, and see what he can do!" Luzita exclaimed.

"But, Luzita," Señora Cabrillo interjected, "do you know if the general will speak to you? Do you think you can get his help? They say he is so well protected nowadays that one cannot even approach him without getting shot."

"No, Señora Cabrillo. As you know, we grew up with him. Inside, he is the same person he has always been."

As Romulo rode into the rancho with his captors, several men stepped out on the road. His horse came to a stop. Captain Alfonso was a short man dressed in the same manner as his soldiers. He wore a big sombrero and had a large, black mustache that covered his top and bottom lips. The only way one recognized he was a soldier was from the ammunition belts that crossed his chest, along with his pistol and rifle. Captain Alfonso stood waiting for the doctor to arrive with his men. As he approached the horse Romulo was on, he displayed a wicked smile and said, "Dr. Rodriguez, I am glad to see you. I think we have some business to tend to. I am Capitán Alfonso. We have not met in person, although I sent you a few messages. Did you receive them?" Romulo knew what he was speaking about, but he wanted to act as though he did not. "What messages, Capitán?"

"I talked to your rancho foreman, Antonio. I told him what I wanted from you. Did you not receive the messages? If you did not, then we will have to go and find Antonio. He will be punished for not delivering my messages. But what does that matter to you, Doctor, right? He is but a mere peasant; and who cares about them, right, Doctor?" Captain Alfonso asked sarcastically.

Romulo took a deep breath. He did not want to put Antonio in any danger. He knew Antonio was just doing his job and acknowledged he should have taken charge of the situation. No one, only him, should have to take the blame. "Yes, Capitán, he gave me the messages."

"Well, Doctor, where is the maíz? We came out here, and we are unable to find anyone. Not even one person! It seems as if the maíz has disappeared or has been taken away," Captain Alfonso alleged. He waited for Romulo to respond.

Romulo did not know what to say. Should he say he did not know anything and that his wife was in charge of the maíz? If he did, he might put Luzita's life in jeopardy. He did not want to do that. "Do you want the maíz capitán? Is that what this is about?"

"Is that what this is about?" Captain Alfonso repeated, sounding agitated. "Take this man down from his horse!" he commanded, looking over at one of this men. "No, stop! I will take him down!" the captain said as he stepped to the side of Romulo's horse. He pushed Romulo over, making him fall. Romulo's hands were still tied. He tried to catch himself, but it was difficult to move his arms to protect himself. He fell solidly on the ground and felt pain all over his body. As Romulo hit the ground, the frightened horse jumped and almost trampled him. He lay on the road dazed, not knowing if he could get up.

"¡Oíga! Doctor," the captain called as he stepped around the horse. Romulo did not answer. He was moaning in pain. "¡Oíga! Doctor! I am speaking to you!" the captain repeated, irritated. Again Romulo did not respond, knowing he could not give the captain what he wanted. He did not know where the maíz was hidden. Captain Alfonso kicked Romulo with his heavy boot, striking him on the head. Romulo's head instantly started to bleed.

He rolled with the blow, thinking he was not going to survive this attack. He wanted to get up and strike the captain but knew there was not much he could do with his hands tied and the captain's men all around watching.

"Doctor, I want to know where the maíz is right now! Tell me or you will be hung! I have the notion to hang you anyway, even if you tell me. If you cooperate, I will give you your life in exchange for the maíz."

Romulo looked up at the captain and all his men standing around him. He wanted to tell him where the maíz was, but that was impossible. "Capitán, I do not know where it is. I am a doctor, and I do not take care of the rancho. I have no interest in what goes on here. I really do not know."

"¡Desgraciado!" the captain shouted as he kicked Romulo once again in the torso. He looked at his men and pointed to a tree nearby, yelling, "Tie him up to that tree!" He looked back at Romulo and said, "Doctor, I will give you one hour to think about your life. I want to know where the maíz is. If I do not get an answer in one hour, that is the tree you will be hung from. If you want to live, you will think about this because no one can save you now. You will die, Doctor!" He glared at his men and yelled, "Tie him up! Mario, I want you to send some men around the area to see what they can find. See if there are any traces of the maíz, and tell them to be back in one hour. In one hour we will hang this inútil (good for nothing) doctor. Then we will leave!" Captain Alfonso turned and walked back to where he was sitting when they arrived.

"I need to see the general right away!" Luzita demanded.

Two soldiers who stood in front of the general's door asked, "Who are you, señora? Aren't you the doctor's wife?"

"Yes, I need to see Señor Díaz right away. I mean, General Díaz!" Luzita said loudly.

"I will see if he will speak to you, señora." Just as he said this, General Díaz came to the front door.

"What is it?" he asked.

"General, you have to help me, please!"

The general stepped outside. "What is it, Luzita? What has happened?"

"They took Romulo away! You have to help us!"

"Who took Romulo away, the federales?" he asked, confused.

"No, it was some of your men, a Capitán Alfonso! He took him and said he was going to hang Romulo!"

"Why? What did Romulo do? Did he kill one of our soldiers or a horse? Did he help the federales in anyway?"

"No, General. He did not do anything. It is my fault! The capitán went out to the rancho and told my foreman to tell us he wanted our maíz. However, as you know, General, my husband, he does not know anything about the rancho. I take care of all the business out there. I could not just give the maíz away! So I hid it from the capitán. Romulo does not know where I hid it. He does not know anything, and they are going to hang him for nothing," Luzita explained as she started to cry. "General, I need your help! Please intervene! Please! I do not want my husband to die," Luzita begged as she covered her face and started to weep more intensely.

General Díaz looked at his men standing by his house and ordered them to get their horses and his. "We will stop this right away! I never liked Capitán Alfonso. He has always tried to do things his way, and I do not like it. Now he wants to hang one of my friends! I will stop him! I have had enough of him!" Just as he was saying this, the general's men brought his horse and one for Luzita. Ten other soldiers joined them. They mounted their horses and rode off.

CHAPTER SIXTEEN

BLUE BLOOD

"All right, Doctor, your time is up. Do you want to tell me where the maíz is?" Captain Alfonso asked.

"Capitán, if I knew, I would. I really do not know where it is. I have nothing to do with the rancho. I am telling you the truth. I work in the pueblo as a doctor, and that is my business!" Romulo claimed as he sat tied against the tree, hoping he would be believed.

"Mario, throw the rope over this branch. This is where the doctor is going to die!" Mario was the arresting soldier who brought him out to the rancho.

"Sí, Capitán," he said as he walked by Romulo. He gave Romulo a hard stare as if he were going to enjoy hanging the rich man. Mario had always hated the rich, classifying them all the same. He grew up on a hacienda in slave-like conditions while the owners lived in luxury. They never cared for him or any of the campesinos (laborers). He joined the revolution to put an end to the unjust conditions in all of México.

The captain knew Romulo was a doctor and that people spoke well of him, but he did not believe it. He felt the doctor was deceiving everyone because he felt the wealthy were all alike.

As he threw the rope over the large branch, the captain looked at Romulo and gave him a wicked smile. He stared at him knowing he had seen Romulo before, pressing himself to remember from where he knew the doctor. At first he could not recall.

Captain Alfonso stood up and stepped over to Romulo. "This is your last chance. Do you want to tell me where the maíz is?"

"I am sorry, capitán. As I told you, I do not know."

"All right," the Captain said as he looked over at Mario. "Hang him! He deserves to die like a dog!"

Just then two of his soldiers rode their horses toward them. They came to a stop. One of the men was holding a cob of maíz. "Capitán, we found it! There is a lot of it, all stored away in some old ruins not far from here."

"Well done, muchachos. Take some men, find a wagon, and start loading it up. We do not want to waste anymore time here."

Just as he was saying this, Mario was staring at Romulo. It clicked. "Capitán, I remember where I saw the doctor! This is the doctor who shot Capitán Juan Hernández!"

Captain Alfonso looked at Romulo and said, "You are the one who shot my friend!"

"I have never shot anyone, Capitán. I do not know what you are talking about," Romulo said truthfully, saying what he really believed.

Mario looked at Romulo and reminded him, "It was a few years ago that you and another man were out on the road. You shot the capitán. I shot your friend, and you got away."

Romulo's mind went back to the night his best friend was shot; he felt a great sadness. He looked at Mario and thought he could kill him with his bare hands if he were untied. Romulo said, "You are the devil who shot my friend! If I could, señor, I would kill you right now! You are a snake and deserve to die! I always dreamed of avenging my friend Daniel."

Romulo realized saying this was not going to help his situation, but he did not care. He knew things were not going to go well with him, and he wanted this man to know how much he was hated.

The captain looked at Romulo and said, "So, Doctor, you are the one responsible for the death of my friend Capitán Hernández. Now you will pay for it. We will have to hang you even though we found the maíz."

The other soldiers were getting ready to leave to pick up the maíz and were standing around listening to the new development. The captain said, "Get him, and put the rope around his neck. He will be hung!"

Two men untied Romulo from the tree. Mario stood only a few feet away. The men pulled him up, one on each arm. Romulo broke away and leaped at Mario, hitting him with such force that Mario flew back. Romulo continued toward him, reaching with his tied hands to grab Mario's head. Soldiers were trying to pull Romulo away from Mario. Romulo knew he did not have much time. He wanted to inflict as much injury as he could in the next few seconds. He had his big hands around Mario's head and took his thumbs and gouged them into his eyes. Even as he was being pulled away, he did not let go. He felt his thumbs pene-trate into the man's eye sockets.

Mario was screaming with terror. As the men were pulling Romulo off and away, he would not let go of Mario's head. He wanted to hurt him as much as he possibly could. He knew he was going to be hung or shot. As Romulo was being dragged away from Mario, his hands were dragging Mario. One of the soldiers punched Romulo on the center of his back with the butt of his rifle. Romulo felt the pain, but it was not enough to make him let go. As far as he was concerned, he was not going to release Mario until he lost consciousness or if his arms were broken. All he could see was his best friend Daniel's face. Romulo probed deep into the sockets of Mario's eyes and moved his thumbs around with all his strength. He wanted to do as much damage as he could. Again the soldier let Romulo have it, this time on the back of his head. Everything went black.

Romulo felt himself being dragged. The men dragging him threw him several feet. As he hit the ground, he regained consciousness. He looked up, trying to remember where he was and what was happening.

He saw Mario coming toward him with his arms covering his eyes and his gun drawn. "¡Te voy a matar! (I'm going to kill you!)" He came up close and pointed his gun at Romulo's head. Romulo uttered his last prayer for his wife and children and asked God to forgive him for any-thing he had done immorally in his life. Romulo felt he was in good standing with God because of all his goodwill toward humanity.

"Mario! Stop!" Captain Alfonso yelled as he raced over to him and grabbed the gun out of his hand. "Mario, we will hang him and make him suffer. It will be better than a bullet. A bullet is just too quick!"

Mario tried to look at the captain, but his eyes crossed and teared. The muscles in his eyes had been damaged badly.

Romulo picked up his head, looked at Mario, and said with a vicious glare, "If you get too close to me, hombre, I will tear your eyes out and then kill you!"

Mario pulled his leg back and gave Romulo a kick in the ribs. Romulo rolled in pain as two men stood him up and lifted him onto a horse. He could hardly keep himself upright. A noose was put around his neck. He knew it was going to be over soon.

"Doctor, any last words?" the captain asked.

Romulo gazed at the captain, not saying anything. He had stated all he was going to say.

The captain was preparing to fire his gun to scare the horse away and leave Romulo dangling, hanging from the tree. He heard a shot in the distance. The captain and all the soldiers looked in the direction of the gunshot and observed riders approaching them. He was determined to fire his gun; however, one of his men said, "It is the general!"

The captain lowered his gun and looked, squinting his eyes. He saw a woman riding with the general and his men.

When they approached, Luzita dismounted and ran to the doctor. "No! What do you think you are doing, mujer (woman)? Leave him alone!" Captain Alfonso yelled out.

"Help her!" General Díaz ordered his men.

Three men ran to Luzita's side as one moved to take hold of the other end of the rope. They helped Romulo off the horse. Luzita loosened the noose from around his neck and removed it.

"What is this, Alfonso?" General Díaz asked, staring at the captain.

"This is the man who shot Capitán Hernández!" Captain Alfonso explained.

"Who is Capitán Hernández?" General Díaz asked.

"He was the capitán who was shot on the road a few years back. He was my friend."

"The murderers of Daniel!" Romulo said angrily as he embraced his wife.

General Díaz remembered the incident well. He also was a friend of Daniel, having grown up with him in San Bartolomé de los Llanos. General Díaz stared at the captain with indignation and asked, "How do you know?"

"Mario is the one who shot his friend, General," he said as he pointed to Mario.

"Alfonso," the general asked, "why did you bring the doctor here in the first place?"

"He hid the maíz, but we found it. Now we have possession of it."

The general stood in deep thought, wondering how he was going to handle the situation. He dismounted, walked toward Mario, and drew his pistol. He raised it to Mario's head and fired. Everyone was watching and saw the side of Mario's head blow off as if a bomb blew up inside his brain. Mario's body pulled away from where the gun was fired, and he dropped like a puppet. All were shocked to see the general kill Mario without hesitation. He then stepped over to Captain Alfonso and raised his gun to his head. The captain had an expression of shock, not really believing the general was actually going to shoot him as he had shot Mario.

The captain thought the general was only trying to scare him, but then the general pulled the trigger. The bullet went through his head and burst out the other side as the captain darted in the direction of the blast. It seemed as if his head were emptied of its contents. The general stood and gazed at the captain as he hit the ground. He turned and looked at all the soldiers and said, "I am General Díaz. I want you to pick another capitán, and I want all to know the doctor is my friend. I do not want anymore harm to come to him. Do you understand?"

The soldiers stood silent for a few seconds. They were all in shock in seeing their captain executed. They knew they had better agree with the general, or they might find themselves lying next to Alfonso and Mario. One of the braver soldiers answered, "Sí, General Díaz. Whatever you wish! We are at your orders."

The general stepped over to Romulo and put his arm in Romulo's arm. He assisted Romulo to his horse and helped him mount it. He wanted all to know that Dr. Romulo Rodriguez was his friend, and he did not want anyone to give him anymore trouble. The general turned and to looked at the soldiers. He told them to pick up the maíz they found and take it where it was needed.

Romulo, now on his horse with Luzita next to him, looked at the general, never believing he would do such a thing to defend him. The general smiled at Luzita and Romulo and said, "I would like both of you to come to my house at your next opportunity. We can talk. Will that be all right?"

"Sí, General," Luzita said as she turned her horse and rode away with her husband.

On the way home Luzita stopped a few times to let Romulo rest. He had taken a bad beating. She told Romulo she was sure they had only found one of the two storage cellars of the maíz. They would wait for a while to recover the one they did not find. As far as Romulo was concerned, he wanted nothing to do with the maíz.

Upon arriving in town, Romulo and Luzita went home and tried to recoup from the experience they had just survived. They still could not believe the general shot the two men so easily.

Romulo and Luzita knew General Díaz all their lives and never imagined he could shoot people without hesitation.

That night as they were in deep thought and as they both lay on their bed resting, Luzita stated, "Romulo, I think I will now start to call Señor Díaz, General Díaz."

The following morning they went to the general's home as he requested, even though Romulo and Luzita were still in shock from all that had occurred. Romulo was still very sore from his beating.

When they stepped into his kitchen, they could not believe how the general was acting. He was laughing, had a piece of chicken in his mouth, and was holding a drumstick in his hand when he greeted them. He asked them to sit down and help themselves to food. They sat, but they did not eat because they still felt shaken by their experience.

The general was not the same person with whom they had grown up. The boy they once knew could not hurt a fly. The general seemed as if it were an everyday occurrence. He went on to tell them about the war and what the revolutionaries wanted to accomplish in the next few months. Since he saved Romulo's life, Romulo and Luzita did not say much. They let the general do all the talking.

When they were married, Romulo was forty-two; and Luzita was twenty-six years old. Before the incident with the general, Luzita already had two children, Marina and Jorge. Later that year she bore her son Pancho. In the following years their family continued to grow. Luzita had Luis and then José. When Luis was two years old, he became ill and died. The next son was given the same name, Luis. Following Luis were Gloria, Rolando, Ramiro, and Martha, the youngest.

México was in chaos and fighting an aimless war. In the years that followed, things were changing for the nation. From President Francisco Madero, who died in 1913, until Alvaro Obregón, who was elected in 1920, México had ten presidents. A few, such as Victoriano Huerta and Venustiano Carranza, left their marks for better or for worse. Most of the others had short reigns with little consequence. This made things difficult for all sides who were waging the war.

In September 1916 President Carranza ordered a convention that considered what changes in the Mexican constitution the revolution made necessary. This changed the way a lot was to be handled in all of México and also for the future of Rancho U-Chem. One of the constitution articles affected the Rodriguez family. The article empowered the government to take over private land or resources for the "general good of the people."

In 1917 the new constitution was in effect. It gave meaning and purpose to the previously aimless revolution. Not all its articles were strictly enforced; but there they were, in black and white. If México was to move ahead, the articles had to mean pretty much what they said. In time the rancho would be taken over by others.

Within just a few months following the incident with the maíz, Romulo received papers regarding Rancho U-Chem. They informed the Rodriguezes that the land they owned was going to be taken from them to be distributed to the people. Romulo and Luzita understood. Because of the conflict in México, the changes might or might not actually happen. They did not want to take any chances working the land and losing their investment; therefore, they sold whatever they could and no longer cultivated the land. Romulo continued to work in his medical practice and continued to have a good relationship with all in the community.

One lazy Saturday evening Romulo was drinking with his friends whom he invited for a late supper. "Mi armor (my love), get Arlette to prepare food for Señor Caballero and Señor Chevarria," Romulo asked. The three men sat at the kitchen table.

Luzita stepped into the kitchen, greeted the visitors, and kissed her husband. She had Arlette prepare a quick supper. The men kept drinking and talking until early in the morning. Luzita did not mind if Romulo's friends visited; she enjoyed entertaining them.

Once they ate and left, Arlette went to bed. Romulo continued to drink his whiskey. Luzita sat with her dear husband and listened to him recite his favorite poems. He had written many poems, some especially for her.

In a short while he started with his philosophies of the purpose of life. Consequently, Romulo started on the subject Luzita hated.

"Luzita, enlighten me. How do you feel and how has your experience been, being part of a noble familia?"

Romulo was an educated man and spoke with elegant words. But when he was drinking, he slurred and did not speak gracefully.

"What royal familia, Romulo?" Luzita asked, her pleasant tone changing to one of resentment.

Romulo was not happy that his wife never acknowledged the superiority of his family's lineage. Romulo glared at her, wanting her to pay attention. "Luzita, you know, the children and I have blue blood running through our veins, right? You understand it, true?"

Luzita did not respond. She had heard enough of his boasting through the years. Romulo continued to lecture her about his blue blood. She sat there pondering to herself, wondering how she could put a stop to all of Romulo's insignificant-lineage talk. Romulo went on and on about his blue blood. He wanted his wife to accept his philosophy that blue blood makes a person superior to others.

"Romulo, stop it! You are loco! I do not even want to talk about it! So that is enough!" she insisted, raising her voice as she stood. She stepped over to the hot stove and looked inside to see if it was still burning.

"Luzita! You must understand who we are! And furthermore, Luzita..." Romulo turned and saw that she had left the kitchen. He filled his glass with whiskey and took a long, hard swallow. He heard footsteps re-enter the kitchen. "Luzita!" Romulo raised his arm as he did on many occasions to show his wife he meant what he was saying. "In these veins there is blue blood! Do you understand, Luzita?"

Romulo waited for her to respond; all he heard was rustling behind him. He raised his glass and took another big gulp of his whiskey. "Mi armor, do you understand?" he questioned as he turned to look at her. "I possess papers to prove it to you!" he repeated as he consistently did when he was drunk. He was even willing to get his Monkey Box containing the precious documents. As he was speaking, he saw the Monkey Box in his wife's hands. The lid was open.

Luzita stood with the stove door open. "Romulo, now you have no proof. There is your blue blood!" she declared, pointing to the stove as the papers burned. She continued, "Now what are you going to do without your papers to prove your blue blood?"

Romulo could not believe what his eyes were seeing. He stood, wanting to strike his wife. As he stepped toward her, she put her arms up to protect herself, believing she was going to be beaten.

"What have you done, Luzita? What have you done?" he cried hurtfully. He looked in the stove and saw the priceless papers quickly burning; they were so old. He grabbed the Monkey Box from her hands to save whatever was left. Romulo looked inside the box and saw it was empty. He stared at Luzita in shock. His family lineage was lost forever! His children and their children would never have these documents!

Luzita knew in that instant she had done more damage than she realized. Romulo left the house and did not return for a few days. Once he returned, he never spoke to Luzita about the papers again, even though it was a tragedy for him, his offspring, and the generations who followed. In time even the Monkey Box was lost forever.

As the years went by, Romulo's children continued to do well. He was a busy man, unable to spend a lot of time with them. Regardless, they still loved and respected their father very much. He left the raising and disciplining to his wife. He was very mild with his children and did not approve of his wife spanking them. Luzita had to discipline the children while he was away.

Romulo began to develop symptoms of sugar diabetes, and within time it became very serious.

All of Romulo's sons were receiving a good education. Once their basic education was completed, they were sent to school in San Cristóbal de Las Casas.

José was the most difficult of the children, always wanting to do things his way. From a very young age, he showed signs of disobedience. At first his father and mother thought he was going to be a bad son; he had been a very difficult child when he was young.

At the age of eight years, he was very mischievous with his mother. One day Luzita had enough of it.

"Josecito, go into the house! You are not allowed to play with your friends!" she yelled.

"Mamá, I did not do anything. It was not my fault!" José tried to explain.

"Te voy a pegar, muchacho, (I'm going to hit you, boy) if you do not mind me! Now get into the house, and go to your room. If you continue, you are going to get the belt!" Luzita threatened.

José stepped inside and looked back to see if his mother was following him. Luzita was in the street talking. José was furious; he felt he was treated unfairly and did not like it one bit. It seemed to him he was always mistreated. His brothers were never picked on as he was, and he felt something should be done.

José stopped and turned at the doorway of his mother's bedroom.

He looked back again toward the front of the house to make sure his mother was not following. He hesitated a few seconds. Entering her bedroom, he looked in the closet for her favorite dress, one she had made for special occasions. Luzita had become one of the best seamstresses in the area. People were paying her a fair price to make nice garments. However, this dress was one she made for herself. She was planning to use it for the next big fiesta.

José stepped back to the front door to check to see where his mother was. He wanted to repay her for always nagging him and to teach her she needed to leave him alone. Luzita was still speaking to the same woman. It seemed as if she was walking away from the house with the lady.

He went to where his mother kept her sewing tools and found a large pair of scissors. Walking toward his mother's bedroom again, he hesitated before entering. He wanted to make absolutely sure she was not around; he did not want to be caught.

Assuring himself of this, he turned and walked once again to his mother's bedroom. He stopped and wondered if he was doing the right thing, of the times his mother made him work for being disobedient, such as separating beans and rice if she could not find other work. "No way out! I have to do it to teach Mamá a lesson on how to treat me," he resolved.

He pulled down her beautiful dress. To him it did not look as pretty as his mother and all her friends had said. He took the scissors out of his back pocket and was about to take the first cut. He realized this was not the dress he had in mind; it was a different one. This dress did not have the ruffles around the neck and sleeves.

He looked back to where her clothing hung, scanning the garments. Stepping over to the closet again, he found the dress. He pulled it down, sat at the end of his mother's bed, and started to cut through it. The dress was white with attractive laces around the shoulders. It also had bright colors throughout.

"Next time Mamá beats me with the belt, she will think twice about it," he whispered to himself as the scissors cut across the dress. He felt himself hot and angry, thinking of all the beatings his mother had given him for no reason. The last beating he received from her, she called him a little devil for the way he behaved. "I am not a devil, and she will think about it the next time she makes a dress like this one," he thought as he kept cutting.

Once he was done, he rose from the bed. He peeked out of the bedroom door, wanting to make certain his mother had not returned. Glancing back into the room, he saw the mess. At that moment he knew things were not going to go well for him.

José tossed the scissors into the room and made his getaway toward the front door. Looking out at the street, he saw many people standing and talking; the street was busy with people as always.

He left the house and thought about what he was going to do and where he was going to go. He did not think about what could happen. He tried to forget about the dress and went to his cousin's home a few streets away.

"José, how are you?" his tía asked.

"I am fine, Tía. Is Agusto home?" he asked, standing and waiting for her reply. If he was not home, he would go to another cousin's or a friend's house.

"Yes, he is here. He is in the house. Go on in."

"Thank you, Tía," José said as he stepped inside. He found his cousin sitting in the backyard, carving out a new toy. The backyard was as most were in the small town. It was full of greenery and surrounded with walls from other homes. If one needed to escape from this particular home, there was no way out but through the house.

All the children in these small towns made their own toys, mostly out of wood. Agusto was making a slingshot. He had a few of them, as did most of the boys. Sometimes they would use them as toys and sometimes as weapons against one another in fights.

Usually José's younger brother Luis would accompany him wherever he would go. Luis always liked being with José. In the event of any trouble with other boys, he would protect Luis. José was the hottest tempered of all the Rodriguez brothers. His older brothers always wondered what was wrong with him. He always seemed to get into trouble, and trouble always seemed to find him.

As José was asking Agusto what kind of rubber he was going to use for his new slingshot, he heard talking in the house. At first he did not pay attention, thinking his tía had visitors. He then heard his mother's voice and dreaded what was going to happen next.

"Yes, Luzita, he just arrived. He is in the backyard with Agusto. What is wrong? What happened? You do not look well, Luzita."

Luzita was angry. She could not believe José could do such a thing. It took so long to make the dress. She had taken her time and had given it so much attention. She knew it was José because he was the only one home at the time, and she knew he was the only one with the disposition to do such a thing. As far back as she could remember, she always had problems with him. He had a bad attitude and was always the son who spoke back to her. Luzita tried to direct him in the right way, but it just seemed as if she was never able to get through to him.

José heard his mother approaching and stood up. He knew it was big trouble for him and knew his mamásita was really angry. As she stepped out to the backyard, he looked at his mother and said, "Mamá, hola."

"What do you mean, 'hola'; malcriado (spoiled brat)!" she yelled as she grabbed him by his shaggy hair and pulled him up on his toes. "What did you do, muchacho? What did you do? You really did it this time, José! Come home so you can make me another dress!"

José's tía had never seen Luzita act this way. "Luzita, what did he do? Ay, Josecito, what did you do this time?" she asked as she looked down at him. She held her hands clasped together near her face in a praying position. She knew all of Romulo and Luzita's boys; he was the roughest and most difficult to handle.

José did not say anything to his tía. He knew he was in for the biggest spanking he would ever receive. One thing he did not realize was that this incident would be referred to all of his life. José was not a rebel, just a child who wanted to do things his own way.

As they became older, Jorge and Pancho were already moving forward in their education. Jorge had his heart set on being a doctor like his father. Pancho always marveled at his father as he helped people with their legal papers. He wanted to follow a law career. José and Luis did not really know what they wanted at this point; they were still too young.

During this time Romulo was approaching his sixties and was becoming increasingly ill with sugar diabetes, along with all its side effects. Because she was much younger than Romulo, Luzita was still vibrant. She worked hard in her trade as a seamstress.

Luzita often reflected back to her mother and father who had already passed away. They lived a good life. Her parents had a deep love for each other. In a way she wished she had remained single to help her mother and father more in their senior years.

Luzita loved her husband regardless of the pain he caused her through the years. She had heard stories of Romulo being with other women. However, he always came home and did not spend the nights elsewhere. She never felt this was a threat to their relationship and decided it was not worth making an issue of, even though it pained her. She did not know if the stories were true or not and really did not investigate them.

Once the two younger boys completed their primary school, it was time for them to follow their brothers and move to San Cristóbal de Las Casas to attend boarding school. Their father had done the same many years before when he was a young man.

José never changed his character. Although he wanted to have a good life and appreciated the education he was receiving, he was always ready to be bold and to take chances.

José wrote his ill father in 1937 and expressed to Romulo the love he had for him. He related how he always appreciated his love and the concern shown to him by his parents. He expressed that he wanted to pursue a medical career, caring for people as Romulo had always done.

At this time Romulo was no longer working and was unable to walk because of his illness. He received his son's letter with great joy and wanted to express his feelings. As he always did with his elegant writing, he wrote José the following.

> To My Beloved Son, Josecito,
> I received your letter and am pleased with your intentions. You have such good ways. I know the birds of heaven recline on the goodness of your heart and wish that the poison of the world not stain nor contaminate you. Conserve your well-meaning intentions all the days of your life. In that way they can serve as a trophy or a flag for you.
>
> Keep moving forward to reach your goal. If you define a road for your future, you will possess a goal that will be full of beautiful and hopeful accomplishments.
>
> Look at the grand architect, the One who created you. Pay attention to Him all your life. With all the good things He has given you, observe them in your heart. Return this goodness to society and to those you love. In fulfilling this you will please the

Director of Nature.

I am tired of wrestling with all the unpleasant problems of life. I have suffered with the poisons of this immoral system and have been a prisoner of them. Even though I am drained from the toxic taste of the world, I keep marching forward.

Study, my son. Do not waste the capability of your mind and the desire to learn what the Grand Inventor has given you. If you persist, you will be successful. The privileges God has given you, take them, appreciate them, and conserve them with love, embracing them always. If you do this, you will establish firm convictions and develop a name for yourself. You will also be a role model. When humanity reads your title, they will have respect and admire you. Also see that your brothers take advantage of all this.

Your mother has made a grand sacrifice in leaving her familia for the sake of having her own household. She set a pattern for you. Your mother should always be regarded as sacred to you and your brothers. Take care of her, my son, as long as she lives; repay her a hundred times. You must never ignore her value but treasure it and return it with goodness.

I agree with your recommendation for yourself. My deepest desire is that all you yearn for you will receive. Reap the fruits of this. I wait for the future day when it will all come to pass.

Give hugs to your brothers for me. Take care of them. In this way they can travel the favored road of life. Guide them there with your noble and sweet heart. Love your bothers without envy.

Your father who loves you, Romulo

José received this letter with much joy. He felt his father gave him the responsibility of caring for and seeing after his mother and brothers. He treasured the letter, was proud of it, and kept it all of his life, passing it on to his children.

CHAPTER SEVENTEEN

IN JOSE'S HONOR

José and Luis were in school together. Jorge and Pancho were now in México City attending the university. Pancho was pursuing a career in law, and Jorge was studying to be a doctor. José and Luis were not really sure what they wanted at the ages of almost fifteen and sixteen and were still attending school in San Cristóbal de Las Casas.

José had many friends, including numerous girlfriends in San Cristóbal de Las Casas. One day he was visiting María, a girlfriend who was one of the nicest young women he knew. María was seventeen years old, and her father was a wealthy man. She was thin, very pretty, and prieta (dark complected). With long, black hair with a slight natural curl to it, she also had beautiful, large, brown eyes. She liked to dress in colorful clothes; and also had a stunning smile with white, straight teeth. José admired her smile so much that when she looked at him and smiled he became speechless with her beauty.

María informed José she was having a fiesta at her home. Her father had approved it, and the party was going to be held in José's honor. He was flattered by her thoughtfulness. With her own money she was going to pay for the marimba music.

Luis accompanied José wherever he went. He told José he had heard of many who were attending the fiesta, and he believed it was going to be a big gathering. There was one group of young men José and Luis did not care for because they followed a guy named Tómas. José and Luis knew the day was coming when they were going to have trouble with him.

José and Luis were dressing in their living quarters. Their room consisted of one dresser for both boys, a small desk they shared for their studies, one closet, and two small cots where they slept. They kept their personal belongings in boxes next to the dresser. The room had a small window with a view of the school's courtyard. Both José and Luis were neat and kept things tidy in their room. Each helped the other when it was needed. If either José or Luis were in a hurry and did not have time to pick up after himself, the other would clean the room.

Luis felt María must really care for his brother because she was having a party in his honor and was covering all the expense of the fiesta. He asked José what his intentions were with María. "José, what are you going to do with her? Are you going to marry her? Do you think you love her?" Luis asked as he stopped dressing, turning to observe José as he answered.

José looked at his brother, stopped dressing, and laughed, "Luis, what is wrong with you asking me something like that? You know that is not the case. I really like María, but she is just a girlfriend. Besides, I have many girlfriends. I have all of my life to find the woman I want to marry. Someday I will find the girl I will marry. When I do, she will be the mother of my children and the only one. I will love her as I have loved no other girl. But hermanito (little brother), that is a long way off. I have to have my share of muchachas first!"

"So, José, you are saying you will stop having other girlfriends once this happens? Right?" Luis asked, not believing his brother would be able to commit himself to one woman only.

"Ay, Luis, I did not say that. You are putting words in my mouth that I did not say," José said, laughing and continuing to dress.

"Good!" Luis laughed and also continued dressing. As he was buttoning his shirt, he added, "I am glad, José. I was a little worried you were falling for her and would change your plans and the plans Papí has for us. I know our father will never approve of us having a serious relationship. You know how he is and how he feels about our education. He does not mind if we have all the girlfriends we want. He does not want us to give up anything for them, at least not until we are finished with our schooling."

"I know, Luis. I cannot count how many times our father instructed us that way. I know what I am doing. I am old enough to know better," José declared, feeling confident and believing he was a grown man at his young age.

"I am glad, José. I do not want to see you get in over your head with María. It is very easy to do. Look what happened to Anna and me. I almost lost it! I will never do that again as long as I am in school. I will have chamacas (girls), but I will not fall in love with them until I am out of school. Just think about all the stories we have heard about our father and all the women he had. Even though he had all that fun, look at what he has accomplished."

"Ay, Luis, hermanito (little brother), you will have to learn how to play and not fall in love. Do not worry. You will learn when you are smart like your older hermano (brother)."

Luis answered jokingly, "You mean like Jorge?"

"No, Luis, like me!" José declared. "I think God made girls for us to have fun with. I can love them and then leave them. We might as well enjoy them while we can. That is what I say! I do know one thing for sure. I am going to have fun tonight!" José proclaimed as he fixed the cuffs on his pants and straightened his collar. He reached for his gun and placed it in the back of his belt. In this part of México, most boys carried guns during this time; there were a lot left from the revolution.

"Do you think you should take that tonight, José?" Luis asked, concerned for his brother and knowing he did not like Tómas. Luis thought Tómas and his friends would be at the fiesta that night. Luis hoped there would not be trouble between the two.

"Hermanito (little brother), you know I cannot go anywhere without my baby. Without it I feel as if I am not dressed. Where I go, my baby goes," José declared with a sarcastic smile. When he had this smile, it was on one side of his face. He always showed this expression when he thought he was being funny.

"All right, hermano, you know best. I sure hope there is no trouble at María's house," Luis asserted.

"Luis, what if there is?" José asked.

Luis paused for a second and replied, "If there is, I sure hope no one gets killed." Because his brother liked fighting, Luis felt that one day his aggressiveness and violence was bound to ruin things for them. They stepped out of the room, Luis following José, not saying anything more for awhile.

Arriving at the fiesta outside of town, they noted the beauty of the rancho of María's father. The rancho was always beautiful; however, José had never seen it at night. An almost-full moon lit up the earth with such splendor that one had to stop and take a deep breath, appreciating being alive.

The yard was decorated with party ornaments nicely arranged all over the fiesta area. There were many candles and torches around the vicinity. In the center of the yard was a large gazebo where the marimba band was setting up their instruments. As one stepped down from the gazebo, there was a nice floor made of white bricks; the area would be used for dancing on this night. The large dancing area was lined with chairs. Approximately twenty guests were already present.

José heard someone yell out that Luis and he had arrived. María's heart jumped as she heard the announcement. She felt she really loved José and hoped he felt or would feel the same for her. She believed she had found the person of her dreams and wanted to spend the rest of her life with him.

María was speaking to a band member and looked up to see José and Luis. José looked just as she had imagined him. He smiled at her, and she returned his smile. He dressed handsomely tonight, just as he always had. She discontinued her conversation with the band member and stared at José with amazement at how he carried himself. She also thought of how handsome he was and felt that one day he would belong to her. José could feel her smile. He continued to smile as he approached María, feeling very flattered that the party was being held in his honor. She felt as if she could melt from the way he was looking at her.

"José, I am glad you are here early. We will have time to talk for awhile before the marimba starts to play and before the other guests arrive."

José, María, and Luis all sat down and began small talk. José asked, "María, do you have any refreshments for my brother and me?" He meant alcohol and hoped he could start to feel "a little high" before the music started.

"I do, but you must not let my father see you. I will go and get a drink. Pour it in your punch, but do not let anyone know. I will get some for you and your brother. I will be right back," María said as she walked away.

José felt important. He knew he was going to have a lot of fun this evening. If she did not have anything strong enough to get high with, then José and Luis would have to drink the whiskey they brought. They did not really want to do this because it would show disrespect to María's gesture in having José as the guest of honor.

Within just a few minutes, María returned with two glasses of refreshments for José and Luis. They sat together for a while and talked. José drank his drink very slowly, knowing it was going to be a long and fun-filled night.

María showed José how she felt in the way she looked at him. She knew she was going to marry him and also knew she would have her father's approval because José was a good person. More importantly, he came from a distinguished family. However, José had no intentions of marrying María. He made it a practice to have girls fall for him, enjoying their company as long as it lasted. María was one of his favorite girlfriends. She was very beautiful, and he felt as if he were beaming when she accompanied him. Even though he felt this way, he would not give up his other girlfriends for her. Because he was the son of Romulo and knew the stories he had heard about his father's love affairs, he thought it was not a big issue to continue to have female friends, even after marriage.

As people arrived at the fiesta, they greeted María and José as they passed them. They thanked her for the invitation. In a short time the marimba started to play. José asked her if she wanted to dance the first dance; she accepted without hesitation.

José was a very good dancer, and the girls admired this about him. At times he would show off when he danced.

As José and María were dancing, he noticed Tómas and three of his friends enter the fiesta area. From the very first time José met Tómas, he never liked him. He was a big muchacho, big as in tall and broad shouldered. His appearance was messy. He had straight, black, shaggy hair that did not seem as if he ever combed it. When Tómas was not smiling, he had a mean expression. Eighteen years old, he was a big bully with all the younger and wimpy muchachos. José was tempted in the past to become involved in fights that Tómas had with younger muchachos. However, he always thought that one day he was going to show Tómas how tough he really was.

"María, did you invite Tómas?" José asked, knowing a lot of the girls did not like him and would not have invited him.

"No, José, I think he came with Miguel. My brother is friends with him and said he was going to invite him. Miguel is the muchacho in the green shirt with Tómas," she answered. She looked in the direction where Tómas, Carlos, Miguel, and one other unfamiliar muchacho stood. They had stopped and were talking to some of the other guests who were arriving.

José and María now slowed in their dancing and were speaking and gazing at Tómas and his friends. Tómas looked in their direction and noticed they were staring at him. He sensed José and María were speaking negatively about him. Tómas smiled sarcastically at José and tilted his chin up as if he were saying, "¿Que pasa (What's happening)?" José looked at María, and she looked at him. He smiled at her, indicating it was of no importance what Tómas thought. María returned José's smile and gazed in his eyes as he swung her around the dance floor.

The dance number was over. José and María returned to their seats. As they sat, the band started to play the next song. Tómas stepped over to José and María. Luis was talking and mingling with other guests. "Oralé, José," Tómas greeted. He turned and looked at María and continued, "María, you look very beautiful tonight."

"Thank you, Tómas," she answered, glancing at him for just an instant. She knew José did not care for him and did not want to give his compliment any attention.

"That is a beautiful song they are playing, María," Tómas said, observing the marimba band. He turned and faced her again and asked, "Would you like to dance with me? I would be honored if you would." Tómas put his hand out to take hers.

María looked up at Tómas and responded negatively. "No, thank you," she answered as she looked at José.

"All right, María, maybe later," Tómas answered in a harsh tone, taking a dim view of her answer.

At that point José knew he and Tómas were going to clash that night.

As the evening progressed, José and María had a pleasant time, dancing almost every number. José tried not to give Tómas any attention, not wanting to ruin the fiesta.

Everything seemed to be fine. José thought maybe it was going to be all right and that he would not have to confront Tómas for stepping out of line.

María and her sister brought out a cake and wanted to make an announcement. "José, can you get everyone's attention for me?"

"Everybody! May I have your attention everybody?" José asked loudly. The noise level dropped so María could speak.

She placed on the table the large cake her mother's servants had baked. Then she turned and looked at everyone as she led José by his arm so that he stood beside her. "I would like to say the following. As most of you know, this fiesta is for my special guest José." María turned to him and continued, "José, I want to thank you for being who you are. You are always showing consideration to everyone you come in contact with. You are a very generous person who is always willing to do what you can to aid others. Thank you, José."

José was a generous person and did try to help others who were having difficulty. He had a kind heart. María had heard of his many good deeds and how considerate he was to the poor. It was unusual for a young person like him to be this way. She knew and heard of his wildness, but she felt his good qualities outweighed the bad ones. María's announcement continued, "The marimba is concluding their night here; so if you want to dance, you might as well find a partner and dance now. It is your last chance. They will be done in about an hour."

As the night progressed, José and María continued to dance. They enjoyed themselves very much. Of course, María had planned for another group to play music at her party after the marimba was finished; however, the new group did not compare to the marimba.

One of the numbers came to an end, and José and María thought it was good to rest. They had danced continually for quite awhile. José noticed Luis standing and waiting anxiously for him. He stepped over to where Luis was waiting. As José approached, Luis whispered in his ear, "José, Tómas is going to all the guests and asking for contributions to keep the marimba going. I do not think María or her familia know he is doing this."

José turned and scanned the surroundings for Tómas. He saw him standing over a young muchacho with his hat positioned upside down. It appeared he was trying to make the young muchacho put money into the hat. José felt it was an insult to María and her family to be asking for donations when it was not his fiesta. Tómas was not the guest of honor. If María wanted the marimba to stay longer, all she had to do was ask her father. He would have paid the band for more hours. María believed her father had contributed enough for the night, and she was satisfied.

"I am going to tell him to stop," José said with his eyes fixed on Tómas. He started to make his way toward him and brushed by Luis as he proceeded. Luis saw the expression on José's face and knew his brother was angry. He knew he would have to help José if anything happened in the next few minutes. Luis was not a fighter; however, he would back up his brother if it came to that point.

María saw Luis whisper something to José and then saw José look toward the opposite side of the dance floor. When she scanned the area to see what caught his attention, she saw Tómas having an argument with Edmundo, one of Maria's guests. As Luis followed José, she followed behind Luis.

Tómas had Edmundo by his collar. Edmundo was a clean-cut, well-mannered, young muchacho who was small in size. Tómas was telling him to put pesos in his hat or he was going to kick Edmundo out of the fiesta.

As José approached Tómas, he came to a stop just a few feet from him. José said, "Oralé, Tómas, what do you think you are doing?"

Little Edmundo was relieved that someone came to his rescue. He thought he was in for a beating because he did not bring any pesos to the fiesta. Edmundo tried to tell Tómas this, but he did not believe him and demanded he contribute pesos for the marimba.

The noise level had dropped somewhat when Tómas tried to force Edmundo to contribute money. However, now that José was speaking aggressively to Tómas, and with María standing behind him, the fiesta became more silent. Even the marimba played more softly.

Tómas turned around, looked at José and Luis, and said, "What do you want?" Tómas' voice had a slight slur, indicating he had been drinking. He did not like that José was becoming involved with something he felt was none of his business. José felt it was his business, and he had to put a stop to it.

"I asked, what are you doing? ¿No oyes, muchacho? (Can't you hear, boy?)"

"What do you care, José? This is none of your business!" Tómas replied angrily.

María stepped in front of José and told Tómas, "Take your hands off Edmundo right now! What do you think you are doing?"

"And? So what? What are you going to do about it, María?" Tómas asked with a sarcastic smile. He released Edmundo and turned his body toward them.

Irritated, María answered, "Are you trying to pick a fight with little Edmundo?"

Tómas laughed and looked at Edmundo. His laugh changed to a

harsh and wicked one. "So, that is your name, Edmundo."

Edmundo sat down, not saying anything, not wanting trouble with Tómas. He knew he was no match for him. Tómas continued, "So are you going to give your share or not?"

"Tómas, I want you to leave right now!" María demanded.

"Leave? Why María? I am trying to help you out by not letting people like this Edmundo get a free ride," Tómas replied, still looking at him. He turned to María. "I do not want to leave. I was invited here like everyone else," he declared, getting angrier and speaking more roughly to her.

María did not appreciate the manner in which she was being addressed. She put her hands on her hips and insisted, "Tómas, leave! Right now!"

"Who do you think you are to tell me to leave?" he asked.

María was really upset at this point. "Tómas, if you...."

"Tómas," José interrupted, stepping in front of María when he saw him change his posture. He seemed to want to take a swing at her. José continued, "What are you going to do?" Tómas glared at José with an expression that could kill.

Tómas pulled his shoulder back as if he were going to take a swing at José. José did not take any chances. In the past he saw those who hesitated in a situation like this, and it was disastrous for them.

José reacted as fast as he could, letting go with a hard blow, wanting to knock Tómas out. His blow struck its mark, and Tómas fell back and to the ground. His friends raised their hands in a fighting position. Luis took a step forward to stand next to his brother. Tómas held his nose as blood poured from it. He was trying to get to his feet. Other muchachos went running and stood next to José. They wanted to show their support for him and their hostess María. At this point the marimba stopped playing to observe what was occurring.

Tómas' friends knew if they jumped in and helped, they would be outnumbered. José saw Tómas' with his face full of blood; he knew he was in a lot of pain.

Tómas was now standing, wanting very badly to make José pay for what he had done to him. José did not believe in a fair fight but did whatever was necessary to win. He did not want Tómas to recover and come back at him.

Just as Tómas was about to stand erect again, José reached back and plastered him once more. José hit Tómas with such force that he again hit the ground. This time he could not stand.

José felt his fist hurting. He stepped over to Tómas and with one hand grabbed him by his black, long, shaggy hair. He grabbed the back of his shirt with the other. Tómas was forced to come to his feet. He was still trying to hold his nose and was moaning at the same time. José marched him to the entrance of the property that was not far from where they were. Once they arrived to the rock fence, José pushed Tómas past it. He took a few steps and fell to the ground, still dazed from the two blows.

"Tómas, I do not want you to step foot in the fiesta again. If you do, I will make this seem like a small beating!"

José turned around to see who was watching. He saw most of the guests observing them; all were flabbergasted at what had just taken place. Even the marimba band stopped playing and joined the others to watch. José stepped over to Tómas and said in a low voice close to his ear, "If you come back in, it will be the last fiesta you go to! Do you understand?"

Tómas looked at José and knew he had to answer affirmatively for the present time. "Yes," he said as his eyes looked at José. He quickly lowered his look to the ground.

José straightened up and walked back to where Tómas' friends stood. "And you," he said to the two who raised their fists to fight earlier, "go get your camarada (friend); and get him out of here! We do not want you here either! Do not come back!"

They did not say anything. Instead they walked away toward their friend Tómas who was lying on the ground in front of the property. They picked him up and left.

José took María's hand and walked toward the other side of the dance floor. María looked at his right hand and noticed it was hurt. "José, are you all right? Look at your hand. It is bleeding."

The marimba group had gone back to their instruments and resumed playing.

Jose raised his hand and looked at it. "It is nothing. It is only scraped from Tómas' ugly face. Look," José moved his fingers to show her they were all right. They hurt a little, but it was not bad enough to make a big deal of it.

"Ay, José, thank you for getting Tómas out of here. I think it was sad for poor Edmundo to be pushed around. You know, his father does a lot of business with my father. I am sure glad you did not get hurt."

"María, here comes your father; and he does not look happy," José said as he stood, wanting to show respect to Señor Hernández.

Señor Hernández did not appear as if he was in a good mood as he approached María and José. He was a tall man with a big, white mustache and broad shoulders. He also wore a big, white hat that appeared very expensive to José. The hat made him look taller than he actually was.

"María, what happened here? I was told there has been trouble. Is it so?" Señor Hernández was still walking towards them. He came to a stop.

José wiped his hand on the back of his pants then extended it to shake Señor Hernández's hand. "Hola, Don Hernández. How are you?"

Señor Hernández reached for José's hand and greeted him, saying, "Hola, José. I am fine. How are you? I was told you had a problem here? Is that true?" As Señor Hernández squeezed José's hand, he felt the pain and wanted to pull away.

José did not know what to say. He had to find the right words for Señor Hernández, not wishing to upset him. María interrupted, "Papá, Tómas came to the fiesta and was not invited. I do not know if you know him, but he came and started to fight with Edmundo. I told him to leave Edmundo alone. Then Tómas was going to hit me. That is when José stepped in to protect Edmundo and me."

Señor Hernández appeared angry. He replied, "He what? He was going to hit you?"

"Well, I don't know if he was going to hit me; but it sure looked as if he was."

"Why was this Tómas picking on little Edmundo?" Señor Hernández asked as he looked back at José.

José now knew it was going to be all right with Señor Hernández. "Because, Don Hernández, Tómas wanted the marimba to keep playing. He wanted little Edmundo to pay for a few more hours."

María looked at José. She really was not aware of what had transpired earlier. She now knew what Luis had whispered to José and why he went to where Tómas and Edmundo were. She went along with José's story. "Yes, Papá, he had no right to try to make Edmundo pay anything." Señor Hernández listened to the young people and wondered if maybe they were leaving something out. He knew youngsters.

Edmundo saw Señor Hernández speaking with María and José. He knew María's father was questioning them about what had just occurred. Edmundo stood up and walked over to where they were. All of the guests were observing the situation, knowing María's father could put an end to the fiesta in a second.

When Edmundo approached them, he stated to José, "I want to thank you for coming to my defense. I did not understand why that muchacho thought I had pesos to pay for the marimba. He said I had to pay him, and I knew he was not in charge here." He then looked at María and continued, "María, I know if you had wanted me to give pesos to keep the marimba going you would have asked me yourself. I am so glad you had someone like José to throw him out. I just hope he does not bother me in the next few days."

Señor Hernández now seemed irritated. "I will have that muchacho placed in jail. I will speak to the polecia in the morning and have them warn him to leave you alone, Edmundo. I do not ever want him here again. You said he was not invited. Who did he come with, María?"

"I am not sure, Papá. But I think maybe my hermanito (little brother) had something to do with it," María answered in a worried tone, not wanting to get her little brother in trouble.

Señor Hernández turned and looked for his son. When he saw him on the other side of the dance floor, he walked away from José and María. He stopped, turned, and said to José, "Muchacho, gracias."

"You are welcome, Don Hernández." José was glad María's father did not throw him out for fighting with Tómas. He knew the next time he saw Tómas he would have a fight on his hands. He thought of his baby in his belt and felt he could handle anything Tómas had in mind.

José and María danced for the remainder of the evening. The rest of the night went very well. Luis met a girl and was with her the rest of the night as well.

CHAPTER EIGHTEEN

A BARREL OF A GUN

The following morning José woke and sat up on the side of his bed. He rubbed his face and stretched. He felt good even though he drank heavily at the fiesta.

José looked at his brother who was still sound asleep. He knew he was going to sleep late.

From where he sat, the window was facing the courtyard to the school. He could see the activities of the street. People were talking and moving around. Some were setting up their stands and shouting out what they were selling. José could hear marimba playing somewhere nearby. Just about every morning someone hired marimba musicians for their loved ones, sometimes for birthdays, other times for marriages or anniversaries. People who lived in the town of Chiapas woke to such pleasant music, giving them a sense of happiness and pride in being Chiapanecos (people from the state of Chiapas).

Without waking his brother, José dressed and left the room. As he stepped into the street, he felt the movement of the people. The street was very lively even though it was early in the morning. Women were walking hurriedly with baskets under their arms to purchase their daily supplies. José stopped and looked around. It delighted him to see so many people moving around busily.

He wore a green-sweater vest with khaki pants. He carried his gun under his belt in the front left side as he did most of the time, especially now that he knew Tómas was going to be looking for him.

As José started to walk up the cobblestone street, he reflected on the night before and thought, "I need to be ready all the time, just in case Tómas wants revenge." He glanced behind and then scanned the buildings and rooftops.

José walked two blocks and arrived at a small restaurant where he ate on a regular basis. As he approached, he saw Francisco inside behind the counter. José thought, "Francisco must have just opened. Good!" Francisco was a man in his late forties, overweight, and mostly bald.

"¡Hola, José! Sit! Sit! José, it is good to see you. You are my first customer. Now I have someone to talk to."

The restaurant had no front wall and was open to the street. There were six wooden tables with colorful tablecloths. The floor was made of brown brick. There was a small counter, and behind the counter was where Francisco cooked the food. Next to the counter was a stack of firewood he used to heat the stove.

"Good morning, Francisco. How are you this morning?"

"I am fine. You are here early. You are my first customer. Do you know what that means, José?"

"Well, let me think. Maybe I will get my meal for free!" José said as he laughed and pulled out a chair to sit.

Francisco also laughed and said, "No, José. It means you will have good luck today. All who come here and are first to be served have good luck for the day! That is what they tell me anyway. I am sure it will be the same for you."

"I need all the luck I can get, Francisco."

"What will you have this morning, José?"

"I will have huevos (eggs), frijoles (beans), and a steak. I think you make the best frijoles in this pueblo." José had to have frijoles with every meal.

"Thank you, José. That is what my vieja (old lady) says. She will eat my frijoles before her own," Francisco said proudly as he stepped back behind the counter.

"The other day you said you were going to a fiesta to be held last night. Did you go?" Francisco asked as he was fixing José's plate.

José thought it was remarkable that Francisco remembered. "Sí, it was all right. María had a nice fiesta with marimba. We danced all night," he answered as he lay back on the chair, stretching and with his arms falling behind him. He did not want to brag and tell Francisco he was the guest of honor. In a few minutes José asked, "Do you know a big muchacho named Tómas? He was raised here I think."

"Tómas? Tómas?" Francisco asked himself in deep thought, trying to place him. "Do you mean a big muchacho with long hair?"

"Sí, he is very big and has long, black, shaggy hair. I have only known him for a short time."

"Yes, he comes in here once in a while; but he is not from this area. He is from the coast, Tapachula," Francisco responded as he walked over to José to serve his breakfast.

Francisco set José's plate on the table. He looked at it and then at Francisco. "Gracias, Francisco. It sure looks good. I will see if it tastes as good as it looks." He picked up his utensils and started to cut his meat. Before putting the piece of meat in his mouth, he took a tortilla, served frijoles on it, and placed it in his mouth. He made a sound of pleasure as he chewed. With the fork he placed the meat in his mouth. He looked at Francisco. With his mouth full he said, "It is very good. You are such a good cook, Francisco."

"You are welcome, José. You can thank me when you pay." Laughing, he went behind the counter again.

José served more frijoles onto his tortilla and put it in his mouth. Francisco was facing the wall as he cleaned the back counter. José was enjoying his food; his mouth was full. He was attempting to swallow while trying to tell Francisco what happened with Tómas at the fiesta.

Just as José swallowed his food, he turned his head and saw Francisco with his back toward him. He felt someone grab him around the neck. José did not know what was happening. Someone had a tight grip on him with his arm. Whoever it was, he had clinched him so firmly that José could not move to break loose. He was going to swing his body around with all his might when he felt the barrel of a gun next to his head. He worried that he might make the gun fire. José sat, not moving a muscle. The seconds before the person spoke seemed to drag by very slowly. Then he heard Tómas' voice say, "If you move, I will blow your head off." With these words José knew he was facing trouble.

Tómas continued, "You think you are tough, do you? Well, we are going to see how tough you really are!"

"Tómas, what do you think you are doing? Do you know you will be in big trouble for killing me here where everybody can see you?" José responded quickly, thinking fast and trying to get Tómas to reconsider his actions. He felt that if he could stall for just a minute, he might be able to reach for the gun in his belt.

"Now let us see what kind of man you are!" Tómas threatened, wanting to terrify José for the insult of the night before.

José laughed as he said, "Oh yeah, you have a gun to my head;

and I am eating with utensils in my hands." José was still holding the knife and fork as he was going to cut his steak. He did not want to move them and end up with a bullet hole in his head.

"That is right, big shot, José! You are not going to ever use those utensils again because I am going to kill you!" Tómas screamed as he squeezed José's neck tighter, trying to hurt him.

José knew he had to make his move right at that moment. With all his might he pushed up with his feet. At the same time he dropped his knife and fork.

With his left hand José reached up to grab Tómas' gun. With his right hand he reached down to grab his pistol, hoping Tómas would lose control of the situation. José's hand was only inches away from his gun when he saw a fireball explode next to his head. José felt as if his face and jaw had been ripped apart by the blast. A great numbness overcame his face and the side of his head. He was blinded from the explosion. The bullet ripped through one side of his face, next to his ear on the upper part of his jaw, and exited on the other side through his lower jaw.

José could not see anything. He struggled to turn his body around, holding onto Tómas. He had a hold of Tómas' gun. Tómas did not intend for the gun to go off. His plan was to frighten José and to make him beg for his life.

He was trying to push José away from him, so he could make his getaway. Blood was everywhere.

José was able to pull the gun away from Tómas. As he did, Tómas grabbed for it. It was released and fell to the ground. José reached up with both hands and choked Tómas with all his might.

He walked in and shot José all in a matter seconds. Francisco turned when he heard Tómas talking. He did not see Tómas walk into his restaurant because he came in through the back door. Francisco did not know what to do when he saw the gun at José's head. He reasoned that if he tried to do anything Tómas might get upset with him, and he might be the one to receive the bullet. Francisco did not wish to give up his life for something that was between José and Tómas.

José's legs were beginning to collapse as he tried to tighten his grip on Tómas' neck. He was in pain now, but he still put all of his strength in trying to kill Tómas. Tómas was fighting for oxygen. He did not know from where or how José was getting his strength after being shot.

As José was struggling with Tómas, he remembered the gun in his belt. He released Tómas' neck and reached for it. Tómas gasped for oxygen. José took the gun, aimed it at his face, and pulled the trigger. It did not go off. José pulled the trigger again. Tómas had an expression in his eyes, one that said he knew he was going to die. Again the gun did not go off. José turned the gun around; and with its butt he started to bang on Tómas' head repeatedly, as hard as he could. Over and over again he hit him. José did not stop striking him. Finally he felt Tómas become weak. He wanted to do as much damage to him as he could before he blacked out. José heard Francisco yell out, "Stop! Stop!" This was the last thing José remembered.

A doctor was rushed to the restaurant. José was semiconscious. Tómas was unconscious from the blows he received to his head.

The next day Luzita was told her son was shot. There was only one bus that left Venustiano Carranza to San Cristóbal de Las Casas. In 1934 San Bartolomé de los Llanos' name was changed to Venustiano Carranza, a president's name during the revolution. When Romulo heard his son was injured by a gunshot wound, he also wanted to be by his side; however, he was too ill to make the trip.

When Luzita arrived, she stayed with José until he was able to make the trip home to recuperate. Tómas, on the other hand, was charged with assault. When he recovered, he was sent to prison.

Within three months José fully recovered and went back to school with his brother.

One day, during the same year, José and Luis received a letter informing them their father's health had deteriorated to a very dangerous point. Luzita told them they needed to return home at once. Immediately they boarded a bus and returned home. During this time, instead of being a journey of two days on horseback, it took four hours in a motor car or a bus to travel on the dirt roads. José's other brothers were also informed in México City, and they also traveled home.

"Mamasita, it is good to see you," José greeted Luzita as he gave his mother a big hug.

"Josecito, I am glad you and Luis came at once. Your father is very ill. He has been asking for you. Where is your hermanito?" Luzita asked, looking around.

"He is coming. He stopped to talk to Jessica." Just then Luis stepped into the parlor. Jessica was one of Luis' girlfriends.

"Hola, Mamasita, how is my papí?" Luis asked as he also embraced his mother.

"Not well, mi hijo (my son), not well at all," Luzita answered with a worried and sad expression. Luzita loved Romulo so very much. She just could not imagine living without him. He took care of her and the children very well. The people of the town also loved him very much. Through the years Romulo always showed compassion for them, the rich as well as the poor.

José's sisters, Marina and Gloria, stepped into the parlor. "José, Luis! You are here!" Marina exclaimed. Marina was the oldest of all of Romulo and Luzita's children. Gloria was a year-and-a-half younger than Luis.

"Yes, we are, mi hermana. How is our father?" José asked his sister, knowing what her answer was going to be.

"He is not very well, José. He has asked for you several times," Marina answered sadly. She continued, "He is very weak now, and we do not know what is going to happen to him. We love him so very much, José." Marina was now sobbing as José was holding her in his arms. "We are glad you came right away to be with him and us," Marina stated as she wept. Luzita was standing, watching her oldest daughter expressing herself. Marina's words were for all of them.

Luzita had her arms around Gloria and Luis. José looked at his sister Gloria who was also crying.

Marina was married at this time and lived with her husband but was spending a lot of time with her family.

José took a deep breath and said, "I want to go in and be with my papí now." He looked in the direction of his father's bedroom. He stepped over to the entrance of the room. He stopped and looked at his mother, sisters, and brother. They all had very sad expressions. José would remember those expressions for the rest of his life.

Romulo was lying in his bed asleep. He appeared frail. He had been suffering with his sickness for the last few years. Romulo had always been a large and tall man. José noticed how thin and weak his father now looked.

He sat on the side of his father's bed. Romulo opened his eyes and looked at his son. "Josecito, mi hijo," he whispered.

"Yes, Papí, I am right here."

Josecito, I, I...." Romulo paused, not having the strength to speak the way he wished. Romulo forced himself to speak. "Josecito, I want you to take care of your mother. Hijo, you have so much goodness in your loving heart. I...." Romulo closed his eyes for a second and rested. Then he opened his eyes, raised his hand, pointed his skinny finger at José's chest, and said, "I always knew you were the one with the biggest heart, Josecito. So," Romulo coughed and rested without saying anything for a minute. José waited patiently, knowing his father was trying to say his peace. "So, with your big and sweet heart, mi hijo, I want to give you the responsibility of looking after your mother. I know you are," Romulo paused again, trying to rest. He had been waiting for José to arrive to express his wishes. "Muchachito, Josecito, I know your heart," Romulo whispered, trying to raise his head. His head dropped back down to the bed, his eyes closed, and he fell asleep.

José looked at his father and wanted to cry. He had a difficult time releasing his emotions and felt it was unmanly even though he was only seventeen years old. He sat there for a few minutes holding his father's hand. José heard low crying behind him and turned to look. He saw everyone standing at the doorway watching and listening to what his father had just said to him. He tried to smile at them as if he were saying everything was going to be all right. Luis could not help himself and also had tears rolling down his cheeks. José sat with his father for the remainder of the evening.

Early the next morning Romulo asked for Luzita. "Yes, mi armor, I am right here." It was just unacceptable to Luzita to live without Romulo.

Romulo opened his eyes and looked at his wife; Luzita was sitting next to him on the bed. He whispered hoarsely, barely getting the words out, and at the same time picking up his head a few inches, "Luzita, I love you. I... I... I want you to keep moving... forward...." Romulo stopped talking, lay his head back, closed his eyes, and took a deep breath. His chest filled with oxygen one last time. He released his breath, lay silent, and was still.

José sat close to his father and picked up his frail body, resting him on his lap. He held him in his arms. "!Ay, Papí! !Ay, Papí!" José started to cry. Luis, Gloria, and Marina were also in the room; they also began crying.

Luzita still could not accept that she was losing her true love. "Romulo! Romulo! Ay, Ay, Ay, Romulo! I cannot live without you, mi amor!" she cried. "Please, Romulo!" Luzita pulled him out of José's arms and held him tight, rocking him back and forth while weeping and wailing. People on the street could hear Luzita's wailing and knew Dr. Romulo Rodriguez was gone.

In the months that followed, life became very difficult for Luzita as well as for her children. She was depressed and felt lost without Romulo. Even though Romulo was sick for a long time before his death, she always had him to talk to. Romulo was a good listener and gave her moral support.

José and Luis, as well as their brothers, continued their schooling. Luzita continued to work as a seamstress. She still had a little money left from Romulo, but it would only last for a short time.

Once José completed school in San Cristóbal de Las Casas, he left for México City to continue his studies. He started school to become a doctor, just as his father and brother Jorge had. However, he could not accept the high level of responsibility, having to be on call twenty-four hours a day. He acknowledged after viewing his first autopsy, when he fainted, that being a doctor was not for him; therefore, he discontinued his education. In his studies he also took accounting courses. José was later employed as an accountant and was paid a decent salary.

Because he felt a need to help his mother financially, he sent most of his money to her and returned home periodically to see how his family was doing. He saw things were not going well for her and knew he had to take her out of the town to help her out of her depression.

José was living in México City when he wrote his mother and told her to prepare to move. He was going home and would take her and the children to live in Tuxla Gutierrez, which was the capital of Chiapas at that time. On the way home José stopped in Tuxla Gutierrez and secured a place for his mother to live, not far from other relatives.

José continued to send money to his mother from México City. The money she received from José and the little she made as a seamstress were enough to manage.

CHAPTER NINETEEN

A TINY CASA

When Luis completed school, he wanted to travel north on an adventure. Luis invited José to join him. José, however, did not think it was wise at the time. He was working and believed it best to stay and continue to care for his mother.

Luis left on his adventure. Several months later he wrote to José and invited him once again. Luis told him he had a job for him that paid better than his position as an accountant. He could get him employment at the same company where he worked. Luis liked his job at the American Can Company in San José, California.

In one year Luis returned to Mexico City to visit. He told José he left his job on a leave of absence and asked José to return to the United States with him. He told his brother to consider it an adventure. If he did not like living in California, he could always return.

Once José thought it over, he agreed. They left Mexico City and arrived in Mexicali, a border town on the Mexican side. They obtained jobs as border police officers, inspecting people and vehicles on the Mexican side. Luis worked in this position for a short time until he was able to arrange for his documents to return to the United States.

Upon arriving in San José, California, Luis asked his employer if he was willing to give his brother the job they had discussed a few months earlier. The employer was unable to provide a position until the busy season arrived. Luis wrote José and informed him of the job situation; José replied he was coming anyway and would look for another job in the meantime.

In two months José crossed the border. Upon arriving in California, he found employment in Watsonville, just a few miles from San José.

José worked on a strawberry ranch for a rancher named Mr. Wilson. Mr. Wilson liked him very much and gave him a place to stay on the ranch. After a short time José found he did not like working in the fields; however, he knew it was going to be temporary.

Three months later he found himself working at the American Can Company. He enjoyed working at the company with Luis, even though it was hard work. José worked in the noisiest part of the plant where large machines fabricated the cans. He then moved to the warehouse where it was still noisy but not as much as in the factory. José's job in the warehouse required using a large wooden fork, forking cans into large boxes and loading boxcars. He got along with everybody and was well liked.

He found life in California enjoyable and felt he could live there for the rest of his life.

One summer evening in 1947, José went to the popular Rainbow Ballroom with his friends. He was twenty-three years old. The Rainbow Ballroom was a very nice dance hall; the best big bands in the area played on Friday and Saturday nights. The music was an alternate of big band music, such as Glen Miller, and Mexican music.

Most of the people who attended were from the United States. José was one of the few who was from Mexico. Some dressed casually and some sloppily, but José stood out for his clean-cut appearance. He often wore slacks, a white shirt, and a sport coat.

José and his friends arrived at the front door of the building of the ballroom and climbed up a flight of stairs to the second floor. A table with a girl was set up at the top of the stairs to sell tickets to enter. Guys paid, and ladies were admitted free.

José danced continually with girls who were also good dancers and always enjoyed himself. He was sitting out a dance number when he noticed a very pretty girl. Mildred had curly, short, light brown hair; deep-set hazel eyes; and was hüera (light complected). She also had a small, dainty nose and small, thin, rosy lips. Mildred was nineteen years old.

"Ay, ay, ay," José said to himself. He turned to one of his friends and pointed to her. "Look at that gringa," he said in Spanish.

"What gringa, José?" Charlie asked, also in Spanish, looking in the direction José was pointing.

"Esa (that one), over there. The pretty one, Charlie," he replied as Mildred looked in their direction. She saw him saying something about her as he pointed to her.

José was embarrassed that the hüera saw him pointing to her and speaking about her.

Mildred wondered if José was going to ask her to dance. She knew if he did, she was going to have a difficult time. She was not a good dancer; it was very seldom she went out dancing. Her father Ben was a very strict man. In fact, to be there on that night, Mildred had to sneak out of her window and go with a friend.

Mildred was the oldest of her two sisters and four brothers. She was born in Albuquerque, New Mexico, and moved around a lot, depending upon where her father located work. He spoke a mix of Spanish and English. Mildred and her brothers and sisters understood a few words in Spanish but could not speak the language.

José stepped away from his friend and walked toward Mildred. As he approached, she looked at him, knowing he was going to ask her to dance. José asked in Spanish, "Would you like to accompany me for this dance?"

"What? Are you asking me to dance?" she asked as she smiled.

José, with the limited English he was trying to learn, understood the word dance. "Sí, dance?" he asked as he pointed to the dance floor. José carried around his English/Spanish dictionary and always opened it when he needed to find a word he did not understand or could not speak.

As they danced, José could not take his eyes away from her. He thought she was the most beautiful girl he had ever seen. José did not notice that Mildred was a poor dancer. Her nice smile made up for her two left feet.

The dance number came to an end, and Mildred turned to return to her table. José took her hand and asked again, "Dance?" Mildred smiled and nodded her head affirmatively. They danced the next three songs together.

Mildred really enjoyed herself. She had met other young men before, but there was something special about José. She thought it was the way he looked at her and smiled. Every time José looked at her, she felt a happy feeling. Before the fourth dance number started, they both stood on the dance floor admiring each other.

The band started to play. It was a slow dance. As they came together, Mildred felt José's arm reach around her. It gave her a feeling of security. She was intrigued by José's cologne. Not knowing what was happening to her, she felt very happy with José, something she had never felt with anyone else. She did not know why these feelings had arisen, especially since she had just met him.

"My name, José."

Mildred looked up at him and said, "My name is Mildred. Nice to meet you, José."

She thought he was the handsomest guy she had ever met. Her heart was beating faster than normal. She knew he felt the same way as she did.

The rest of the evening went very well. José asked Mildred in Spanish and in sign language if she would return to the dance the following week. Mildred did not understand what he was asking, so she called her friend Lisa who was talking to friends at another table. "Lisa, what is José trying to tell me?"

Lisa looked at José and asked, "¿Qué dices (What are you saying)?"

"¿Si Mildred volverá el fin de semana que viene?"

"He wants to know if you are coming back next weekend?"

"Tell him I don't know. He will have to come and see if I'm here."

Lisa interpreted for Mildred and also told José that Mildred's father was very strict. She told him this was why Mildred did not know for sure if she was going to be present. She advised José to be there Friday night in case they were able to return.

All week at work José thought about her. He had only met her one time and knew he had met the girl who was meant for him. Mildred also thought of José and could not wait for the following weekend.

On Wednesday evening Mildred was helping her mother correct papers at their home on Mabury Road, off King Road in San José's east side. Francis, Mildred's mother, was a schoolteacher at Mayfair Elementary School. She had Mildred and her younger sister Annabelle help her during the week. At one point Mildred stopped marking with her red pencil; her thoughts drifted. She dreamed about marrying José and having children; four children would be ideal. She saw herself in a small house with her children around her waiting for her husband to arrive home from work. Then....

"Mildred, what is the matter? Are you all right, dear?" Frances asked with her sweet and soft mannerism.

"I'm all right, Mom. I was just thinking, why is Dad so strict? Why doesn't he let me go out to the dances? I'm already nineteen years old. When is he going to let me do what I want? I don't know why he doesn't trust me."

Ben would not let his girls go out dancing. He told them if they ever went out and got pregnant they would find themselves in the street. They were so naive, they believed a kiss could impregnate them.

"Oh, honey, your father means well. You know that. He just doesn't want you to go out and get mixed up with the wrong people. That is all." Frances always did what her husband wanted. She was very submissive.

"What do you mean the wrong people? Where? At the dances?"

"Yes, at the dances."

"Why does he think there are bad people at the dances?" Mildred asked, trying to see how her mother felt. She believed that maybe her mother could help persuade her father to let her go out; therefore, she would not have to hide.

"Because he knows. He has been to dances and knows what kind of people go there."

"Is my father a good person or one of those people?"

"Why, he is a good person. You know that," Francis responded. She then realized where Mildred was going with her question.

"Mother, that means there are good people as well as bad people there. Since there are good people, I should be able to go. Mom, tell me again how you met Daddy."

Francis put her red pencil down and looked at Mildred. She knew she had told Mildred in the past how her husband and she met. However, it seemed Mildred wanted more details.

"Well, I was a school teacher in Cuba, New Mexico. I went to live with my aunt, so I could teach there. I taught in a large, one-room schoolhouse. As I told you many times in the past, all the children came and were taught together. Anyway, your father came and would visit me there all the time. I remember when he would come. His shoes were in such bad condition. I felt sorry for him, so I bought him a pair of shoes. Well, after that we fell in love; and that was it. We married."

"What did your family think about Daddy?"

"Oh, my father did not approve of my marrying him. They said he was poor. They were completely against it. However, I told my father and my family I was going to marry him because I loved him and no one was going to stop me."

Mildred did not say anything. She picked up her pencil and started to correct again. She was in deep thought. Francis knew something was up with her oldest daughter but did not really know what it was.

The following Friday night Mildred fixed her bed, snuck out, and met Lisa. They again went to the Rainbow Ballroom. Mildred did not go often. However, now that she had met José, she would go as often as she could.

She danced with José and sat at his table. From that night on they met everyday, even if it was just for a few minutes. Sometimes she would meet him when she went to shop downtown. Sometimes it was at the corner store. As the next few weeks went by, they began to understand each other better, even with the language difference.

One day Mildred told her mother she had a boyfriend. "Who is he, Mildred? Do we know him?"

"No, Mother, you don't. He is Mexican, from Mexico. His name is José Rodriguez."

"I see, and what do you think your father is going to say about your having a boyfriend from Mexico?"

"It doesn't matter what he says. I'm not going to stop seeing him. I care for him very much, and I'm going to continue to see him no matter what anyone says."

"Well, dear, you should talk to your father; so he will know how you feel."

Mildred was in love and knew she had to tell her father. She was worried what he would say. However, she knew that regardless of his feelings it did not matter. She was going to continue to see José.

The following day her father, Ben Wiggins, came home from work. He entered the living room, sat down, and removed his shoes.

Ben Wiggins was a partially bald, well-built man who worked in construction. When Ben was two years old, his mother died. His father could not take care of a small child; therefore, he gave Ben to his sister who was married to a man from Mexico. The man only spoke Spanish. This man, Gómez, adopted Ben. Ben grew up speaking Spanish. He was never sent to school and never learned to read and write. When he spoke to his children, he spoke in incorrect English.

"Hi, Daddy, how was work today?" Mildred asked nervously.

"Good," Ben replied, looking at his pretty daughter. "Whatsa matter, Mildred?" Ben asked, knowing his daughter so well he knew something was occurring.

"Well, Daddy, I want to speak to you."

Ben did not respond. He let Mildred continue. "I want to tell you I met a young man. I really like him, and I want to bring him home to meet you and mother."

Ben wondered who this young man was. Mildred had her father's full attention, but Ben had a feeling he was not going to like what he was about to hear. He knew if Mildred wanted to bring him home, there was more to it than just being a friend. "What? Who he is? Where do you know him from?"

The way her father stared at her, Mildred wished she had never brought up the subject. "He is very nice, Daddy. I met him downtown." Mildred was not lying to her father because the Rainbow Ballroom was downtown. "His name is José, and he is very nice," she repeated.

"Where he from? Who is his family? We know them?"

"No, Daddy. His family is from Mexico, and he is from Mexico."

Ben did not like the sound of it. He saw many Mexican men come to the United States. They married American girls and had a child just to receive their legal status. They would then bring their families over.

"No! No, Mildred! I not think itsa good idea for you have boyfriend from Mexico. Sometimes them come for justa look for a wife then hit them. No, not good. Itsa way they are. No bueno. Not good! Sometimes have wives in Mexico, too. No good to see him anymore!" Ben demanded. He felt it was not going to be a problem because Mildred always complied with his wishes.

Mildred now knew her father was not going to be understanding of her feelings. She knew she had to tell her father she was in love and was going to be married; José and she were already discussing marriage in their conversations. They felt they did not have to wait because they were in love, and that was it. "Daddy, I am not going to stop seeing him. I am telling you right now. I love him, and that is the way it is!"

Ben froze in his chair and did not know what to say. He had never heard Mildred speak to him like this before. He stood. He had thoughts to taking off his big belt. His hand was already on his large belt buckle. Raising his voice, Ben said, "What? Whatsa you say? ¡Muchacha, no me hables asi (Girl, don't talk to me like that)! You do likea I say to you and that is it! I no want to hear about it no more! You understand? Do you?

Answera me!"

Mildred's father had not yelled at her for a long time in the tone he was addressing her now. As Ben was yelling, she imagined José smiling at her. No, she could never give in and stop seeing José. She did not care what happened to her or what her father would do. She looked at him in the eye and said, "Daddy, I am going to see him if you like it or not. You are not going to stop me!" Mildred then ran out of the living room to the front yard. She walked down the street to the store at the corner of Mabury and King roads.

Ben did not know what to say. Frances stepped in the living room from the kitchen, wearing her colorful, full-length apron. She had heard the whole conversation. She sat on a chair and did not say anything for a few minutes, knowing her husband was upset and needed time to cool down. Wondering what he was going to do, Ben walked back and forth. He knew he really could not beat her with the belt because she was already nineteen years old. He had never seen Mildred act in this manner. He knew from the way she looked at him and spoke that he was going to have a difficult time stopping her from seeing José.

"Ben," Frances said as she sat very still with her hands together on her lap. Ben did not say anything. He knew what his wife was going to say. Frances always spoke calmly and always with persuasive words.

"Ben, remember when we met?" She did not think she had to say too much to her dear husband if he just thought back twenty years.

Ben sat down where he was sitting earlier. He was in deep thought. Nothing was said for a few minutes. Then he spoke in Spanish. "What I will do is tell Mildred she can bring the boy over. If I do not like him, I will put my foot down!"

Frances knew her husband would do the right thing. That was exactly what she was going to propose to him.

In an hour Mildred returned from her walk. She was anticipating another fight with her father, perhaps even being beaten by him. But she did not care; she was willing to take whatever came. She hoped her father was in the shower or his bedroom when she entered the house. She also wished her mother was more outspoken with her father, but she knew her mother would do whatever he wanted without question.

Mildred entered the house and saw her father sitting in the same chair. It seemed he was doing nothing but waiting for her. "Mildred, sit." She sat down and wondered why her father was not furious.

He did not say anything for a few seconds. Then he said very calmly, "I wanta meet your boyfriend. Tella him to come here for supper tomorrow. Where he-a works?"

Mildred was shocked. She could not imagine her father was going to budge on the issue. She was lost for words, thinking she had not heard correctly. Answering, she said, "He works at the American Can Company, Daddy."

Ben knew working at the American Can Company was a very good job, one that paid well. "That is good. Ask him come here for supper tomorrow. O.K.?"

"Oh yes, Daddy, I am sure of it! I will call him in the morning at work to tell him. That will be really nice. I know you are going to like him, Daddy," Mildred said, still in shock that her dream was coming true.

The following morning Mildred called the company and asked for José. José's supervisor really liked him and did not mind going out to the warehouse to call him. José never received calls from anyone, and the supervisor thought it might be important. He picked up the phone, "Bueno?"

"José, this is Mildred." During the two months José and Mildred had been seeing each other, they began to understand each other much better. "My father wants to meet you. My daddy," Mildred repeated, hoping José would understand.

"Sí, your papá."

"Yes, come over for supper today. SUPPER, EAT!"

"¿Comer? Eat? ¿Donde (Where)? House?"

"My house, mi casa!"

"¿Tu casa? Your house?" José answered to make sure he had it right.

"Sí, mi casa. ¡Mi papá, mamá!" Mildred said, feeling good about her Spanish.

"OK, sí, tiempo, aw... clock?"

"At 6:30. 6:30. Three zero."

"Bueno, seis y media. O.K., bye."

Frances was in the kitchen, cooking with Annabelle's help. All were anticipating seeing Mildred's boyfriend. Mildred's teenage brothers, Ben and Wilfred, also wanted to meet him. They saw someone walking up the sidewalk.

José was slender. He had black hair and a thin mustache. He was wearing a white dress shirt with a tie; had nice black slacks; and black, shiny shoes. If José was not working, he always dressed with nice clothes.

He knocked at the front door even though he could see people inside through the screen.

"Pasa, muchacho (enter)," Ben said. The way José looked, Ben had a feeling he was going to like him.

"Con mucho gusto, Señor Wiggins," José greeted him as he reached out to shake Mr. Wiggins' hand.

Ben said in Spanish, "You can call me Ben. So you are José." Ben did not like being called señor, a respectful term. It made him feel distant, and he wanted their relationship to be friendly. From this point on, Ben and José always spoke in Spanish with each other.

That evening went well. Ben truly liked José. He showed a lot of respect to Ben and Frances. Even the boys liked him. José treated them well, knowing they were going to be related in a matter of time. On that evening Ben gave José permission to date his daughter.

A month later José and Mildred made plans as they had a few times before, to walk to Alum Rock Park, three miles from Mildred's home. Before leaving, José went to her house and visited with her father and mother for awhile.

Leaving her home, they stopped at the corner store on King and Mabury roads and bought Cokes. Later they would stop and purchase snacks at the next store that was on White Road and Alum Rock Avenue. They walked, holding hands as they told each other stories and experiences of their lives as they grew up. At times they did not understand each other, so they would laugh and try again. It did not matter that they did not understand. They were in love and were going to enjoy every minute of their time together.

They arrived at Alum Rock Avenue. From Alum Rock Avenue, going west towards town, the street was paved. Going east to Alum Rock Park, the street was constructed of beautiful, red brick. Every so often they would find a place to stop and rest. There were some fields on Alum Rock Avenue, but there were mostly homes that lined the street. They walked on the south side of the street because it had a gravel sidewalk. José carried two white handkerchiefs. One was for him to use. The other was when they stopped to rest; he could put it down very neatly for Mildred to sit on. He did not want her to soil her pretty dress.

As they walked up Alum Rock Avenue, Mildred told José about her grandfather Gómez. "When my dad and mom were married and I was little, we lived with my aunt and uncle; but we knew them as grandparents. My grandma Concha had only one leg. On the other they originally amputated her foot. In time they amputated to her calf, to her knee, and then to her hip. No one ever knew what was really wrong with her."

"¿Y tu grandpa Gómez?" José asked, wanting to know about Mildred's family.

"When I was a little girl, I don't know how old I was, but I remember we were all eating chicken at the table, all of a sudden my grandpa fell to the floor. He was choking on a bone. Everybody was rushing around trying to remove the bone from his throat, but they couldn't. He died right there on the kitchen floor. It was a sad day for our family. My daddy loved him so much. He was good to my daddy and raised him as his own son."

"Ay, Mildred, I sorry," José expressed as he held Mildred's hand tightly, really caring for the way she felt.

As they were nearing the foothills and the country club that was there, the road became a little steeper. It was not really a difficult walk as long as they walked slowly.

José went on to tell Mildred about his father's death and how much his family and the entire town loved his father. He told her his mother was still living and had been depressed since his father's death. He explained that it was a different world where he once lived. He described a beautiful place of dense jungles; green, grassy plains; and raging rivers. He told her that although it was beautiful he would much rather live in the United States, especially now that he found her.

Alum Rock Avenue had a bend where the street stretched along the back of the country club before it entered into the park. At the bend of the road, a large home was being built. It was only the frame. José and Mildred decided to rest in the big-frame home that faced San José. It had a nice view of the small city. José again put his handkerchief down so Mildred would not stain her dress. They opened their Cokes and snacks and looked at each other with dreamy eyes, loving every moment of their time together. José loved Mildred and knew he was going to have a happy life with her. He knew he would do anything for her. Mildred knew she would never find anyone she loved more than José.

"Millie," José called her. He had a difficult time pronouncing her name, so he started to call her Millie. "When esta casa is done, yo te la compro, buy it. It will be you casa."

"Oh, thank you, Joe. That would be nice; but I will be happy with a little, tiny casa," Mildred answered. She liked calling him Joe instead of José.

Mildred smiled at José and thought all she wanted was to be happy with him. She imagined having her own family with him. "I want to have four children, Joe. How many do you want?" Mildred asked, smiling lovingly.

"Four, like you," he answered, putting up his fingers.

They both sat and smiled, dreaming the happy, contended visions of young lovers. Mildred visualized her four future children: Eddie, Arthur, Mildred, and Victor. They were married one month later with the blessing of Ben and Frances.

In the years that followed, their children had many stories of their own.

(*East Side Dreams* continues the story and history of the Rodriguez family. Read it and enjoy it.)

View my Picture Album at www.EastSideDreams.com

SUEÑOS DEL LADO ESTE. . .

Viaje usted con Art Rodríguez, conforme sueña su pasado. Art experimenta una desagradable niñez, llena de obstáculos difíciles que pudieron haber disminuido sus oportunidades para desarrollar una vida normal. La vida aparece para él como una vida sin esperanza durante esos años de la juventud cuando se esfuerza para descubrir quien es realmente, al mismo tiempo que vive una continua batalla con un padre dictatorial. Viaje con él y acompáñelo a través del sistema carcelario de California, la cárcel para jóvenes delincuentes.

No obstante que creció bajo semejante estado general de tensión, él encuentra todavía disfrute y alegría al crecer en San José California, acompañando a sus amigos adolescentes en Virgnia Place, en el lado Este de San José. Experimente con él su niñez, conforme recuerda los tiempos pasados de infelicidad y los momentos agradables. En esta historia capaz de hacerlo llorar y de reir; tanto los jóvenes como los adultos pueden encontrar ánimo sabiendo que cuando la vida parece desolada y aparenta no haber esperanza, las circunstancias pueden cambiar. Existe escape de una situación desesperada. Vea como una mala relación entre un padre y un hijo puede cambiar, desde el resentimiento a una relación afectiva.

Esta historia es un estímulo para los jóvenes y para los adultos porque en ella pueden descubrir como Art deja su vida de delincuente y se impulsa hacia un futuro con promesas.

En 1985, Art Rodríguez comenzó un exitoso negocio en San José, la ciudad en la que nació. ¿Cómo pudo este hombre, un ex delincuente, comenzar un negocio con semejante pasado? Descubra junto a él y acompáñelo en el relato de su vida y experimente el sufrimiento, la privación y luego el éxito de su nueva empresa.

ORDER THE MONKEY BOX. . .

Take a journey back in time with Art Rodriguez as he traces his family's past.

In the 1800s Art's great, great grandfather was not only a duke in Spain, but he was also a priest. He had an affair with a young woman, and it became public knowledge when the young lady died at childbirth.

The church was taking steps to excommunicate the priest, and the family was very humiliated because of the situation. His family offered an inheritance as well as family lineage documents for him to leave the country with his daughter Lydia.

As time went by in Mexico, the documents were stored in an airtight box that was carved with beautiful monkeys. What happened to the documents and the love story that followed 16-year-old Lydia? How did the family end up in the United States? This journey will reveal Art Rodriguez's family story.

ORDER FORGOTTEN MEMORIES. . .

"Turbulent Teenage Years! But Life Goes On!"

Are you having difficult teenage years? Does life go on? Travel with Art Rodriguez as he takes you through his teen years. You will see that life does get better, even though it appears confusing and harsh at times. You will enjoy his stories of growing up in San Jose, California. He will take you for a stroll; as he does, you will experience with him fun times and hard times. You will enjoy this sequel to East Side Dreams.

You may order Forgotten Memories through Your local bookstore or from the last page of this book.

ORDER FORM

Give a person a Gift.

No. of Copies:

_____**East Side Dreams by Art Rodriguez.** (Inspirational Story About Growing Up.)
. . . . $12.95

_____**The Monkey Box by Art Rodriguez.** (Romantic Family Story.) $12.95

_____**Forgotten Memories by Art Rodriguez.** (Sequel to East Side Dreams.) . $12.95

_____**Sueños del Lado Este by Art Rodriguez.** (East Side Dreams in Spanish.) . $12.95

Shipping & handling, first copy $4.00 plus $1.00 for each additional copy.
Five books or more, Shipping & handling, NO CHARGE. *We are prompt about sending books out.*

If you are paying with a credit card, you may fax or send to address below.

❑ Visa   ❑ MasterCard   ❑ American Express   ❑ Discover Card

Card Number _____

Expiration Date _____

Signature _____

Check No. _____
Make checks payable to **Dream House Press**.

Your Name _____

Street _____

City _____

State _____Zip _____

Phone (_____) _____

Send to:
Dream House Press
P. O. Box 13211
Coyote, CA 95013
Phone: (408) 274-4574
Fax: (408) 274-0786
www.EastSideDreams.com

Dream House